The
Classical Mandolin

The Classical Mandolin

Paul Sparks

CLARENDON PRESS · OXFORD

1995

Oxford University Press, Walton Street, Oxford OX2 6DP
Oxford New York
Athens Auckland Bangkok Bombay
Calcutta Cape Town Dar es Salaam Delhi
Florence Hong Kong Istanbul Karachi
Kuala Lumpur Madras Madrid Melbourne
Mexico City Nairobi Paris Singapore
Taipei Tokyo Toronto
and associated companies in
Berlin Ibadan

Oxford is a trade mark of Oxford University Press

Published in the United States
by Oxford University Press Inc., New York

British Library Cataloguing in Publication Data
Data available

Library of Congress Cataloging in Publication Data
Sparks, Paul.
The classical mandolin / Paul Sparks.
p.   cm.
Includes bibliographical references (p.   ) and index.
1. Mandolin. I. Title.
ML1015.M2S63 1995   787.8′4—dc20   94–30665
ISBN 0–19–816295–2 (acid-free paper)
1 3 5 7 9 10 8 6 4 2

Typeset by Graphicraft Typesetters Ltd., Hong Kong
Printed in Great Britain
on acid-free paper by
St. Edmundsbury Press
Bury St. Edmunds, Suffolk

Preface

This book completes the work which I began in *The Early Mandolin*, and studies the history and repertoire of the instrument from 1815 to the present day. The mandolin (in its various forms) can be traced across four centuries but, although it has enjoyed several periods of enormous popularity in both classical and popular music (including the present era), it nevertheless remains a much-misunderstood and frequently denigrated instrument. Despite its numerous appearances in operatic, chamber, and symphonic works, it is still widely viewed by musicians as an eccentric intruder into the concert-hall, while its huge repertoire of original works remains almost entirely unknown, except to aficionados of the instrument.

A century ago, the situation was very different. Throughout much of Europe and North America, the mandolin was one of the most widely owned and played of all instruments, its popularity amongst amateur musicians probably being equalled only by that of the piano. Enormous quantities of mandolin music were published, much of it undemanding and ephemeral, but some of it of great technical complexity and undeniable artistic worth. Verdi, Mahler, Webern, Massenet, Schoenberg, and many other leading composers included the mandolin in orchestral and operatic works, and establishments such as Trinity College of Music and the Guildhall School of Music in London accepted it as a legitimate instrument of study. In most towns and cities, there was at least one mandolin orchestra regularly rehearsing and performing, with the best of them competing at huge national and international festivals.

The impetus for this upsurge in interest was provided by a number of virtuoso performers, mostly Italian, whose compositions and recordings demonstrate that they brought the art of mandolin-playing to a perfection which has seldom been equalled since. Nowadays, one searches in vain through the 'Mandolin' entries in music dictionaries for the names of Raffaele Calace, Carlo Munier, Ernesto Rocco, Leopoldo Francia, and Silvio Ranieri, but it was these musicians (and their contemporaries) whose brilliant recitals established the instrument in the concert-hall, doing for the mandolin in the years before World War I what Andrés Segovia later did for the guitar. Although the Italian lyrical style in music had largely fallen out of favour with the concert-going public by the 1930s, the best works of these composers (especially those of Calace) are of lasting worth, and deserve to be better known.

This book chronicles the rise and fall of the Italian style, and the distinct styles of playing that subsequently evolved in Germany, the USA, Japan, and South America, as well as the use of the mandolin in contemporary music by composers such as Henze, Petrassi, and Boulez. Although primarily concerned with the classical mandolin, the instrument's tremendous importance in folk and popular music cannot (and should not) be ignored, and is also dealt with here. While this book is not intended as a tutor for the instrument, the final chapter looks at technical and practical aspects of playing and writing for the mandolin, and also gives brief definitions of some of the bewildering variety of fretted instruments akin to the mandolin that have been developed since the late nineteenth century.

Until the mid-nineteenth century, mandolinists made no systematic distinction in nomenclature between the six-course and four-course instruments, usually calling them both by the same name. In *The Early Mandolin*, James Tyler and I made a distinction by calling the former MANDOLINO, and the latter MANDOLINE, and I have continued to make that distinction during the first chapter of this book. However, during the first half of the nineteenth century, both instruments were extensively redesigned and standard names gradually began to be assigned to them—the six-course (now single-string) instrument became generally known as the Milanese or Lombardian mandolin, and the much more popular four-course instrument as the Neapolitan mandolin (or, simply, the mandolin)—and this book follows that standard practice in its discussion of the instruments from the mid-nineteenth century onwards. For reference, the tunings of the two instruments are given here, both in stave and in alphabetic notation, as in the example.

g	*b*	*e'*	*a'*	*d''*	*g''*		*g*	*g*	*d'*	*d'*	*a'*	*a'*	*e''*	*e''*

[Ex a] Milanese mandolin   Neapolitan mandolin

Over the past century the very ubiquity of the mandolin has, ironically, caused it to be marginalized within the classical-music world. Although the quality of a well-made mandolin bears comparison with that of any other concert instrument, the average specimen offered for sale has usually been of a very poor standard of manufacture, leading many musicians to consider all mandolins to be inherently tinny and permanently out of tune. There are many fine pieces in the mandolin's repertoire, but the huge quantity of facile light music published for the instrument has tended to overshadow them. And, while numerous recordings (especially those made during the early decades of the twentieth century) testify to the astonishing technical and musical skills of many professional players, the mandolin has always held a particular appeal for amateurs because of the ease with which simple pieces can be performed upon it, leading some musicians to form low expectations of the instrument's potential, even in expert hands.

Fortunately, however, the mandolin's fortunes have considerably improved during the past decade, thanks to a rising generation of gifted performers, the continuing rediscovery of the seventeenth- and eighteenth-century repertoire, and an increasing number of new compositions for the instrument. It is my hope that this book will also play its small part in furthering the appreciation and rehabilitation of the classical mandolin.

Acknowledgements

Because the study of the mandolin has existed largely outside the formal academic music world, it would have been impossible to write this book without the help of countless mandolinists and mandolin organizations world-wide, who have kindly provided items from their private archives or given me the benefit of their expertise over the past decade. I have tried below to acknowledge all those who have helped with the writing of this book, and apologize to anyone I have inadvertently overlooked.

In Germany, Gertrud Weyhofen-Tröster, Marga Wilden-Hüsgen, and Gerda Wölki; in Britain, Barry Pratt, Nigel Woodhouse, Doug Parry, and R. H. Davis of the Brotherton Library, Leeds University; in France, Marcelle Gros Domergue, Christian Schneider, Marie-France Collerie de Borely, Françoise Granges, Didier Leroux, Jean-Paul Bazin, and Franc and Françoise Huber-Hulin; in Denmark, Mette Müller of the Musikhistorik Museum og Carl Claudius' Samling, Copenhagen, and Tove and Peter Flensborg; in Belgium, Robert Janssens, and Henri Gamblin; in Austria, Herta Habersam, and Ulrike Greiner-Eckhart; in Australia, Stephen Morey, and Kurt Jensen; in the USA, Neil Gladd and Norman Levine of Plucked String, Tony Williamson of Mandolin Central, Torrey and Calvin Burnett of Medway, Massachusetts, Hajime Kanehara of Ridgewood, New Jersey, David Grisman, and James and Joyce Tyler of Los Angeles; in Japan, Ken Tanioka, Rikio Ichige, Mrs Shiori Kobayashi of the Kunitachi Music College Library, Tokyo, Sanae Onji of Takarazuka, and Tetsuro Kudo; in Italy, Giovanna Berizzi, and Arena Anna ved. Calace; in Brazil, Paulo de Sá.

I would also like to thank my supervisors in the music departments of Sussex University (Jonathan Harvey, David Roberts, and David Osmond-Smith) and the City University (Malcolm Troup, Eric Clarke, and Richard Langham-Smith) for their assistance and encouragement during the early 1980s, when I first began my research; the late Marco Roccia for his mandolin restoration work, and for his many memories of his days in charge of the Clifford Essex workshops; Keith Harris for many helpful suggestions after his reading of the first draft of this book; the Japan Mandolin Union for making many items available to me in Western languages; Cisca van Heertum for heroically plugging the numerous gaps in my linguistic competence; my parents, Harry and Joan Sparks, for proof-reading the manuscript; and the late Hugo d'Alton, whose excellent performances and lifelong dedication to the mandolin attracted many musicians to the instrument, and first inspired me to begin my research. Lastly, my thanks to my wife, Tobey Burnett, for everything.

P.S.

West Knapton, Yorkshire
October, 1994

Contents

List of Illustrations

List of Music Examples

1

1815–1878

1.1 *The Decline of the Mandoline and Mandolino as Concert Instruments*

During the comparatively peaceful and prosperous decades that followed the end of the Napoleonic Wars in 1815, the mandoline and mandolino disappeared almost entirely from the major concert-halls of Europe. The last of the Italian mandolinists in Paris had already fled at the onset of the French Revolution. Bartholomeo Bortolazzi had left Vienna by the end of the wars, and only two resident mandolinists, both amateurs, are known to have continued performing there: André Oberleitner, who also composed some light music for the instrument, and Signor Fr. Mora de Malfatti, Beethoven's physician and the recipient of Hummel's *Grande sonata* for mandoline and piano. There was only one performer during the next thirty years who enjoyed an international reputation: Pietro Vimercati, a virtuoso whose family had been manufacturing stringed instruments since the mid-seventeenth century, first in Venice and later in Milan. After performing in Florence in 1808, Vimercati began touring Italy (often playing in the entr'actes at the Teatro Re in Milan), and made several European tours between 1823 and 1840, with regular concerts in London, Paris, and Vienna.[1] Although primarily a mandolino player, he often performed on the mandoline:

The King's Theatre, London. On the 8th of May, the night of Signor Curioni's benefit, Signor Vimercati, who was just arrived from Paris, performed an air with variations on the mandolin. This instrument is strung with wire, and is played with a plectrum, or piece of wood, held between the thumb and fore finger. The tone has not the sweetness that is yielded by catgut strings, but is more penetrating, and therefore better calculated for a capacious theatre, or large room. Signor V. has obtained great mastery over his instrument, and does wonders with it: the French

---

[1] Wölki (1984: 16), and the relevant entries in Vannes (1951) and Fétis (1873a). Wölki gives his date of birth as 1778.

accounts which we have received of him, are therefore not exaggerated. (*Harmonicon*, 1823: 85.)

Vimercati acquired a high reputation as a mandolin virtuoso. The influential Viennese critic Eduard Hanslick dubbed him 'the Giuliani of the mandoline', noting concert appearances in Vienna in 1820, 1826, and 1829.[2] Gustav Schilling called him 'the Paganini of the mandoline', and mentioned that he often performed violin concertos by Kreutzer and Rode on his instrument.[3] In his memoirs, the pianist and composer Ignaz Moscheles recalled a conversation he had once had with Rossini: 'He then talked of the specialities of the different instruments, and said that the guitarist [Fernando] Sor and the mandoline-player Vimercati proved the possibility of obtaining great artistic results with slender means. I happened to have heard both these artists, and could quite endorse his views.' (Coleridge 1873: ii. 271.)

In 1824, he performed again at the King's Theatre, and at the oratorios in London.[4] During his stay in the city a further concert took place at the New Argyll Rooms on 21 June, in which the 12-year-old Franz Liszt performed 'Di tanti palpiti' 'as a concertante with Signor Vimercati on his little mandolin'.[5] Vimercati toured Holland and Germany in 1835, Berlin and Weimar in 1836, and Russia in 1837, although he continued to live and teach in Milan, composing church music in addition to pieces for mandolin.[6] Many of his performances were reviewed by the *Harmonicon* which, although acknowledging his talent, usually offered equivocal praise:

M. Vimercati . . . is now exhibiting in Paris. He has already astonished Italy and Germany by the rapidity and grace with which he executed violin concertos on his instrument, the mandoline. The French connoisseurs, who were led by curiosity to visit him, found themselves irresistibly detained by admiration. (*Harmonicon*, 1823: 42.)

Vienna, Karnthnerthor Theatre . . . Signor Vimercati, the celebrated virtuoso on the mandoline, delighted the public with a series of variations composed by himself, to the Sicilian canzonetta, *Bandiera d'ogni vento*. The effect which he contrives to give to his apparently insignificant instrument is truly surprising; and he met with very warm encouragement. (*Harmonicon*, 1826: 227.)

Concerts of M. Hummel at Paris . . . M. Vimercati received the same applause for a very different sort of merit,—he executed a concerto on the mandoline. True connoisseurs are inclined to allow but little to the mere conquest of difficulties. The

---

[2] Hanslick (1869: i. 257). The comparison is with the celebrated guitarist Mauro Giuliani.
[3] Schilling (1835–40: vi. 773).   [4] Sainsbury (1825: ii. 507).   [5] Loesser (1954: 350).
[6] Schilling (1835–40: vi. 773).

composition of M. Vimercati was not in good taste. Why has he not dedicated to the harp, or even to the guitar, the immense time which he must have employed upon the mandoline, an ungrateful instrument, whose sharpness he will never soften, and whose dryness cannot be overcome. (*Harmonicon*, 1825: 99.)

These ambivalent reviews are symptomatic of a general lack of interest in (and widespread decline in the concert use of) all plucked instruments during the second and third quarters of the nineteenth century. The lute and harpsichord had been completely eclipsed, the guitar could boast only a few professional performers, and even the harp was seldom included in symphonic or chamber music, surviving mainly as a drawing-room instrument. The stringed instruments that now dominated the concert-hall were either struck or bowed—pianos and the violin family. Developments in piano design had resulted in instruments of formidable range and power, while the sustaining qualities of bowed strings ideally suited the extended melodic lines favoured by Romantic composers. Large public halls were built in great numbers, and composers wrote strident, powerful music to be played in them. In these altered circumstances the mandoline and mandolino fell completely out of favour with the art-music world.

In eighteenth-century opera, the mandoline had carved a niche for itself as the ideal accompaniment for the serenade, most notably in Mozart's *Don Giovanni*, a work whose continuing success and frequent staging ensured that the instrument was never completely forgotten. The Act II canzonetta 'Deh, vieni alla finestra' was, and still is, widely regarded as one of the most sublime moments in all operatic music and, in 'Namouna' (1832), Alfred de Musset analysed the song's enduring fascination, dwelling on the apparent dichotomy between voice and mandoline:

> Do you know, reader, the serenade
> That Don Juan sings, in disguise, beneath a balcony?
> A melancholy and piteous song
> Exuding pain, love, and sadness.
> But the accompaniment speaks with a different voice.
> How lively and joyful it is! With what agility
> It skips about!—One would say that the song caresses
> And covers with languor the perfidious instrument;
> Whereas the mocking air of the accompaniment
> Turns in derision on the song itself,
> And seems to jeer at it for proceeding so sadly.
> All this however gives extreme pleasure.—

> It is all true,—that one deceives and that one loves;
> That one weeps while laughing;—that one is innocent
> And guilty at the same time . . .

This appearance of Don Giovanni serenading beneath a balcony in Seville was, for most music-lovers of the time, their one overriding image of the mandoline, and was largely responsible for the widespread belief that the mandoline was a Spanish instrument rather than an Italian one, a misconception that was to be reinforced by events later in the century. But although Mozart's opera remained as popular as ever, the status of the mandoline plummeted, even in Paris where it had once been in such favour, as Berlioz (an accomplished guitarist and one of the few major composers of the period to show an interest in plucked string instruments) poignantly noted in 1843:

> The mandoline is today so neglected that, in the theatres where *Don Giovanni* is staged, it is always a problem to execute the Serenade. Although after a few days' study a guitarist or even a violinist can ordinarily familiarize himself with the fingerboard of the mandoline, there is so little respect in general for the intentions of the Great Masters, when it a question of the least departure from old habits, that it has become allowable almost everywhere, even at the Opéra (the last place in the world where one should take such a liberty), to play the mandoline part in *Don Giovanni* on pizzicato violins or on guitars. The timbre of these instruments does not have the piercing delicacy of that for which they substitute, and Mozart knew well what he was doing when he chose the mandoline to accompany the erotic song of his hero. (Berlioz 1843: 88.)

Georges Bizet was almost alone amongst opera composers in writing for the mandoline at this time, including it in one number of his early *opéra comique Don Procopio* (1859), but he also foresaw difficulty in finding a player, and allowed for substitution by a pizzicato violin. The large body of eighteenth-century mandoline music was neglected, and most composers now considered the instrument suitable only for a serenade, a plaintive, nostalgic form that found no sympathetic resonance in the progressive mid-nineteenth century aesthetic. In opera-houses the instrument was often reduced to the level of a mere theatrical prop, a plight aptly demonstrated by this extract from Act I of Daniel Auber's *Fra Diavolo* (1830):

> MATTEO [*takes down a mandoline from the wall and offers it to Zerlina*]. There child.

ZERLINA [*puts it beside her on a corner of the table*]. Thanks father; I would rather sing without it.

By mid-century, the mandolino was a forgotten instrument in most of Europe, while the mandoline was regarded as quaint and antique, although the latter's history had actually been a fairly brief one. Although rarely heard, it now became a symbol of a far-off age of pastoral simplicity and chaste seduction, and often appears in that guise in poems and songs of the day. 'That Mandolin Girl!' (London, 1861),[7] a setting by S. Nelson of a lyric by Edward J. Gill, is a rather clumsy attempt to conjure up a distant world of chivalry, damsels, and troubadours:

> I tell of love that pines away,
> Weeping with sad heart alone;
> While songs have I for wooers gay;
> That smile tho' love and truth are flown.
>
> With my merry Mandolin,
> Oft I sing of glory bright;
> Deeds of war that bring renown,
> Plumed helm, and belted knight.

A much better example is 'Mandoline, Sérénade', the second of *Six mélodies* (Paris, 1863)[8] by Gaetano Braga, an Italian cellist and composer who worked mainly in Paris and London. Eugène Bercioux's words evoke a bitter-sweet nocturnal world of unrequited love:

> Ah! A lone voice in the shadows sweetly raises itself,
> And sings in the night of its joy and its torment.
> Listen, in the sombre night; the voice of your beloved
> Whispers its song in the shadows, its joy and its torment.

In 1860, the great French poet Paul Verlaine had been deeply impressed by an exhibition in Paris of *fête galante* paintings by Jean-Antoine Watteau, and his own *Fêtes galantes* (1869) contains impressionistic paraphrases of many of the pictures, replete with pastoral serenading, innocent love-making, and references to figures from the *commedia dell'arte*. In Watteau's early eighteenth-century paintings the serenades were accompanied by guitar, but in Verlaine's work the instrument has become the more exotic mandoline:

---

[7] Voice and piano. Copy in the British Library, London: H. 1323. a (4).
[8] Voice and piano. Copy in the British Library, London: H. 1774. a (13).

Mandoline

The serenaders and their beautiful listeners
Exchange banal remarks beneath the singing boughs.
There is Tircis, there is Aminta, and there the eternal Clitander,
And there is Damis, composer of tender verses for cruel ladies.
Their short silk jackets, their long-trained dresses,
Their elegance, their joy, and their soft blue shadows
Swirl in the ecstasy of a pink and grey moon,
And the mandoline chatters among the trembling of the breeze.

The prevailing status of the mandoline was, in general, accurately summarized in this entry in a British encyclopaedia:

Mandoline—A musical instrument of the lute kind, but smaller, having four strings which are tuned as those of a violin. The mandoline is still met with occasionally in Italy, but has fallen into disuse in most other parts of Europe. (*The Penny Cyclopaedia*)

However, as we shall see, 'still met with occasionally in Italy' was a considerable understatement.

1.2 *Italy and the Creation of the Modern Mandolin*

In 1815 Italy remained a geographical and cultural entity, rather than a political one, with the north composed of several small states (some autonomous, others under Austrian rule), while the whole of the south comprised the Kingdom of the Two Sicilies, ruled by a Spanish branch of the Bourbon dynasty. However, during the period of French rule (1796–1814), Napoleon had briefly united these fragments into a single country, giving Italians their first glimpse of nationhood since the fall of the Roman Empire. Subsequently the desire for a sovereign, democratic Italy grew and, until Unification was achieved in 1861, became the overriding aspiration in the lives of most Italian artists and intellectuals.

Owing to the extreme political repression in most of the Italian states (which forced republican societies to meet in secrecy), opera became the principal rallying point for nationalist aspirations, achieving such popularity that it was no longer simply entertainment, but an integral and vital part of people's lives. There were opera-houses in some two hundred Italian towns, and the larger cities had performances almost all year round. Although not overtly political, many of the most popular operas dealt with the struggle for freedom from oppression, or retold stories of Italy's past greatness, sentiments that the population never tired of hearing. The operas of Rossini, Bellini, Donizetti, and Verdi (whose name became a nationalist rallying cry in the phrase 'Evviva Verdi', an acronym for 'Evviva Vittorio Emmanuale Re d'Italia') dominated cultural life, their sensuousness and natural expression making a direct appeal to Italians and unifying them in a way that literature could not, since the country then lacked a single common language.

This preoccupation with opera led to the almost total neglect of instrumental music, which had become the principal means of expression for most northern European composers. The French writer Stendhal was already noting during a visit to Italy in the 1820s that 'the art of instrumental music has wholly taken refuge among the peaceful, patient folk beyond the Rhine',[9] a state of affairs that continued throughout the century. Like many other foreign visitors, he was appalled at the poor standard of orchestral playing he encountered in a country where only the voice was now of interest, but was fascinated by the natural melodic fluency of the Italians: 'I have met with a score of young Neapolitans who could compose a song as unconcernedly as young men in London write letters, or young men in Paris pen sets of verses'.[10] Scarcely any significant Italian composer of the nineteenth century showed more than the most fleeting interest in orchestral or chamber music, regarding instruments mainly as a means of accompanying the human voice. Even Paganini, the most celebrated violinist of the century, often met with apathy in Italy. Faced with such indifference, it is scarcely surprising that Pietro Vimercati chose to spend much of his performing career abroad, touring in countries where instrumental music aroused more interest, although he did sometimes perform in Italy, usually between the acts of operas:

> Milan, Teatro Canobbiana . . . We had a visit from one of the first mandoline players of our time, Signor Vimercati, who has recently returned from his travels in France and England. He played a concerto between the acts, which obtained considerable applause, though this instrument is by no means a favourite here, and many a regret was expressed, that such talents should be wasted upon so inefficient an instrument. (*Harmonicon*, 1826: 61.)

---

[9] Stendhal (1956: 10).   [10] Stendhal (1956: 8–9).

Illustration 1. Giovanni Vailati playing a Milanese mandolin (from Bone 1972).

Apart from Vimercati, there were few others to bring the instrument to the attention of the concert-going public. Luigi Castellaci, a guitarist and man-dolinist from Pisa, began to tour Europe in 1820 and spent many years in Paris, where he apparently published pieces for both instruments.[11] Cavaliere Carlo Antonio Gambara, a composer who studied in Parma, is said to have composed a quintet for mandolin, harp, violin, viola, and cello during this period.[12] But the only mid-century artist worthy of comparison to Vimercati was Giovanni Vailati (Illustration 1), a blind mandolino player from Crema, near Milan.[13] This sympathetic review of an appearance in Florence shows how unusual it had become, by 1855, to hear any type of mandolin in the concert-hall:

Teatro Pagliano . . . An honourable mention is also due to Prof. Vailati, who played on the mandolin a beautiful fantasia on *Sonnambula*. Exceptional, not to say unique,

[11] Castellaci: b. Pisa, 1797, d. Paris, after 1845, according to Bone (1972: 75–6).   [12] Bone (1972: 128).
[13] Vailati: b. Crema, n. Milan, *c.*1813, d. Crema, 25 Nov. 1890. According to Janssens (1982: 33), Vailati lost his sight at the age of 15, but the *Gazzetta musicale di Firenze* (19 July 1855: 21) states that he had been blind since birth. The *Banjo World* (Dec. 1896: 21) mentions that he appeared in a number of London theatres *c.*1876, per-forming transcriptions of various overtures, including the one to Rossini's *William Tell*.

is the ability of this artist who, from what is certainly not the most obliging of instruments, draws delicate sounds, and passionate, enchanting melodies. It is not an exaggeration to assert that one is not only surprised but affected to think one is listening to the neglected mandolin, and to feel it the most agreeable of the stringed instruments. The pianissimo which he executes is incredible, and was perhaps not sufficiently appreciated in the excessive vastness of the theatre; no less a merit is the sustaining of the instrument's voice like a violin, a thing that seems impossible, yet it is not so for Vailati. The reception on this evening was very flattering, following which we prophesy even greater. (*Gazzetta musicale di Firenze*, 28 June 1855: 12.)

From a financial standpoint this prophecy was cruelly mistaken, as Vailati found out when he staged a benefit concert in Florence a few weeks later, on 14 July at the Sala dell'Arte. However, the reviewer was clearly even more impressed by his artistry on this occasion, and the *Gazzetta* devoted its front page to an extended tribute:

The Teatro Pagliano already knew of his ability, and a large audience deservedly applauded him. Last Saturday evening Vailati put on a benefit concert; but his expectation was disappointed, because the hall was almost empty. Oh Art! when so little encouraged or protected . . .

The performer magnificently executed a grand fantasia composed especially for the mandolin on themes from *Trovatore*. Sig. E. Testa made his beautiful tenor voice heard in a romanza. Next Vailati played *Il Carnevale di Venezia*, a piece in which he drew out many beautiful effects. Following this, sig. Ettore Corti performed to applause the baritone aria from *Luisa Miller*.

The second part opened with the aria from *Trovatore* beautifully sung by signora Laura Giordano, an artist well known through her appearances at the Teatro Pagliano. The *concertista* then, with the mandolin *on one string only*, played variations on *Sonnambula* with true mastery.[14] The signori Capriles and Corti sang the duo from *Puritani* very well. The concert ended with the *concertista* playing 'Casta diva' perfectly.

We finish this report with a wish that signor Vailati meets with better luck in the future, as he deserves. (*Gazzetta musicale di Firenze*, 19 July 1855, 21.)

This story of the mandolin's progress in the nineteenth-century concert-hall has so far been rather a bleak one, with a few Italian virtuosi performing transcriptions of violin concertos and sets of variations on operatic melodies,

---

[14] *La sonnambula* is an opera by Bellini. The playing of elaborate variations on a single string (usually the *g*) was a favourite virtuoso violin technique, originated by Paganini.

battling away on behalf of their instrument in the face of general public indifference. To see a healthier picture of the instrument's fortunes, we need to turn our attention away from the formal concert world, and look instead at how it was incorporated into the recreational music-making of ordinary Italian people.

In central Italy, it was customary for young men to perform *stornelli* and *rispetti* (traditional forms of Tuscan song) to young women as part of the courtship ritual. The *stornello* was a three-lined poem pleading for love, usually sung in a minor key to a mandoline accompaniment on a summer evening. There are many traditional *stornelli*, although the performer often made up his own or modified existing ones to suit the needs of the moment. The *rispetto* was a longer form (most commonly six lines), a respectful greeting from the lover to his beloved, sung to an improvised guitar or mandoline accompaniment. The more uninhibited and gregarious went even further:

> In the Tuscan mountains at all seasons, even in winter, the Serenata or Inserenata are common. This means that a party of youths armed with guitars, mandolines or violins will set forth after sunset to sing of the love, hopes or sorrows of one of their number under the window of the girl he woos. The verses are alternated with brief instrumental melodies, brightly decorated with shakes and arpeggi. In many districts these melodies are called Passagalli, a characteristically Tuscan word to designate this method of playing the violin, guitar or mandoline to fill in the short pauses between the singing, that allow time for the Improviser, for these verses are usually improvised, to collect his thoughts and ideas. Such parties of singing swains have been known to continue their exercises from sunset to sunrise. (Zimmern 1906: 253.)

The further south one moved though Italy, the more frequently one encountered festivals which, while Christian in intention, were in practice little more than excuses for revelry. The Danish painter Wilhelm Marstrand captured this carefree spirit splendidly in his *October Festival Evening outside the Walls of Rome* (Illustration 2). The local peasantry are dressed in traditional costumes, and a couple dances to the rhythm of tambourines, with harmony and melody supplied by guitar and mandoline (the latter's construction appearing identical to the original Neapolitan design of almost a century earlier). Twenty years later Denis O'Donovan described the frenzy of the Roman Carnival, and noted how lower-class girls saved throughout the year so as to appear well attired and travel in style during these important days of the social calendar:

> Often no less than ten of these fair ones may be seen packed into one open carriage—two seated on the reversed cover, and one—she to whom the palm of beauty

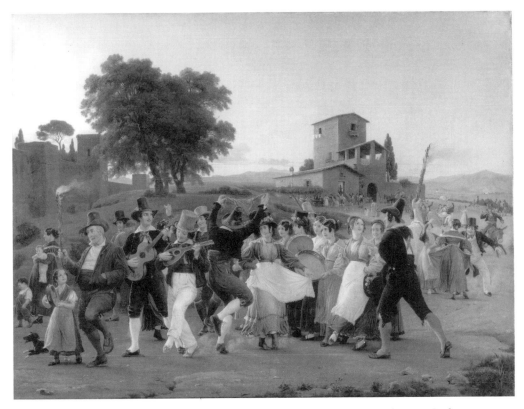

Illustration 2. Wilhelm Nicolai Marstrand (1810–73): detail from *October Festival Evening outside the Walls of Rome* (Rome, 1839; photograph courtesy of the Thorvaldsens Museum, Copenhagen).

is adjudged—enjoying the post of honour beside the coachman. And as these decimal bevies flash gaily by with music of mandoline or basque-tambour, they form a delightful accessory to the general brilliancy of the spectacle. (O'Donovan 1859: 122.)

A decade later, the young French composer Émile Paladilhe published 'Mandolinata (souvenir de Rome)' (Paris, 1869),[15] a fine song that atmospherically captures the hopes and fears of a group of serenaders. The front cover (Illustration 3) depicts a male quartet making music beneath a balcony[16] while two women look down, and one lets a flower drop to the ground. The words of the song relate the emotions of the performers:

[15] There are copies of two versions for voice and piano in the British Library, London: H. 1774. g (15 & 16). The latter has Italian words by A. P***, the former a Fr. adaptation of them by R. Bussine J[ne.]

[16] Despite the title of the song, the unknown artist has depicted what appear to be types of colascione (a long-necked southern Italian lute), rather than mandolines.

Illustration 3. Title-page of Émile Paladilhe's 'Mandolinata (souvenir de Rome)' (Paris, 1869). Photograph courtesy of the British Library.

> Friends, the night is fine, the moon will shine.
> By its light, in liberty, friends, we will dream.
> The love that calls us tells us we have to love;
> Sighs and tears, sadness and pain, we throw flowers on them all!
>
> Soon we'll see the curtains start to open as though a zephyr were blowing,
> And her shadow will glide by in the distance, like a sigh.
> A lily will fall, run! The flower is over there.
> Which of us shall have it, look for it!
> The lover will know where it is, look for it!
> The lover will know where it is, only he will know, and won't stop singing!

The piano accompaniment is imaginatively arranged by Camille Saint-Saëns, who takes every opportunity to evoke still further the authentic sounds of this nocturnal scene. The bare opening chords are marked 'the arpeggios very dry, almost like struck or plucked chords', and later this imitation of the simple strumming of a guitar in the bass supports a rapid tremolo mandoline-style melody (Ex. 1).

Ex. 1. Paladilhe: 'Mandolinata', bars 80–90

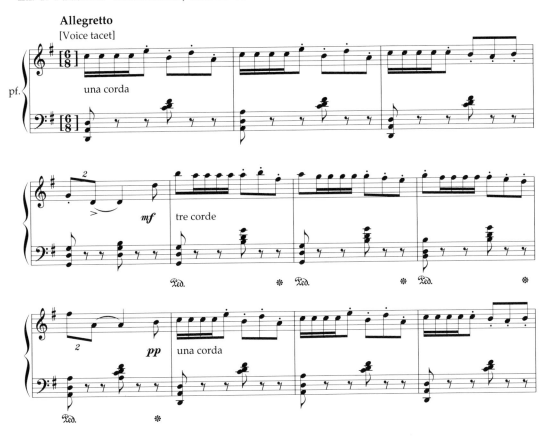

South of Rome lay the Kingdom of the Two Sicilies and its capital Naples, the largest and wealthiest city in Italy and the home of the mandoline (which had been developed by Neapolitan luthiers during the 1740s). The Bourbons still ruled their lands on feudal lines, lavishing vast amounts of money on their favourite city at the expense of the rest of their subjects. While the peasantry starved throughout the rural south, the Kingdom of the Two Sicilies became richer than all the other Italian states put together, and Naples developed into one of the most modern and fashionable cities in Europe. Street lighting, railways, an undersea telegraph, and a host of other modern amenities were installed long before any other part of Italy acquired them, while huge subsidies ensured that the San Carlo opera-house maintained its international reputation. No British aristocrat could claim to have completed the Grand Tour unless his itinerary had included a lengthy stay in Naples.

One unfortunate aspect of life on which visitors frequently remarked was the huge number of *lazzaroni* or destitute beggars they saw in the city (estimated at 40,000 out of a population of 300,000 in 1830).[17] To quell potential unrest in the capital, state grants were paid to these urban poor, leaving them idle but not hungry, a policy that fostered Naples's already mixed reputation as a city of street musicians and petty criminals. While the latter were a source of constant irritation to travellers, the former added greatly to the city's piquancy for foreigners, whose first impression was often of singing, noise, and a teeming mass of humanity. Peter Gunn offers this description of daily life alongside the Porto di Santa Lucia in the 1850s, near the Caffè di Europa where fashionable society would relax after hearing an opera at San Carlo:

> ... the raucous cries of the street vendors, the shouts of the *lazzaroni* who seemed unable to carry on a conversation except at the top of their voices; the music that was heard everywhere, from wandering mandolins and guitars or from street and military bands; and the clamour of bells from a hundred churches and convents. (Quoted in Seward 1984: 289.)

The Swedish novelist Fredrika Bremer spent the summer of 1858 in Naples, at the Villa Pisani, where she was often entertained by these musicians:

> Our villa acquired also new life from the wandering troubadours who came in the evening with their guitar or mandolin and sang Neapolitan songs, or played to the boys who danced the tarantella. These natural singers have neither pure nor beautiful voices, but they are often strong, and always full of expression; and they sing the fascinating folk-song, 'Santa Lucia', with a passion which made the heart beat, spite of the false notes of the song. ... The bright side of the natural and popular life of Naples is expressed in the words and music of this song. (Bremer 1861: ii. 302.)

In addition to traditional folksongs and operatic excerpts, street musicians performed Neapolitan popular songs, a genre which was closely identified after 1835 with the annual summer festival of the Madonna at Piedigrotta, a village just outside the capital. Both amateur and professional composers entered the contest there each year, and the winning entry was certain to be sung for many years to come, not just in Naples but throughout Italy. The style owed much to street song and to Lieder, with strong melodies that juxtaposed simple lyrical passages with sudden dramatic moves to remote tonalities, and

---

[17] Leeds (1974: 27).

accompaniments that were often harmonically surprising, with a taste for chords built on the flattened supertonic or flattened submediant. Popular subjects were the pleasures and pains of love, the glories of the sun and the sea, the splendour of Naples and its surroundings, and the sadness of having to leave the beloved city. Printed editions of these songs were intended for drawing-room performance and therefore usually had a piano part, but their natural habitat was a Neapolitan street, where they were performed from memory to the accompaniment of a mandoline or a guitar, very much like folksongs, for which visitors like Bremer often mistook them. Teodoro Cottrau, composer of 'Addio, mia bella Napoli' and the world-famous 'Santa Lucia' (1849), was perhaps the most successful Piedigrotta contestant of the mid-nineteenth century.

The instruments in general use at this time were similar to the first mandolines designed by the Vinaccia family in Naples in about 1744, and copied by many other makers: ten frets on a fingerboard lying flush with the table to which some additional frets were glued, three pairs of brass strings and one pair of gut, all tuned with wooden pegs and plucked with a quill. Although the export market for these instruments had disappeared by 1815, Gaetano Vinaccia continued to make mandolines in this style for local consumption, in the old family workshop in the rua Catalana, until his death after 1831. It fell to his son Pasquale to bring the mandolin into a more modern age, redesigning it and producing a new type of instrument that would appeal to concert artists as much as to street singers.

There are many ways of describing the evolution of art music during the nineteenth century, but perhaps the simplest observation is that it got a great deal louder. Not only did orchestras double or triple in size, but nearly all the individual instruments were redesigned to produce a greater volume of sound and to extend their upper range. The violin fingerboard was raised and extended, its body was strengthened to support higher-tension strings, and a heavier, longer bow was used. On the piano, strong metal frames replaced weaker wooden ones and, by the early 1830s, advances in industrial processes had produced a high-tension steel which could be used to make durable and powerful strings. The guitar too was changing, adopting an extended fingerboard and higher-tension strings and, from the early 1820s, replacing wooden tuning-pegs with more accurate metal, screw-thread machine heads. Over the next few decades these new features became the norm, as makers copied each other and new instruments gradually ousted old ones.

Pasquale Vinaccia was influenced by these alterations in violin, piano, and guitar construction when he designed the modern Neapolitan mandolin in about 1835. He raised and extended the fingerboard, increasing the number of frets to seventeen and the mandolin's upper limit to *a'''*. He deepened the bowl for greater resonance, strengthened the body, increased the size and weight of the whole instrument, and was then able to fit strings made from the new high-tension steel, the upper two courses plain, the lower two wound with copper. Machine heads, essential when tuning such sensitive strings, were also adopted. A quill was not robust enough to pluck the thin steel and was replaced by a plectrum made from tortoiseshell, a commodity readily available in southern Italy, where it had long been an important export. This was Pasquale Vinaccia's revolutionary design and, although individual makers have since modified many of its details, it has remained the standard form of the mandolin in Europe for the past century and a half.

For several decades the mandoline and the new mandolin coexisted in Naples, with the latter gaining in popularity at the expense of the former. Given the comparative poverty of most of the indigenous players, and the natural conservatism of musicians, it seems probable that most mandoline players would have continued to use their existing instruments for as long as possible. However, the greater volume of sound produced by the new mandolin, and the more extrovert style of playing that it allowed, must have gradually overcome the reservations of those used to the older, more intimate instrument. Just as many old wooden-frame pianos were accidentally destroyed in this period by performers attempting to play them more loudly than their makers had ever intended, and many old violins imploded when fitted with high-tension strings in a quest for extra decibels, so many old mandolines must also have come to an untimely end during the next few years, as their owners overstrung them in the hope of equalling the volume of a new Vinaccia mandolin.

Although almost no written mandolin music from the seventeenth and eighteenth centuries used the tremolo[18] other than as an occasional ornament, we know that this distinctive and idiomatic technique had long been common amongst street musicians. For instance, the Parisian mandolinist Giovanni Fouchetti had noted in 1771 that there were players in Italy (whom he called *Pétacheux* and likened to village fiddlers) who constantly used tremolo.[19]

---

[18] Alternate up and down plectrum-strokes on a single note, performed very rapidly to give the illusion of a sustained tone.

[19] Fouchetti (1771: 6). See also the discussion in Tyler and Sparks (1989: 118–21).

During the first half of the nineteenth century, when the instrument was neglected by the art-music world, the large repertoire of notated instrumental music for mandolino and mandoline was completely forgotten, as was the single-stroke style of playing. Mandolins continued to be played tremolo-style by street musicians, the adoption of steel strings encouraging still further a legato, cantabile style with a powerful tone containing more high harmonics than were obtainable from a gut or brass string. By mid-century, no mandolinist would think of playing any but the shortest notes of a melody without tremolo.

Although the Vinaccia family also made guitars, they were particularly associated with the manufacture of mandolins. For a long time no other Neapolitan maker could rival their instruments, but another dynasty emerged to challenge their supremacy as the century progressed. Nicola Calace, the son of Michele (a pharmacist), was born in 1794 in Pignolo near Cosenza, in the far south of Italy. He belonged to the Carbonari, a secret republican society which took part in an unsuccessful uprising against the Bourbons in the 1820s, as a result of which he fled north in about 1825 to the small island of Procida, just off the coast of Naples. There he established a workshop, making mostly guitars and some mandolins until his death in 1869. His son Antonio, born on Procida in 1828, moved the business to premises at Strada mezzo-canone no. 32 in Naples, and acquired a reputation as a fine maker of guitars and mandolins. He was awarded a silver medal at the Palermo Exposition in 1872, and died in 1876 after fathering two sons (Nicola, born 1859, and Raffaele, born 1863), of whom we shall hear much more in due course.[20]

In the north of Italy, the mandolino was also undergoing a transformation. Its double strings were replaced with six single ones and, although these were still made from gut (or metal wound on silk for the lowest courses), their weight and tension was increased. Frets were now always made from metal rather than from pieces of gut tied around the neck, the fingerboard was hollowed out so that the spaces between frets were slightly concave, the body became fatter, and the resonating chamber increased in size. The most notable makers (although it is uncertain whether they were the first to redesign the mandolino) were the Monzino family of Milan, hence this new instrument became known as the Milanese (or Lombardian) mandolin. The family had

[20] Biographical information on the Calace family throughout this book has been taken from various sources: correspondence with Arena Anna ved. Calace; *Dizionario biografico degli italiani*; Vannes (1951); and *Enciclopedia della musica*.

Illustration 4. A Portuguese guitar, a bandurria, and a Milanese mandolin (an advertisement from Bone 1914).

first come to prominence there in 1750, when Antonio I founded a workshop for mandolinos and guitars in the Contrada della Dognana. After his death in 1800, he was succeeded by Giacomo Antonio II, a violinist and guitarist, and by Antonio III, who seems to have been largely responsible for building up the reputation of the Monzino family business.[21] The single strings were less conducive to a smooth tremolo than double courses, and the Milanese mandolin also lacked the volume of the steel-strung Neapolitan instrument. But, while it was never to become anything like as popular as its southern relative, it was widely played in the northern Italian states and, as we have already seen, was Vailati's chosen instrument (Illustrations 1 and 4 depict a Milanese mandolin).

The course of the mandolin's history was to change in the wake of the dramatic events of 1859–61, when the Austrians were expelled from the north, the Bourbons from the south, and Italy finally became a unified kingdom. Although this revolution was welcomed by liberals everywhere, many Neapolitans saw it not as liberation but as annexation, a conquest of the rich south by the

[21] Vannes (1951).

envious north, while many northerners regarded the south as a backward, primitive region, fit only for plundering. Under the new national government, based in the north, Naples rapidly fell from being the most advanced and prosperous Italian city to one of the poorest, with too many inhabitants and no clear role in the new nation. Its people already had a long tradition of emigration—for example, the opera-houses of Europe had relied for centuries on the seemingly inexhaustible stream of itinerant Neapolitan singers, composers, and musicians who sought their fortunes abroad—but after 1860 this process accelerated, with huge numbers of mostly unskilled people leaving to escape from starvation, epidemics, and poverty, and with no intention of ever returning home. By 1870 there were about a million Italians (mostly southerners) living abroad,[22] chiefly in the USA, South America, and northern Europe, and the numbers kept increasing. Naturally these emigrants took the most readily transportable parts of their culture with them: their distinctive, nostalgic Neapolitan songs, and the mandolins and guitars necessary to accompany them.

After Unification, Italian intellectuals and liberals sought ways to unite the fledgeling nation culturally as well as politically, and the woman who came to personify the artistic aspirations of the new Italy was Princess (from 1878, Queen) Margherita of Savoy. Victor Emmanuel II of Sardinia had been crowned king of the new Italy in 1861 and, when the beautiful and artistic Margherita married his son Umberto I in 1869, she utterly captured the hearts of a nation desperate for a symbol of its own identity. The historian Benedetto Croce said that she 'possessed, in addition to her warm sympathy and enchanting smile, a love of poetry and the arts. She seemed indeed to be herself a poem, a true incarnation of the ideal Queen of Italy, land of the arts and of all things beautiful.' (Croce 1929: 81.)

Although modest royal accomplishments are sometimes exaggerated by tactful commentators, there is no doubt that Princess Margherita was an extremely cultured and knowledgeable woman, with a particular talent for singing, and for playing plucked instruments (this latter skill was celebrated by the leading Italian poet Giosuè Carducci in his poem of 1889, 'Il liuto e la lira'). She is thought to have possessed a mandolin as early as 1865, constructed for her by the Roman maker Petroni,[23] and her interest in the instrument seems

---

[22] Gallengha (1875: 298–300).

[23] This instrument has (unusually for an Italian mandolin) a Portuguese style of radial screw-head, of the type depicted in Illus. 4. It is now held at the Victoria and Albert Museum in London (924–1902), together with its wooden case bearing the royal coat of arms.

to have grown after her marriage to Umberto I. The newly-wed couple spent most of 1869 and 1870 in Naples, during which time Pasquale Vinaccia built a mandolin especially for the princess. In 1870, when Rome finally became part of the kingdom of Italy, the couple moved to the Quirinal Palace, and during these years she kindled an interest amongst the upper classes of both cities in what had hitherto been considered a lowly instrument: 'To her lively interest for the instrument we owe its popularity in Italy. At first the ladies of the court took it up as a fad but soon the fondness spread to all classes, high and low took pleasure in playing.' (*Mandoline: Internationales Musik-Journal*, 14 Mar. 1904: 2–3.)

Curiously, although the south was held in low esteem in the new Italy, many aspects of pre-Unification southern culture were greatly admired throughout the country. For all their many faults, the Bourbons had at least lived permanently in Naples and ruled the south as an autonomous kingdom, thereby ensuring a continuity of tradition. The north, by contrast, had consisted mostly of small states, frequently changing hands between various foreign rulers, each of whom imposed aspects of their own culture on to the people. The south had little political power now, but it was felt to be the custodian of the values of the true Italy, and possessor of the authentic and unadulterated voice of the nation. The increasing popularity of the humble but quintessentially Italian mandolin, played in the singing tremolo style associated with Neapolitan street musicians, was one manifestation of this: '. . . it met with more approval and in Rome Bertucci, called "Ragazzino di Borgo" because he was a child of the lower classes and lived in one of the Borghi, worked at its improvement.' (*Mandoline: Internationales Musik-Journal*, 14 Mar. 1904: 2–3.)

Constantino Bertucci had begun playing the mandolin as a child, studying with another Roman, Francesco Finestauri (popularly known as 'Checco de Nonna'). Bertucci's reputation was enhanced when Princess Margherita took lessons from him, a favour she also bestowed on Belisario Matera in 1873, and on Giuseppe Bellenghi. Bellenghi, a Florentine, had started his professional career as an orchestral cellist but, in about 1870, he began to teach the mandolin. This instrument became so popular that he was soon giving instruction full-time, and helping to promote concerts that featured it.

Two mandolin-makers who were later to become pre-eminent in their profession were also beginning their careers in Rome at this time: Giovanni De Santis, who had begun as a harp- and piano-maker in Paris before opening his own workshop in Rome making pianos, harps, mandolins, violins, and guitars;

and Luigi Embergher, who came from the small village of Arpino, some fifty miles south-east of Rome, and worked as a cabinet-maker before opening his own musical instrument manufacturing house in 1870.[24] Although this was based in Rome, many of the instruments appear to have been built in a workshop in his native Arpino.

Unification affected the music publishing business in Italy, severely damaging it in Naples (the only Italian city where it had hitherto been thriving) but helping it to flourish further north, especially in Milan. At least two notable teachers published books of instruction for the mandolin during this period: the Neapolitan Carmine De Laurentiis in 1869 (Ricordi, Milan),[25] and Giuseppe Branzoli, who produced a two-volume method in 1875 (Franchi, Milan). Branzoli was a Roman composer and instrumentalist who worked during the 1850s as a viola player in various orchestras, and in 1858 became a member of the Accademia filarmonica romana. He was also a professor at the Accademia di S. Cecilia, a serious academic, and a significant figure in Roman musical life, the mandolin being just one of his many interests.[26]

At the start of 1878, the mandolin remained virtually unknown to most people outside Italy. Nevertheless, it was acquiring a considerable amateur following within that country, and was also beginning to be played for recreational purposes in other countries, in Europe and in North and South America, within their steadily growing communities of Italian immigrants.

---

[24] Vannes (1951) and others give these dates, according to which Embergher must have started his own business at the age of 14.

[25] Grove (1878–90: ii. 205) mentions this tutor, although only Bone (1972: 203) suggests that it was published as early as 1869.

[26] *Dizionario biografico degli italiani* and Bone (1972: 58–9). Only Bone suggests that it was published as early as 1875.

2

1878–1892

2.1 *The Paris Exhibition of 1878*

The second half of the nineteenth century was a time of extremely rapid technical and industrial advances, achievements celebrated at the international exhibitions which were regularly held in major European (and later North American) cities. The Great Exhibition of 1851, which took place at the Crystal Palace in London, had been the first, but those held every eleven years in Paris were probably the most cosmopolitan and varied cultural and commercial events that the world had yet seen. Lasting for several months and visited by millions, these vast exhibitions embraced not only the whole of industry (including all aspects of musical instrument manufacture), but every manifestation of human culture then known to the West, offering Europeans the rare chance to encounter all manner of exotic art, music, and dance.

The Palais du Trocadéro was built especially for the exhibition of 1878, and offered a showcase for musicians to perform to the international public who had gathered in Paris. A few of the growing number of Italian mandolinists were tempted to travel to France and, while there, booked the hall and put on their own concerts. Bertucci gave a successful performance there with a mandolin orchestra, and subsequently achieved considerable popularity in France.[1] Giuseppe Silvestri, a leading Neapolitan teacher and performer, played there in September, attracting a huge crowd and the undiluted admiration of the critic of *L'Art musical*, who spoke of:

> this instrument, once neglected but nowadays back in fashion in Italy. Its sounds, so meagre when produced by other hands, resemble those of the violin or cello when M. Silvestri is drawing them out, and when they mingle with the obedient, satisfying, and protective harmonies from the piano . . .
>
> Italian right through to his fingertips—to those two fingers that with such mastery guide the little point of the tortoiseshell over the double strings of his dainty

[1] Janssens (1982: 30).

instrument—M. Silvestri had chosen, for his Sunday concert, some of the most beautiful pages of the Italian masters; fantasias on *Norma*, on *Lucrezia Borgia*, on *La traviata:* Bellini, Donizetti, Verdi. However, to demonstrate that the virtuoso also doubles as composer, he alternated these great pieces with three others of his own: a concert waltz entitled *Sport*; a *fantasie caractéristique* which he named *Pausilippe et Pincio* in memory of Naples, his homeland, and Rome, his country's capital and cradle of the arts; and a pot-pourri on popular Neapolitan melodies . . .

The audience was really under his spell, they cried 'Bravo!' during the performance of the six encore pieces, they applauded lengthily and noisily at the end.

The concert over, the mandolinist was surrounded, congratulated, acclaimed. The one who complimented him most, and addressed some of the most flattering words, was Commander Correnti, the Italian Commissioner General at the Universal Exposition. (*L'Art musical*, 26 Sept. 1878: 308.)

As a result of this favourable response, Silvestri began to divide his time between Paris and Naples, becoming a celebrated performer and teacher in both cities. Within a few years his popularity was sufficient for an outraged correspondent to *L'Art musical* to object (albeit in somewhat ironically exaggerated language) that he was causing members of the Parisian public to neglect the piano in favour of:

an instrument appreciated primarily in courtyards and in fashionable Flemish taverns at the moment . . .

Apparently this artist [Silvestri] departs each year from Paris, where he spends his holidays, with dislocated limbs and bruises all over his body, so manhandled is he by those who wish to hear him play a serenade or a barcarole. Pupils are on the look-out for M. Silvestri, who comes here to rest, and implore him so much to give them lessons that he is forced to accede to the wishes of the charming ladies making the requests. (*L'Art musical*, 1 June 1882: 171.)

But for us, the most significant performance at the Paris Exhibition was given not by an Italian mandolinist but by a group of bandurria players from Madrid, known as the Estudiantes Españoles, or Spanish Students.[2] Their concerts attracted widespread attention at the Exhibition and, in order to understand subsequent developments in our own instrument's history, it is necessary for us now to examine the contribution that Spanish musicians made

---

[2] The *New York Times* (2 Jan. 1880: 8) mentions their successes at the Paris Exhibition. The bandurria, a Spanish instrument with some similarities to (but a quite separate history from) the mandolin, is depicted in Illus. 4 and described more fully in Ch. 2.2 and the App.

in preparing the ground for the mandolin's general popularity throughout Europe and the Americas.

2.2 *Spanish Influences*

During the eighteenth century there had been close cultural links between Spain and the Neapolitan kingdom, which was ruled by Bourbons of Spanish descent. However, the musical influence was almost entirely one-way, with Italian opera completely overshadowing the native Spanish *zarzuela*,[3] and Spanish composers being expected to write in the Italian style. Italian opera continued to be extremely popular there throughout the nineteenth century but, after the Napoleonic wars, a new generation of Spanish composers strove to re-establish their national musical language by reviving the *zarzuela* and adopting a distinctly Spanish style. One of the most influential of these composers was Francisco Asenjo Barbieri, who had begun his musical career as a humble street musician, and whose singing and bandurria playing remained famous throughout his lifetime; in his *zarzuela Pan y toros* (1864), he became one of the first Spanish composers to use bandurrias on stage.[4]

During the first half of the nineteenth century, the role and status of the bandurria in Spain was very similar to that of the mandolin in Italy; a high-pitched, plucked instrument used by ordinary people throughout the country for serenading, sometimes with tremolo technique, and usually together with the guitar. In Aragon, guitars and bandurrias were used to perform the jota, a rapid triple-time dance, and *rondalla aragonesa* became the name given to any group of youths in the region who sang and played in the streets at night, accompanying themselves on bandurrias and various types of guitar. Further south, the instrument also frequently took part in the accompaniment to the Malagueña (a form of Andalusian song).

In university towns such as Salamanca it was customary, at certain times of the year, for students to dress up in national costume and perform traditional songs with guitars and bandurrias, believing that this would guarantee good luck in the forthcoming examinations; such groups of musicians, roaming the streets, were known as *estudiantinas*. In 1878 or a little earlier, several bandurria-players and guitarists in Madrid formed themselves into a professional

---

[3] A type of musical stage play, incorporating strongly nationalist musical idioms and a Spanish text.
[4] Chase (1959: 135).

group, known as the Spanish Students. They soon became well known local-
ly, and a composition by Isidoro Hernandez, 'Mandolinata de Los Estudiantes:
serenata española', published in Madrid in 1878, was dedicated 'A los Estudiantes
Españoles'.[5] In the same year they began to tour Europe (including the Paris
Exhibition), and they appeared in London in 1879, their instrumentation then
consisting of eleven bandurrias and six guitars.[6] They left London on 10
December 1879, sailing from Southampton to the USA:

> The Spanish student troupe of musicians . . . arrived in this city, from London, on
> the steamship *France*, of the National Line, yesterday morning . . . They were dri-
> ven to the pier of the Fall River Boats, and, at 4:30 o'clock, they took the steam-
> boat *Old Colony* for Boston. There they will appear tonight in connection with
> Abbey's 'Humpty-Dumpty' combination which has been playing for some time
> in the Park Theatre. The troupe will hardly fail to prove a novelty with their
> double-stringed instruments and in the unique costumes of the students of the Spanish
> colleges . . . Their instruments comprise five guitars, nine mandolins,[7] and a violin,
> all of which have double the number of strings of the ordinary instruments, the
> guitars having 14 and 16 strings, and the mandolins 12. The oldest of the students
> is the leader, Signor Ignacio Martin, who is 35 . . . The excellence of their perform-
> ances gave them a wide reputation all over Europe, and they have travelled through
> France, Italy, Austria, Belgium, Germany, Russia, and England, playing in the cap-
> itals and principal cities of each country. Mr Abbey secured their services through
> a London dramatic agent, agreeing to pay their transportation expenses to this
> country, and $1,200 a week salary for the season of 1880. (*New York Times*, 2 Jan.
> 1880: 8.)

The precise number of performers in the troupe varied with almost every
report (averaging about twenty to twenty-two men, with between eleven and
thirteen bandurrias and six or seven guitars), but what is certain is that they
enjoyed a sensational and prolonged success in America. They played in
theatres where entertainment value was more important than artistic merit, yet
their act succeeded in combining the two, captivating audiences with its intrigu-
ing new sound, distinctive national costumes, and a repertoire of 150 pieces
that included sonatas by Mozart and Beethoven, Spanish and Polish dances,
and orchestral overtures, all performed entirely from memory:

---

[5] There are versions for voice and piano, and piano solo. Copies in the British Library, London: H. 1786. c
(24).

[6] Grove (1878–90: ii. 205).

[7] This confusion between the bandurria and the mandolin shows once again how unclear the distinction between
the two instruments was in the minds of most people at this time.

Perhaps the most meritorious and charming of all was that which riveted attention when the Spanish students came upon the scene, in their darkly picturesque attire, performing melodies in which the true soul of music was perceivable. It was this that raised the performance out of the level of mere fun and gaudy splendor ... (*New York Times*, 4 Feb. 1880.)

The second concert, last night, at Booth's Theatre attracted a large audience, and was above the average merit of similar entertainments. The performance of the Spanish Students was an interesting feature. They played an arrangement of the overture to Flotow's 'Marta', which was remarkably well done, and, considering the resources of the mandolin and guitar, was effective. They were, of course, several times recalled and responded with Spanish dance music in their best manner. The unity and finish which these gentlemen show is worthy of praise, though the nature of the instruments they use makes it impossible that they should do more than light and trivial work. The novelty and originality of the music they offered are, however, sufficiently attractive to please an audience, and their proficiency in all they undertake disarms any criticism as to its character. (*New York Times*, 16 Feb. 1880.)

The Spanish Students had various leaders including Denis Granada (who also composed the popular 'El Turia' waltzes), Ignacio Martin, Melquiades Hernandez, and, later, Señor Garcia.[8] The bandurrias were gut-strung and, although only two men in the entire troupe could read music, all accounts testify that their ensemble playing and shading of tone were quite superb. They appear to have returned to Spain in 1881, and then travelled the following year to Mexico, touring both North and South America before finally disbanding in Buenos Aires in 1885.[9]

Their tremendous success made a deep impression on many Italian immigrants, newly arrived in the USA and looking for ways to better themselves. They saw a chance, now that the original performers had returned to Spain, to capitalize on their popularity by pretending to be the Spanish Students themselves, estimating (correctly) that the American public were sufficiently unfamiliar with both nationalities to be unable to distinguish between them. In 1881 Carlo(s) Curti, an Italian violinist who had been performing in the USA since 1866 with Guerra's French Opera Company and therefore understood the workings of the American music business, persuaded a number of other Italian musicians in New York to join him in this somewhat fraudulent,

---

[8] Adelstein (1905: 6) gives the first and last of these; Picard (1901: 15) mentions Hernandez.

[9] Hambly (1977*a*) gives an excellent and thorough account of the Spanish Students and their imitators.

but potentially lucrative, venture. Although passing themselves off as the Figaro Spanish Students, wearing similar costumes and playing a similar repertoire, they preferred to perform on round-back mandolins (which were readily available within the Italian community), rather than flat-back bandurrias, which were unfamiliar and in any case not easily obtainable. Vincent Léon, a trained Italian mandolinist whose family had come to the USA in 1875, joined them in 1881 and later wrote that 'Curti, an Italian violinist, got several violinists together and formed a club of mandolinists. Of course they were obliged to use Neapolitan mandolins because, being violinists, they could master the Neapolitan mandolins more easily than they could learn the Spanish Bandurria.' (*Cadenza*, Aug. 1901: 25.)[10]

Nor was Curti alone in his deception. Over the next few years several bogus troupes of Italian mandolinists, all passing themselves off as the 'Spanish Students', toured the USA, making a good living and helping to popularize the mandolin. These troupes were effectively training-grounds for performers and, by the time that the public had grown weary of both genuine and counterfeit Spanish Students, the USA had acquired its first generation of professional mandolinists, who then reassumed their Italian identity and began to teach and perform in major cities in the north.

The influence of the Spanish Students also added to the belief amongst many Europeans that the mandolin was a Spanish instrument, while those who did make a distinction often referred to the bandurria as 'the Spanish mandolin'. The Parisian critic who praised Silvestri's performance at the Paris Exhibition of 1878 clearly regarded the mandolin as being particularly associated with Spain: '... the modest mandolin, which one thought had been banished to Castille and Andalusia, suitable only to accompany the serenade that an amorous student murmurs beneath the half-open shutters of some Inesilla or some Dolores.' (*L'Art musical*, 26 Sept. 1878: 308.)

As we shall see, when mandolin groups became popular in France they often called themselves *Estudiantinas* and, although the title of Saint-Saëns's beautiful song 'Guitares et mandolines' (1890) may suggest an Italian serenade, the music is absolutely Spanish in style, as are the girls (Ex. 2):

> Guitars and mandolins possess the sounds that make love.
> While munching pralines Pépa allows herself to be charmed

---

[10] Léon states that he was a member of 'Curti's Roman Students', which suggests that, at some point, the troupe dropped the pretence of being Spanish.

Ex. 2. Saint-Saëns: 'Guitares et mandolines', bars 1–26

When mandolins and guitars, brazenly tossing out sharps,
Resonate to disarm her.

Mandolin, with guitar, accompanies the sounds of
The lovers following the beacon of beauty in the night;
And Juana shows, cat-like (guitar with mandolin),
Her mouth and her gleaming eye.[11]

While the bandurria has remained popular right up to the present day in Spain (one of the few Western countries where the Neapolitan mandolin has never been widely played), it was never to achieve widespread use amongst non-Spaniards. Ironically, although the growth of nationalism in Hispanic music began as an attempt to cast off the hegemony of the Italian style, the brief international success of the characteristically Spanish bandurria ultimately served only to whet the public appetite for its Italian counterpart.

2.3 Circoli mandolinisti *in Italy*

Although the mandolin had hitherto always been regarded as an instrument suitable only for serenades and for small-scale music-making, the possibilities of creating entire orchestras of mandolins and guitars now began to be explored for the first time. Within Italy, the mandolin was sufficiently popular for play-ers to start organizing themselves into societies (known as *circoli mandolin-isti*), which usually consisted of a few professional teacher-performers and up to sixty or seventy serious amateurs, sometimes all male, but frequently includ-ing substantial numbers of women. It has already been noted that Bertucci took an orchestra with him to Paris in 1878,[12] but the earliest permanent group-ings of which I am aware were the *circolo* in Perugia, founded in 1879, and the Reale circolo mandolinisti Regina Margherita (Illustration 5), founded in Florence in March 1881 under the patronage of Queen Margherita.[13] Milan, Rome, and Naples all had active and important groupings of mandolinists, but throughout this period Florence was widely regarded as possessing both the finest orchestra and the finest soloists, and we shall begin our survey there.

---

[11] The composer also wrote the words. This is the origin of the phrase 'Guitares et mandolines ont les sons qui font aimer', which has often been attributed to Saint-Saëns by mandolinists, but without giving a full ref.

[12] Janssens (1982: 117) states that Bertucci wrote a 3-vol. method, pub. in 1885 by Ricordi, Milan.

[13] Hambly (1977*a*: 80) and Adelstein (1905: 7–8). While the orchestra in Perugia may have been the earliest, it never became one of the more important *circoli*.

Illustration 5. The Reale circolo mandolinisti Regina Margherita of Florence in 1892. Include: front row (seated, third from left), Luigi Bianchi, (seated, with baton), Riccardo Matini; second row (standing, furthest left), Guido Bizzari, (standing, third from left), Carlo Munier, (standing, furthest right) Amerigo Parini (from Adelstein (1901/05: 11).

Florence

The seminal figure for the mandolin in Florence was Giuseppe Bellenghi who, in addition to teaching the instrument, was an active performer. An early concert of his was held at the Sala Filarmonica in Florence on 10 May 1880, and included a group of ten mandolins and eight guitars playing two of his own light compositions, 'Reverie' and 'Fiorintinella'.[14] He composed a great deal of light music for the mandolin with piano or guitar accompaniment (using the pseudonym of G. B. Pirani for the more trivial works), mainly because there

---

[14] Adelstein (1905: 10).

Illustration 6. Carlo Munier (from his *Scuola del mandolino*, 1891).

was then little else available for the instrument; these pieces are no longer of much interest, although his methods for mandolin and other plucked instruments are still of value today. But undoubtedly his most important contribution was in setting up, in 1882, the specialist publishing house Casa editrice Forlivesi (Forlivesi was his wife's maiden name) which, over the next twenty years, published some 7,000 compositions for mandolin, ranging from solos and duets to quartets and full orchestral works.[15]

The most famous mandolinist ever associated with Florence was Carlo Munier (Illustration 6), the grandson (or great-nephew) of Pasquale Vinaccia[16] and a former pupil of Carmine De Laurentiis. Munier was born in Naples, and entered the city's conservatoire (S. Pietro a Maiella) at the age of 15. As the mandolin was not a permitted instrument for study, he took instruction in piano, harmony, and counterpoint instead, graduating four years later with prizes for composition and harmony. He gave many concerts in Naples, and

[15] After Bellenghi's death, Forlivesi became part of the publishing firm of R. Maurri, still in existence today.

[16] Bone (1972: 253) states that Munier was the great-nephew of Pasquale Vinaccia. However, Munier himself refers to Pasquale as his grandfather in his *Scuola del mandolino* (1895: i. 12), and the dedication of his *Tre mazurke* for mandolin and guitar, Opp. 116–18, reads 'To my dearest uncle, Gennaro Vinaccia' (Pasquale's eldest son).

published his first compositions there, but moved at the age of 22 to Florence, where he was to spend the remainder of his life. Once established there, he quickly acquired a formidable reputation as a virtuoso, and soon became the leading light of the Florentine school, numbering Queen Margherita amongst his pupils.

Like most teacher-performers of the time, he was also a prolific composer for his instrument. We have already noted the general lack of interest in serious instrumental music in Italy throughout the nineteenth century, so it is not surprising to find that Munier's output during the 1880s consisted mostly of light pieces, tuneful but unremarkable (usually for one or two mandolins with piano accompaniment, and mainly published by F. Lucca of Milan). However, even these early, ephemeral compositions give indications of an imaginative musician, striving to move beyond the limitations of a simple dance form or an operatic pot-pourri. When his compositional style matured and developed towards the end of the century, and he started to adopt classical rather than popular forms, he began to produce some substantial works of lasting merit (many of which were published by Forlivesi). Many years later, Silvio Ranieri offered a fair summary of his early contribution to the development of mandolin composition:

> If his music is not always absolutely first-rate, it is always well written for the instrument and produces a good effect . . . He was perhaps the first composer to appreciate that music for the mandolin could be raised above the common waltzes, serenades, and marches which infested the repertoire thirty or forty years ago; his work has in no small measure developed the desire among mandolinists to raise their instrument to an artistic level which would have seemed impossible formerly. (Ranieri 1925: 1994.)

Munier was also foremost in the development, refinement, and teaching of mandolin technique. Most performers of his generation were either untutored musicians who had developed their own idiosyncratic styles of playing, or violinists who were content to adapt violin technique to the mandolin, playing any passage they encountered with only two or three different types of plectrum-stroking. Munier's *Scuola del mandolino* (written in 1891, but apparently not published until 1895) developed some forty different types of stroking, which he insisted should all be practised until they became second nature, so that any piece thereafter could be correctly played, not just technically but also with the appropriate emphasis and phrasing. In the preface to this method,

Munier acknowledges the huge advances made in the study of the instrument over recent years:

> Ten or twelve years ago, the publication of the above method would have been useless, the mandolin being very little known at that time, while now it forms a part in the musical art, and many people study it with great interest—consequently a *Complete Method* is necessary, one that leads without difficulty to a perfect technique. (Munier 1895: i. 11.)

As a performer, although he was one of the most technically advanced mandolinists of the period, his preoccupation was always with musicianship rather than virtuosity. He developed a lifelong partnership with Giorgio Lorenzi, Florence's foremost harpist (he was the professor of harp at the city's Reale istituto musicale) and a composer of several pieces for mandolin, including 'Melodia religiosa', written for the *circolo*. Amongst their earliest concerts together was one given at the cathedral in Fiesole,[17] a recognition by the Church that the mandolin had a spiritual, elevated side to its character as well as a playful, superficial one. Munier led the mandolin section of the Reale circolo mandolinisti Regina Margherita for many years and, in 1890, organized the earliest known plectrum quartet, the Florentine Quartet, which amazed the American mandolinist Samuel Adelstein (Illustration 7) by performing a Beethoven string quartet for him during his visit to the city in April 1890.

The regular members of the Florentine Quartet were also leading performers in the *circolo*: Luigi Bianchi and Guido Bizzari (first and second mandolins), Riccardo Matini (octave mandola), and Munier (liuto and director).[18] The mandola was a slightly larger version of the mandolin (tuned an octave lower) which became popular from the mid-1880s onwards, its rich sonority adding a much-needed middle voice in ensemble playing. Its music was written in exactly the same way as mandolin music (but sounding an octave lower), a system that enabled mandolinists to adapt quickly to the lower-voiced instrument, as they needed to accustom themselves only to a slightly longer fingerboard. The liuto (also known as the liuto cantabile and liuto moderno) had no connection whatever with the Renaissance or Baroque lute; this was a five-course Neapolitan instrument, tuned *C–G–d–a* like a cello, but with an extra *e'* course added. Its ensemble music was usually written in the bass clef, exactly like a cello part, but its four-octave range also gave it great possibilities as

---

[17] Pisani (1913: 18).

[18] On the occasion when Adelstein heard the quartet, Amerigo Parini was playing instead of Bianchi.

Illustration 7. Samuel Adelstein, *c.*1900 (from Adelstein 1905: 2).

a solo instrument, and such parts were generally written in the treble clef with an octave transposition.[19]

Luigi Bianchi was Florence's leading exponent of the Milanese mandolin. Munier admiringly recalled his performance of a polonaise by Vieuxtemps and described him as 'a marvellous concert artist',[20] while Agostino Pisani called him 'the Paganini of the Lombardian mandolin'.[21] Riccardo Matini was the director of the *circolo* and the author of a two-volume mandolin tutor, and often played the piano accompaniment for Munier and Bianchi at their recitals. Like Bianchi, he was an active composer of mandolin music, and also made many of the orchestral arrangements for the *circolo*. The other prominent Florentine composer during this period was Carlo Graziani-Walter, much of whose prolific output during the 1880s was published by F. Lucca of Milan.[22] During the mid-1890s, he succeeded Matini as director of the *circolo*.

---

[19] Further details of these instruments, and other members of the mandolin family, will be found in the App. See also Illus. 9 and 12.

[20] Munier (1909: 4).   [21] Pisani (1913: 65).

[22] Lucca, as well as publishing a great deal of mandolin music during the 1880s, was responsible for introducing Wagner's music to the Italian public. The firm was taken over by Ricordi in 1888, having been purchased for 1m lire from Giovannina Lucca.

Although we are now concentrating on the urban middle classes who refined the mandolin and reintroduced it into the concert-hall, we should not move on without remembering that the instrument's use amongst the general population remained as widespread as ever. The following description of an afternoon in 1885 in Siena (some fifty miles south of Florence) is typical of the picturesque scenes that greeted foreign visitors in Tuscany:

> It seemed to us a very pretty fashion when we saw them holiday making on Sunday afternoon, peasants, priests, officers, townspeople, all out in their Sunday best, and when on the Via Cavour, near the *loggia*, we met two wandering minstrels singing love-songs through the town. One played on a mandoline which hung from his neck by a wide red ribbon, and as he played he sang. His voice was loud and strong and very sweet, and like another Orpheus he drew after him all who heard his music. His companion sold copies of the song, printed on pink paper, gay as the words. He went, bowing and smiling, in and out of the crowd. (Pennell 1887: 48–9.)

Milan

One of this city's leading professional mandolinists was Pietro Armanini, director of the mandolin troupe Compagnia Armanini, which made numerous continental tours during the 1880s. It performed frequently in London, where the most successful item in its repertoire was a solo entitled 'Mostwa', which created a furore when the troupe appeared at the Empire Theatre.[23] The English mandolinist Richard Harrison heard Armanini perform:

> Those who remember the unrivalled playing of the late Prof. Armanini of La Scala can, indeed, bear testimony to the marvellous effects which can be realised on the Mandoline. It is true that the great Milanese, now quoted, was a veritable Paganini, and has never been approached as an executant. He was incomparable—the greatest Mandoline artist in the annals of music. (*Keynotes*, June 1907: 2.)

Armanini (who played the Milanese mandolin) does not seem to have been involved in the creation of the *circolo* in Milan (often referred to as the Circolo lombardo), the only group that could then equal the orchestra in Florence. Ferdinando Francia was a leading member, especially important as a composer and arranger for the orchestra, but his son Leopoldo was soon to become

---

[23] *BMG* (Dec. 1912: 43). The Empire Theatre was then one of London's best venues for high-quality music-hall (vaudeville-style) entertainment.

a much more significant figure. Leopoldo, who studied the mandolin first with his father and then at the Milan conservatoire, later recounted the instrumentation and personnel of

> the mandolin club at Milan, which was then [1892] conducted by Alfredo Antonietti. This mandolin orchestra, which was composed of sixty male performers, included Neapolitan and Roman mandolins, flat-backed mandolins, mandolas, and lutes, Milanese mandolins with gut strings, guitars, mandocellos, one harp, and a flute. Amongst this amateur orchestra the following well-known performers were included: leader of the Milanese mandolins, Professor Angelo Alfieri; leader of the Neapolitan and Roman mandolins, Cattaneo; leader of the mandolas, Professor Tomasini; and first guitar, Professor Bestetti. The conductor, as I said before, was Professor Alfredo Antonietti, and, strange to say, he did not play any of the aforementioned instruments, but was an extremely clever composer and conductor.
>
> In this orchestra I personally played amongst the first Milanese mandolins . . . (*BMG*, Mar. 1911: 84.)

Although the Florentine orchestra could boast Queen Margherita as its patron, the Milan *circolo* had an even more celebrated associate: Giuseppe Verdi, who became an honorary member of the *circolo*,[24] and used several of its members in Act II of his opera *Otello*, first performed at La Scala, Milan, in 1887. The idea of including a mandolin originally came from the librettist Arrigo Boito, in a letter to Verdi dated 17 June 1881,[25] and gradually developed into a full set piece with a chorus of men, women and children, five or six guitars (or harps), bagpipes (or oboe), and five or six mandolins.[26] Early performances placed the instrumentalists on stage with the chorus but, owing to problems with balance and the technical difficulty of the mandolin part, the musicians nowadays usually perform in the wings, while members of the on-stage chorus mime with instrumental props. Originally, the part would probably have been played on Milanese mandolins (which were being manufactured in large numbers by the Monzino family and many other luthiers in the city), and the notes fall easily under the fingers on that instrument. However, as that type of mandolin has never achieved great popularity outside northern Italy, it has almost always been performed subsequently on the much more widely played Neapolitan mandolin, although it requires an expert to play the part at full

---

[24] Bone (1972: 361) states that the *circolo* possessed several letters from Verdi, the last dated 19 Feb. 1888.

[25] Busch (1988: 103–4). According to Janssens (1982: 115), Boito had earlier included the mandolin in his own opera *Mefistofele* (1868).

[26] From the *Otello Production Book*, quoted in Busch (1988: 534)

speed on this instrument. The role of the mandolins (which play in unison) is to accompany the voices, and they remain subordinate to the vocal parts throughout, causing Silvio Ranieri to lament that 'beautiful though it is, Verdi did not obtain all he might from the mandolin had he known the instrument better.' (Ranieri 1925, 1992.) While this may be true, Verdi undeniably included mandolins in a beautiful and memorable moment of a magnificent opera, something which helped enormously in the instrument's subsequent rehabilitation into the mainstream repertoire.

Rome

Giuseppe Branzoli remained the most highly respected mandolin teacher in Rome. His revised *Metodo teorico-pratico per mandolino napolitano o romano* was even more successful than the original edition of 1875, being frequently reprinted and winning gold medals at the International Music Exposition in Bologna in 1888 and at the Palace of Industry in Paris in 1890.[27] Samuel Adelstein, who studied this method with Branzoli himself in Rome, believed it to be the first tutor to explore fully the great variety of possible plectrum-movements, and considered it the original authority for all subsequent methods published in Italy, 'the fountain head from which all derive the fundamental principles of the art.'[28] In addition to the mandolin, Branzoli had a wide range of other musical interests and accomplishments, including the composition of an opera, *Torquato Tasso a Sorrento*, successfully performed in Rome (1860). He also began a collection of period musical instruments at the Accademia di S. Cecilia and, in 1889, organized a historic concert of music by Giulio Caccini and Claudio Monteverdi played on seventeenth-century instruments, a remarkable pioneering attempt to rehabilitate what was then a totally forgotten style of music-making.

The instrument that began to be commonly played in this city and throughout central Italy was the Roman mandolin (Illustration 8) which, although tuned and strung like the Neapolitan mandolin (from which it derived), took the innovations of Pasquale Vinaccia a stage further by incorporating even more features of violin construction into its design. The fingerboard was somewhat curved and narrow, allowing two adjacent courses to be stopped at the same fret with the tip of a single left-hand finger. It extended as far as the

---

[27] *Dizionario biografico degli italiani.*   [28] Adelstein (1905: 19).

Illustration 8. Silvio Ranieri, *c.*1910, playing an Embergher (Roman) mandolin (photograph courtesy of Henri Gamblin).

soundhole on the bass side, but the part beneath the *e″* strings continued for about another inch (across the soundhole), with extra frets fitted into it. The back of the neck was almost triangular, tapering to a fairly sharp edge. The bridge was curved, with the *g* strings clearing the table by a greater amount than the other courses, a design that matched the natural curve of the movement of the right wrist. The body was approximately the same shape as that of a Neapolitan mandolin (with fluted ribs on the best models), but the head was usually scrolled, with mechanized tuning-keys and tuning-barrels (like a modern classical guitar). Some early Roman mandolins had wooden tuning-pegs (like a violin), but these models were quite unsuited to thin steel strings and soon disappeared.

Three people—Luigi Embergher, Giovanni De Santis, and Giovanni Battista Maldura—are credited with refining and redesigning the Roman mandolin to the point where it eventually became the preferred instrument of many famous concert performers. Maldura was a leading mandolinist in Rome who, working together with the luthier De Santis, evolved the basic design of this new instrument in the late 1880s or early 1890s (although his application for a patent for the design of the curved mandolin bridge was not filed until

1896).[29] De Santis won many medals at international exhibitions with this mandolin, but it was Luigi Embergher who further refined the design, ultimately creating what many modern performers regard as the finest instruments ever built. When Adelstein visited Rome in 1890, the instruments he saw had only eighteen frets on the lowest courses and twenty-three on the top course, were strung with rough, copper-wound wire on the third and fourth courses, and were often played with a goose quill plectrum.[30] However, the classic Roman mandolin that was being perfected in Embergher's workshop at about the same time had twenty-nine frets, was played with a tortoiseshell plectrum, and was intended for the same smooth steel and copper strings that were used on Neapolitan instruments.

Amongst the many musicians then associated with the instrument in Rome, two young mandolinists were just beginning their studies; Silvio Ranieri (Illustration 8) and Mario Maciocchi. Little is known about Ranieri's early years except that he spent them in his native city learning to play the mandolin and acquiring a quite astounding technical mastery over it, but we do know that Maciocchi studied with Branzoli and, in 1892, founded a plectrum quintet which he later took to South America. Ranieri and Maciocchi were ultimately to become the most celebrated mandolinists that the city ever produced, although their fame was won elsewhere.

Naples

Although many cities in northern and central Italy were developing their own schools of playing, Naples remained the spiritual home of the mandolin, and instruments built by the Vinaccia family still had the highest international reputation. The core of the family business had occupied the same premises in the rua Catalana since the mid-eighteenth century, until increased demand finally forced most of them to relocate to a larger building in the 1890s.[31] Richard Harrison visited the old workshop of Vinaccia fratelli during the 1880s, and later published this fascinating account:

Rua Catalana is one of the oldest and dirtiest streets in Naples—the narrowest of pavements and the narrowest of roads. The little shop of Vinaccia was on the right side at the lower end of the street. There at the door could be seen an *allievo* or apprentice at work; a small counter, several glass cases containing specimens of

---

[29] *Banjo World* (Sept. 1902: 165–6).   [30] Adelstein (1905: 20).   [31] *BMG* (Mar. 1956: 145).

instruments—one by old Pasquale. A dark passage at the side led to a stone stair-
case, so dark that a workman had to hold a lamp as a beacon. Once upstairs in
the *atelier*, one found Signori Vinaccia[32] surrounded by their workmen and *allievi*,
some five-and-twenty (who are increased in the busy season); and mandolines in
every stage of progress—from the uncarved timber to the magnificent specimens
of inlaid wood ordered for Russia. The Queen of Italy uses a Vinaccia, valued, we
believe, at three hundred pounds. The manufacture of mandolines under this system is very interesting; the selection of the wood, building the body, fretting the
fingerboard, inlaying with pearl and tortoiseshell, polishing and varnishing—all of
which demand great taste and experience, before the instrument is fit for the
player. (Harrison 1898: 159.)

Harrison had gone to Naples to study with Ferdinando De Cristofaro, a
self-taught mandolinist (although he had trained as a pianist at the Naples
Conservatoire) with an outstanding reputation throughout Europe. De Cristofaro's
approach to the mandolin was based on violin technique, and his system for
plectrum-stroking was simple. Unlike the complex plectrum technique of
Branzoli and Munier, he taught only a few different types of right-hand stroking
patterns, and advocated alternate up and down strokes for most passages. In
his recitals, he eschewed popular operatic medleys and flamboyant sets of variations in favour of chamber music by Beethoven, Schumann, Schubert, Chopin,
Sarasate, and Mendelssohn. This policy appealed to more thoughtful and serious mandolin students, and he became much sought after as a teacher in Naples,
and also in Paris, where he spent much of the 1880s.[33] Naples was the one
city in Italy where serious instrumental music was treated with respect during the second half of the nineteenth century. Orchestral and string quartet
societies flourished during the 1860s and 1870s, and, despite the dreadful
cholera epidemic of 1884, instrumental music continued to prosper during the
1880s and 1890s.[34] The profound interest shown by many Neapolitan musicians in the mandolin should be viewed within the context of the general
rehabilitation of non-vocal music during these decades.

When Samuel Adelstein reached Naples in 1890 (as part of his Italian pilgrimage, seeking instruction from the country's leading players), the three mandolinists who impressed him most were Francesco Della Rosa (an orchestral

---

[32] Earlier in the art. he mentions the three sons of Pasquale who were then running the business: Gennaro,
Achille, and Federico.
[33] According to Bone (1972: 87–9), he published a mandolin method in Naples in 1873, and played an instrument made by Luigi Salsedo, a leading Neapolitan luthier.
[34] *RIPM: La musica* (pref.).

Illustration 9. Raffaele Calace with a liuto, *c.*1895 (from Adelstein 1905: 23).

violinist who became an expert performer on the mandolin) and the Calace brothers, Nicola and Raffaele (Illustration 9). Raffaele had studied composition at the Naples conservatoire under Paolo Serrao and Francesco Ancona, then travelled abroad before returning to Naples, taking over the family business and founding, together with Nicola, Calace fratelli, making guitars, mandolins, and violins, many of which were initially exported to Switzerland.[35] As well as making mandolins, Nicola was a fine player and a composer of light but attractive pieces for the instrument (mostly for two mandolins, with piano or guitar accompaniment), but his career became increasingly overshadowed by that of his younger brother Raffaele, who excelled in every area of mandolin activity—manufacture, performance, innovation and design, composition and orchestration—to such a degree that he must be regarded as the greatest single figure in the mandolin's four-hundred-year history. During this early part of his life, Raffaele's main preoccupation, apart from steadily improving the international reputation of the family business, was with the liuto. It is sometimes said that he invented the liuto during the late 1880s (although

[35] According to a letter from Arena Anna ved. Calace, Naples, Jan. 1992.

more probably it was a local Neapolitan instrument, the design of which he greatly improved), and he soon became indisputably the world's greatest virtuoso on it, demonstrating its solo potential by performing violin concertos by Bériot, a feat involving formidable left-hand stretches which, by all accounts, he could accomplish effortlessly. During the early 1880s he also wrote his first compositions, a series of pieces for unaccompanied mandolin (numbered Opp. 1–10), published in 1885 as *Gemine orientali*, Op. 15.

Besides the Vinaccia and Calace families, there were dozens of other mandolin-makers in Naples (usually organized as small family businesses), three of the best being Luigi Salsedo, Giovanni De Meglio, and Umberto Ceccherini. Although the export market for mandolins was steadily growing, most of their output was still destined for local consumption. Mandolin life may have been less well organized in Naples than in many northern cities (there does not seem to have been a formal *circolo* at this time), but the instrument was more widely played here than anywhere else. Adelstein described a typical scene:

> In Naples and vicinity one hears mandolins and guitars all day and nearly all night. All of the incoming and outbound steamers in the Bay of Naples are surrounded by these musicians in their small boats, playing their popular tunes, one of their number holding his hat or outspread umbrella to catch the centissimo that are thrown by the passengers. At the principal hotels in Naples the traveller is serenaded at all hours of the night by these itinerant street minstrels, and in the tourist season it is often difficult for one to have an undisturbed night's rest.
>
> On the steamer from Naples to Capri, with its celebrated Blue Grotto, there was a trio of two mandolins and guitar who played and sang their beautiful Neapolitan airs, 'Santa Lucia,' 'Addio mia bella Napoli,' 'Funiculì Funiculà,' 'Oh Margherita,' etc., etc. On the journey over the azure waters of the Bay of Naples, with the city, Mt. Vesuvius and Pompeii in the background, passing charming Castellemare, lovely Sorrento, with beautiful Capri in the distance, the effect of the music on the water, with these romantic surroundings, was so exquisite that one wished he could listen to it forever. (Adelstein 1905: 8.)

Florence, Milan, Rome, and Naples were undoubtedly the four most important cities for the mandolin, although there were active groups in many other towns, including Bologna, Turin, Alessandria, and Verona.[36] These groups of dedicated amateurs, overseen by a few professional teachers and players, do

---

[36] The Veronese Circolo Margherita was founded in 1890 (*Mandoline*, 15 Aug. 1904: 54); the Circolo mandolinistico di Alessandria in 1890 (*Il mandolino*, 30 Dec. 1893: 4); those in Bologna and Turin were formed before 1892.

not seem to have published any journals or magazines, nor to have been in regular contact with each other before 1892, when the situation was to change radically.

2.4 *The Mandolin Rediscovered*

Outside Italy, the mandolin was slowly developing a modest popularity, especially in Paris, where regular appearances by the Neapolitans, Silvestri and De Cristofaro, were helping with its revival. De Cristofaro's recitals there from 1882 onwards were serious musical events (Charles Gounod was amongst the pianists who accompanied him),[37] and the violinistic approach to plectrum technique outlined in his *Méthode de mandoline* (published in two volumes by Lemoine, Paris, in 1884) made it a popular work, already in its twelfth edition by the time of his premature death in 1890. This uncomplicated right-hand style was adopted by many Parisian players, one of the earliest being Jean Pietrapertosa, who gave concerts throughout the 1880s:

> In a concert given on Tuesday in the Salle Herz, we listened with a real satisfaction and applauded, like the rest of the audience, the Pietrapertosa mandolinists who displayed great talent in a fantasia on *Aida*: the scene with Amnéris in the third act and the final duo, performed on three mandolins accompanied by piano, produced a truly delicious and original effect. (*L'Art musical*, 15 Mar. 1885: 36–7.)

When Adelstein met him in 1890, Pietrapertosa was leading an ensemble of ten mandolins and two liutos (surprisingly, this was then the largest group in Paris),[38] and by 1892, when his two-volume *Méthode de mandoline* appeared (published in Paris by Schott), he felt that the instrument was finally being accepted into the musical fraternity:

> The mandolin has risen enormously in public estimation in the last few years, owing to the virtuosi (amongst whose numbers they kindly include me) having fought valiantly in its favour, in public and professionally. The result of their efforts has been to establish the mandolin firmly in the illustrious family of solo instruments for either concert or drawing-room. The result is now fully confirmed by the large number of pupils seeking counsel and lessons from masters of renown. (Pietrapertosa 1892: i, preface.)

---

[37] *Banjo World* (7 Nov. 1894: 2).   [38] Adelstein (1905: 9).

Two other pioneers in the city were the Cottin brothers, Jules and Alfred.[39] Their parents originally intended them to make their careers in the Church but, after studying violin and harmony with the famous violinist Charles Dancla, Jules and Alfred abandoned the religious life and became virtuoso performers on the mandolin and the guitar respectively. They were much sought after in salons and concert-halls and, when Jules published his *Méthode complète de mandoline* in 1891, *L'Art musical* commented favourably:

> The mandolin has been, during the past few years, one of the instruments favoured by lovers of picturesque music. Top-notch virtuosos, among whom we class the author of the method under discussion, have contributed a great deal to this renaissance. The result is an accepted fact nowadays: the mandolin has an open entry into concert-halls and salons. It is also very popular, and the best teachers have many pupils. (*L'Art musical*, 15 Dec. 1891: 181.)

Although Italian instruments were the most highly prized, large-scale mandolin manufacture was also starting in France, most notably at the town of Mirecourt (in the Vosges), which for centuries had been producing the country's finest bowed instruments. In the early 1890s, Louis Gérôme founded a workshop there, devoted entirely to the manufacture of Neapolitan mandolins; he soon became one of France's largest and most highly respected mandolin luthiers, his success encouraging other makers to set up in business there.[40]

In Britain and many other north European countries, and in the USA, various social factors helped to develop the mandolin's popularity during the 1880s. The rising standard of living of most city-dwellers that resulted from industrialization, greater access to education, and increased leisure time gave people the means and the desire for self-improvement, often reflected in the purchase and study of a musical instrument. Middle-class women started to break free from repressive social conventions, and began to enjoy a wide range of social activities outside the home, including communal music-making. Public transport was improving, and the personal mobility afforded by the bicycle made it easier for people to participate in large-scale musical activities, so long as their chosen instrument was easily portable.

Italian opera, always popular in Britain, became even more fashionable with the advent of *verismo* works such as Mascagni's *Cavalleria rusticana* (1890) and Leoncavallo's *Pagliacci* (1892). Many Neapolitan songs became internationally

---

[39] Biographical details from *Dictionnaire de biographie française*.
[40] *Le Plectre* (no. 0, 1992: 9; no. 1, Apr. 1992: 9).

famous, as did their composers: Luigi Denza, who wrote 'Funiculì, funiculà', settled in London as a professor at the Royal Academy of Music, and Paolo Tosti, composer of many popular songs, became singing teacher to the British royal family. People developed a taste for Italian melody, and were increasingly attracted to the mandolin which, with its distinctive timbre, became identified as a uniquely Italian voice in instrumental music. Amongst dilettante musicians, its modest cost, attractive appearance, exotic associations, and ability to sustain a melody when played with tremolo, the ease with which simple tunes could be performed, and its quiet but pleasant tone all contributed to its growing popularity. Moreover, since it did not carry the substantial cultural weight and expectations of the traditional orchestral instruments, adults could begin studying it without feeling intimidated or inept.

An early teacher in England was Federico Sacchi from Cremona, mandolin instructor to two of Queen Victoria's daughters, Princess Alice Mary Maud and Princess Victoria. He composed many light pieces for mandolin and guitar, and later compiled an English edition of the tutor by Carmine De Laurentiis.[41] De Cristofaro gave recitals in London in 1888 and, when he returned the next year, his concerts included one with Denza.[42] He was also appointed conductor of the Ladies' Mandolin and Guitar Band, one of the first mandolin ensembles in London, composed mainly of aristocratic young women.

A tightening of the copyright laws to prevent piracy led to a huge increase in the number of music publishers and the amount of available music. One London firm specializing in fretted instrument music was John Alvey Turner who, in about 1888, issued Herbert J. Ellis's *Thorough School for Mandolin*, the first tutor written by an Englishman. Ellis[43] was a self-taught musician, and a prolific composer of undemanding music for mandolin, banjo, and guitar. He was also a prominent teacher, and led a banjo and mandolin troupe, whose many performances included a six-week engagement in Paris in 1889.[44]

In the north of England and the Midlands, amateur music-making was strongly associated with choral societies and brass bands, and the first mandolin orchestras were almost all found in London and the south-east of England. One of the earliest was the Luton Mandolin Band, the nucleus of which came together in 1890 and included Philip J. Bone. Much larger was the Polytechnic

---

[41] Pub. by Ricordi.   [42] *BMG* (Dec. 1903: 44).

[43] Bone (1972: 106–7) gives his dates as 1865–1903. However, in *Banjo World* (Mar. 1894: 35) Ellis himself says that he was 'born rather more than thirty years ago'.

[44] *Banjo World* (June 1896: 103).

SIGNOR CARLO D'AMATO.

Illustration 10. Carlo D'Amato (from *BMG*, Apr. 1906: 100). Photograph courtesy of the British Library.

Mandolin and Guitar Orchestra, conducted by B. M. Jenkins, which was formed in January 1891 and gave its inaugural concert at the Crystal Palace in 1892, with fifty performers taking part.[45] The mandolin was accepted as an instrument of study by the Guildhall School of Music, London, in 1891, with Madame Giulia Pelzer as professor of guitar and mandolin, at a fee of three guineas for twelve half-hour lessons.[46] G. B. Marchisio, a mandolinist from Turin, established himself as a teacher in London in 1892, later becoming a professor at Trinity College of Music, where Bone was amongst his students. The instrument also appeared at a Promenade Concert in 1889 (at the old Her Majesty's Theatre), played by Carlo D'Amato (Illustration 10), who (in an interview given some years later) insisted that the mandolin was at its best in the hands of fiery Mediterraneans, rather than the placid English:

> I began the mandolin when I was nine years old. Every child plays the mandolin in Naples—I am Neapolitan—just as every Spaniard plays the guitar. It is part of the local temperament... ['From whom did you learn?'] From no one. Does a

[45] *BMG* (Feb. 1904: 78).   [46] From the Guildhall School of Music Prospectus for 1891.

Tzigane learn to play a violin, does a Neapolitan learn to play the mandolin, does a girl learn to kiss? These three things are innate and natural! ... ['Why does the banjo seem to excite more interest than the mandolin in England?'] In the first place the banjo is much easier and, secondly, as an instrument it is more akin to the Anglo-Saxon temperament. The mandolin is a Southern instrument, and it is responsive to our hot Southern fire. We pick it up, as I said, without teaching. Here, you English *learn*. (*BMG*, Apr. 1906: 100.)

Although unsuited to recitals of serious music, the five-string banjo was the most popular fretted instrument in Britain during the late nineteenth century, with fashion-conscious men and women using it to accompany the latest songs and to play light dance music. Its penetrating tone made it ideal for outdoor music-making, especially in the Pierrot show, a seaside entertainment in which white-faced actors in white Pierrot costumes performed a mixture of songs and humorous sketches. Inspired by the *commedia dell'arte*, and created in 1891 by the fretted-instrument specialist Clifford Essex, the Pierrot show remained a tremendously popular form throughout the Edwardian period.

But it was in the USA, especially amongst urban Whites in Boston, New York, and Philadelphia, that banjo playing became a craze. Brought to America by Blacks in the eighteenth century, its use was largely confined to the South until after the Civil War (1861–5), when the Northern population, having subjugated the South, became fascinated by its culture and adopted its principal musical instrument, exactly as had happened with the mandolin in Italy. Successful though the Spanish Students were, it was the popularity of the banjo that created the fretted instrument industry in America, as George L. Lansing later recalled: 'In the early eighties, the craze for banjo playing spread all over the country. It was the instrument that put us all in the business originally.'[47] Most of the players were women, usually organized into banjo clubs, and by 1891 it was being reported that 'You can scarcely walk down a street in an Eastern city without meeting a lady carrying a banjo.'[48] The first fretted-instrument journals appeared, mostly published by manufacturing houses—the *S. S. Stewart Magazine* (Philadelphia, 1884 – before 1916) and *Gatcomb's Musical Gazette* (Boston, 1887–1897) were among the earliest—and, although initially intended for banjoists, soon began to include items for mandolinists. When mandolin ensembles became popular in the 1890s, they modelled their organizations on banjo clubs, rather than Italian *circoli*.

[47] George L. Lansing (1921: 22).   [48] *Gatcomb's Banjo & Guitar Gazette* (Jan.–Feb. 1891: 2).

By the mid-1880s, the mandolin was becoming popular on the East Coast, not just with Italian immigrants but also amongst fashionable society; in 1886 the *Musical Herald* (Boston) noted that 'The mandolin is the rage at present among fashionable young men and women in New York and elsewhere'.[49] Socially, there was a strong link between bicycle clubs and mandolin clubs, since both offered the opportunity for young men and women to meet each other, and bicycle clubs usually had a banjo, mandolin, and guitar club within their membership.[50] During the 1880s almost all mandolins in the USA were imported, mostly from Italy. Some were from the Vinaccia and Calace workshops but many came from lesser makers, and these instruments often fared badly in the very different eastern climate. Despite this, few indigenous luthiers were then making mandolins, although Joseph Bohmann of Chicago built what may have been the earliest American example in 1883–4,[51] and was the first to establish a reputation as a mandolin-maker.

In contrast to all this social music-making, only a few non-Italian Americans were studying the mandolin as a serious concert instrument. H. Mabel Mann was one exception; she began her tuition with Italian mandolinists in Boston and New York, then travelled to Naples, where she studied with 'one of the greatest mandolinists in the world, Giuseppe Silvestri, with whom she finished the study of her chosen instrument by learning with him the most difficult solos'.[52] There were also a few pioneers on the West Coast. Samuel Adelstein noted that in the mid-1880s it was almost impossible to buy a mandolin in his home city of San Francisco, and that his own composition 'Il mandolina: mazurka espagnole' (1885) was only the second original piece for mandolin ever to have been published in America. He also stated that the first mandolin club organized on the Pacific coast was La lira de Orfeo, formed by Señor Luis Romero in 1887, which gave its first concert on 24 May 1888. On the East Coast, the first group formed for professional work was the Boston Ideal Banjo, Mandolin and Guitar Club (1887).[53]

In Belgium and Germany (subsequently important centres for the mandolin), musicians were just beginning to show an interest in the instrument. In Antwerp, Romain Van den Bosch began to study the mandolin in 1887, and was soon directing the Club des Mandolinistes Anversoises.[54] The first mandolin clubs were also starting up in Germany in about 1890, usually with

---

[49] Quoted in Hambly (1977*a*: 10).   [50] Hambly (1977*a*: 12).   [51] Clarence L. Partee (1912: 148–9).
[52] *Gatcomb's Musical Gazette* (11/2, Oct. 1897: 2).   [53] Adelstein (1905: 8); *Cadenza* (Sept. 1903: 28–9).
[54] *L'Estudiantina* (15 Oct. 1907: 3).

Italian names, such as Santa Lucia, Napoli, and Catania, and often dressed in Italian costumes. One of the earliest teachers was Achille Coronati from Milan, a performer on both the Lombardian and the Neapolitan mandolin, who initially went to Berlin with a concert party in 1888 and settled there permanently.[55] A revival of interest in plucked strings was already under way in Germany, but was then mostly concerned with the guitar (or so-called 'lutes' tuned like guitars), organized in groups such as the Leipziger Gitarrenklub, formed by Otto Schick in 1877. An early mandolin-maker was B. Klemm (Markneukirchen), who took out a patent in 1891 for a family of Neapolitan-style instruments; piccolo-, violin-, viola-, and cello-mandolins, the cello-mandolin having four strings, the others eight.[56] Given the excellence of German piano- and violin-making at the time, it is surprising to find that German mandolins in general had a poor reputation internationally. The reason was that many manufacturers, in attempting to undercut the price of Italian mandolins by mass-producing them, turned out crudely built instruments with a poor tone, causing Richard Harrison to remark contemptuously that 'Those who have witnessed the construction can certify that a really good mandoline is not to be purchased for a few shillings. A German steam factory may produce a "mirage", not the real thing.' (Harrison 1898: 159.)

By 1892 the mandolin was being studied seriously within Italy by large numbers of musicians, while outside that country there were a few dedicated artists, and many more who played it in a casual way, in Europe and the USA. However, an event took place during 1892 that transformed the status and following of the mandolin, initially in Italy, but very soon throughout much of the rest of the world.

---

[55] Janssens (1982: 113) and Wölki (1984: 16).   [56] *Mandoline* (15 July 1904: 44).

3
1892–1918

3.1 *The Genoa Concourse and the Virtuoso Era in Italy*

During the summer of 1892, to celebrate the four-hundredth anniversary of the discovery of the New World by the Genoese-born navigator and explorer Christopher Columbus, Italy and the USA jointly organized a trade and cultural exhibition in Genoa. Amongst the many scheduled events was the first-ever national competition for mandolin soloists, quartets, and orchestras (Primo concorso nazionale mandolinistico), with a distinguished jury that included Camillo Sivori, one of the most celebrated violinists of the century. This concourse finally brought together the numerous groups of mandolinists from throughout Italy, who until then had been developing their art mostly in isolation from each other. The experience had an electrifying effect on many of them, Carlo Munier later describing it as 'the first true concourse, and one which was a revelation.'[1] Leopoldo Francia (Illustration 11) from Milan was amongst the participants:

> In 1892 there was a great concourse of Italian mandolinists, and strangely enough the North of Italy came off with far more honour than the South, although the mandoline originated with the people of the South.
>
> The best performers in Italy took part in this concourse, also mandoline bands from the principal Italian towns. A large orchestra was assembled, numbering 700, and executed a piece under the direction of the composer, Signor Massa, conductor at the Theatre Carlo Felici at Genoa. This was certainly the largest mandoline band of the time. The town of Milan gained most honour for Italy. It carried off the first prize for orchestra, quartet, and soloist. Then came the orchestra of Florence, that took the second gold medal, and also a first prize for solo mandolinist. The quartet took the second prize, and the Milanese mandoline the first. Then Rome took first prize for Roman mandoline; Bologna and Turin third prize; finally Naples took a diploma. Naples sent no orchestra, not possessing one. (Francia 1897: 150.)

---

[1] *Le Plectre* (74, Dec. 1909: 4).

SIGNOR LEOPOLDO FRANCIA.

Illustration 11. Leopoldo Francia, London, 1894 (from *Banjo World,* Oct. 1896: 167). Photograph courtesy of the British Library.

The individual gold medal winners from Milan included Angelo Alfieri, Leopoldo Francia, and Giuseppe Tommasini. V. Curti from Rome took the gold medal as soloist on the Roman mandolin while, amongst the Florentines, Giuseppe Bellenghi was awarded a first prize for his published mandolin method, and Carlo Munier won a soloist's gold medal. Although Francia does not mention it, the Circolo Margherita from Verona also won a second prize.[2]

The important achievement of the concourse was not, however, the awarding of medals, but the awakening of mandolinists to the full range of musical possibilities of their instruments, which were now seen to possess far greater artistic potential than many of the players had hitherto realized. Carlo Munier's gold medal was secured with a performance of his own Concerto No. 1, Op. 163 (in G major, Ex. 3), a full-scale composition with three linked movements and a demanding solo part, probably the most substantial work to be written for the mandolin since Hummel's Concerto of 1799.

Orchestras also had their musical horizons expanded. Up until this point, their instrumentation had usually comprised first and second mandolins, octave

[2] *Il mandolino* (30 Nov. 1892: 4, and 30 Nov. 1895, 4); *Mandoline* (15 Aug. 1904, 54).

Ex. 3. Munier: Concerto No. 1, 1st movement, bars 1–12

Allegro maestoso

mandolas, and guitars. This combination gave composers and arrangers limited scope for creating full and varied textures, and consequently the repertoire
had consisted mainly of simple, short, light pieces. However, the excellent
orchestras from Milan and Florence demonstrated that the addition of other
tenor and bass instruments could enhance the overall tone of an ensemble,
while a *circolo* from Rome astounded everyone by tackling a full-scale operatic overture:

> At the first concourse organized in Italy, in 1892, in the city of Genoa, a group of
> Roman mandolinists audaciously offered the overture to *Zampa* by Hérold. This
> was a new idea because, up until that moment, the repertoire of *Estudiantinas*[3] was
> limited to pieces of lesser importance. The resounding success that this group pulled
> off, in winning both the gold medal and the congratulations of the jury in which
> the illustrious violinist Camillo Sivori was participating, encouraged mandolinists
> to enlarge the means at their disposal. (Ranieri 1925: 1993.)

The concourse ended with a performance of the compulsory piece, 'Amore
e luna', composed by Nicolo Massa. All the contestants took part, playing
mandolins, mandolas, liuti, guitars, and other plucked instruments,[4] after which
they returned to their own cities, fired with a determination to raise the
status of the mandolin family to the level of serious concert instruments.

The initial step towards achieving this goal was taken almost immediately
in Turin, where *Il mandolino*, the world's first journal devoted exclusively to
the instrument, began publishing fortnightly on 15 November 1892. Edited
by Giuseppe Monticone, this periodical immediately established correspondents in all the major Italian cities, and began organizing national competitions for new compositions.[5] Several other magazines, devoted partly or entirely
to the mandolin, also began publication during this period, serving two important functions: firstly, they provided players with a new piece of music in
each edition, and secondly, they recorded a wide range of events that involved
the mandolin. Through their pages, we can obtain a clear view of the wealth
of music-making then taking place in the principal cities of Italy.

---

[3] For reasons explained in Ch. 2, the Spanish word *Estudiantina* has often been used by Fr. speakers to describe
a mandolin orchestra.

[4] *Il mandolino* (15 Nov. 1892: 4) puts the number of performers at 200, rather than the 700 mentioned by
Francia. In *Il mandolino* (15 Feb. 1896: 4) the same piece is called 'Luna e amore'.

[5] *Il mandolino* (15 Dec. 1892: 1). The first competition sought pieces for mandolin and guitar, not more than
2 pp. in length and suitable for amateurs, but later competitions encouraged far more substantial and complex
works.

Florence

Mandolin life in the city continued to revolve around Carlo Munier, who remained unsurpassed as composer, performer, and teacher. Additionally, he directed the Florentine Quartet, whose repertoire comprised a mixture of new compositions and works originally written for string quartet. The two matinée performances which this plectrum quartet gave on 25 and 29 April 1896 at the Sala filarmonica (with Luigi Bianchi playing the first mandolin and Munier the liuto) were typical of their programmes, including a complete Mozart string quartet in G major, a Moszkowski serenata, a Mendelssohn canzonetta, and several quartet movements by Haydn, as well as three pieces by Matini and the first performance of Munier's Third Quartet in C major.[6]

Munier's three quartets are perhaps his most ambitious compositions, and also the most rigorously classical in construction, modelled on the string quartet forms established by Haydn but with a distinctively lyrical vein of Italian melody running through the slower movements. The First Quartet in G major was not published by Forlivesi until about 1903, but is marked Op. 76, suggesting that it was originally composed in about 1887.[7] The opening Allegro begins with imitative entries by all four instruments, but what appears to be a fugue soon turns into a standard sonata form. In the second movement, marked 'Quasi adagio', the central C major cantabile section is framed by brief dramatic, chromatic passages, with an unresolved ending that leads into a light, graceful Minuetto and Trio. A 216-bar Rondò finale, contrasting a Germanic main theme with Italianate cantabile passages, concludes the quartet.

The Second Quartet in D major, Op. 128, is less formal in construction, beginning with an Allegro deciso that develops a simple opening statement in octaves into a sonata-form movement, its cheerful mood darkened only by occasional forays into the tonic minor. A folk-like Canzonetta is followed by a melancholy Andante espressivo, before an exhilarating Rondo in 6/8 (whose continuous quaver movement is marked 'Allegro mosso') closes this short but attractive quartet, one which has remained consistently popular with performers.

The Third Quartet in C major, Op. 203, is the most dramatic of the three works and, in places, the most problematic. A powerful Adagio introduction,

---

[6] *Il mandolino* (30 May 1896: 4).

[7] Munier's *Fantasia on the Stabat Mater of Pergolesi*, Op. 77, and 'Confidenze: Rondò', Op. 79, were both pub. in that year by F. Lucca of Milan.

Ex. 4. Munier: Quartet No. 3, 3rd movement, bars 1–6

with some florid writing for the first mandolin, leads into a Tempo di marcia that requires light and sensitive playing from the lower parts to counter its rather subdued, reserved nature. The second movement, a witty but stately Tempo di minuetto, is followed by a beautiful barcarole marked 'Andantino cantabile', one of the most ravishing pieces that Munier ever composed (Ex. 4).[8] The Finale: vivace can appear disappointingly pedestrian if played at a moderate tempo but, when it is performed extremely fast and delicately, it provides an

---

[8] Originally, all three quartets had liuto parts, although when they were published by Forlivesi (and later by R. Maurri), guitar parts were provided, to maximize potential sales.

effective climax to a substantial composition. After a performance of one of these quartets, the Leipzig journal *Mandoline* remarked:

> We have had the opportunity of hearing an original quartet by the talented composer Munier. The quartet is for two mandolins (1st and 2nd), a mandola and the Neapolitan lute, an instrument with five double strings. Not only its characteristic melody makes the composition very interesting, the different parts are both rich and effective. The style is classical, the melodies clear and simple, and the composition thus really pleases all tastes. Professor Munier's success in applying the rules of classical composition is to be hailed with great satisfaction. (*Mandoline*, 14 Mar. 1904: 7.)

During the mid-1890s, Munier published most of his important didactic material. His *Scuola del mandolino: metodo completo per mandolino*, written in 1891, was issued in 1895 by Lapini (in two volumes and three languages) and received enthusiastically as 'a very serious labour. Munier hopes that it will lead to a real development in the teaching of the instrument. Free of all vulgarity, its principle is to elevate artistically.' (*Il mandolino*, 15 Sept. 1895: 4.) 'It demonstrates that one can make a true and proper school for the instrument, suitable for the academy.' (*Il mandolino*, 15 Nov. 1895: 4.)

As complementary pieces to the method, his *Venti studi*, Op. 216, were published in the next year,[9] as were the four parts of his *Lo scioglidita*, Opp. 199, 213, 225, and 227, designed as exercises in velocity.[10] He also continued to teach mandolin, mandola, and guitar from his studio at 32 viale Margherita.[11] Although Munier occasionally gave concerts outside Italy, most of his performances took place in and around Florence, and were events of considerable importance, as this review of a concert given in the spring of 1904 makes clear:

> This concert, which had been well advertised in the papers and to which the posters had long called attention, was looked forward to with great interest by that part of the public who regularly visit the philharmonic concerts. Carlo Munier is a thorough musician; he has been a member of many musical academies, has travelled all through Italy and also directed concerts in foreign countries. One can easily understand that a concert directed by him attracted much attention; he was enthusiastically received by the audience and the evening's success was quite extraordinary.
>
> Yesterday evening the philharmonic hall presented a brilliant, festive picture. Not only the *crème de la crème* of Florentine society was assembled, even their

---

[9] *Il mandolino* (30 May 1896: 4).   [10] *Il mandolino* (30 Nov. 1896: 4).
[11] *Mandoline* (15 May 1904: 28).

neighbours beyond the Alps had joined their ranks; an aristocratic world of beauty and elegance. This intelligent audience enthusiastically applauded all the artists; encore after encore was demanded, but want of space prevents our enumerating them all; a Phantasy from 'Favorita' (arranged by Munier) in which Signora Marchesini-Guerrini played the harp with great skill, the Original Quartet by Munier, a Phantasy from 'Robert le Diable' [Meyerbeer] and an unpublished waltz 'Giglio fiorentino' by Munier, the melody of which is particularly pleasing, were rendered by the mandolin orchestra with wonderful expression and great accuracy, Munier directing. Carlo Munier performed a solo, a concert-phantasy in a manner wholly worthy of this artist, excellently accompanied by the pianist J. Maglicini. (*Il corriere italiano*, quoted in *Mandoline*, 15 May 1904: 24.)

Of the original members of the Florentine Quartet, only Munier remained by 1905. Bianchi had died[12] and, at a concert given in January 1905 at the Sala filarmonica, the players were now Carlo Munier, Evelina Arias, Pia Pellegrinetti, and Armando Casini.[13] At about this time Munier wrote his best-known composition, *Capriccio spagnolo*, Op. 276 (for mandolin with guitar or piano accompaniment), which, with its mix of exciting Spanish rhythms and Italian melody, quickly became a favourite concert item with performers, and has remained so up to the present day. He also began to experiment with compositions in duo style,[14] a way of playing two or more parts simultaneously with the plectrum and thus dispensing with the need for an accompanying instrument. Amongst such works are the beautiful but technically demanding 'Love Song', Op. 275 (he also made a version with accompaniment), and *Il nuovo stile dei duetti*, Op. 278, six pieces by Beethoven, Donizetti, Munier, and others, arranged by Munier as duets for a single mandolin, with the melody and accompaniment written on two separate staves. These six pieces (dedicated to Samuel Adelstein, one of the American pioneers of duo-style playing) were introduced to the Italian public by Munier:

This new style of 'Duets for Solo Mandolin', already well known and developed in America, is still unfamiliar in Italy. My present work comes, therefore, to fill this lacuna, and I hope that mandolinists of my nation will be seriously interested . . . The greatest difficulty of these duets lies in performing the tremolo notes of the melody while playing the staccato notes of the accompaniment with the same hand. The tremolo must continue unbroken while the small staccato notes are performed, [with the plectrum] jumping from string to string; this must be executed

---

[12] Munier (1909: 4) says that Bianchi was 'taken too soon from the Art', and speaks of him in the past tense.
[13] *Il mandolino* (30 Apr. 1905: 4).   [14] Described in more detail in Ch. 6.2.

with the maximum rapidity entirely to disguise the interruptions, and to give the illusion of two parts that are completely distinct yet fuse together well. (*Il mandolino*, 30 May 1906: 4.)

Munier was often a jury member at the international mandolin competitions that were now regularly being held throughout the Continent. At a contest held in Monaco in June 1906, he had the pleasure of hearing the quartet from the Circolo mandolinisti di Cremona win first prize (and the congratulations of the jury) with an excellent performance of his C major Quartet,[15] and later at the celebratory banquet he made the following speech:

> Gentlemen, allow me to say a few words on behalf of the mandolin, and to drink to its future, a serious artistic future.
>   We hope for two things with every confidence and enthusiasm. Firstly that the great masters wish to take music for the instrument into serious consideration; because it is not the case that the mandolin has to remain a simple instrument for serenades. I can affirm that the art of the mandolin, both in construction and in music, has made great progress over the years. Today one can no longer say that the mandolin is the little, incomplete instrument that it was in centuries past, the folly of dilettantes and street players. The most beautiful effects can be drawn from a plectrum quartet, delicate tremolos and pizzicatos that cannot be obtained from other instruments. (*L'Estudiantina*, 15 July 1906: 2.)

One of Munier's compositions that particularly appealed to classical musicians was his Trio in A major for piano, mandolin, and cello, which he performed in the Sala Maglioni in Florence in 1908.[16] After the performance Antonio Scontrino, professor of composition at the city's Reale istituto musicale and an important figure in the revival of Italian instrumental music, wrote to Munier saying, 'I send to you my sincere compliments for the noble aims of your compositions, namely to elevate the literature of the mandolin to a higher plane than before.'[17] Many other prominent Florentine musicians also praised his compositions and his performance, and lent their support to his campaign for the mandolin to be accepted into the Reale istituto musicale as a legitimate instrument of study. Munier had for some time been director of the first national mandolin and guitar school (a private organization based in Florence and run in conjunction with the Reale *circolo*),[18] but was determined to see the instrument recognized by the city's principal music establishment.

---

[15] *Il mandolino* (15 June 1906: 4).   [16] *Il mandolino* (15 May 1908: 4).   [17] Munier (1909: 4).

[18] *Il mandolino* (30 Dec. 1904: 4).

Giorgio Lorenzi, his lifelong friend and colleague, and professor of harp at the conservatoire, lent his public support to Munier in a letter published in the Neapolitan journal *Musica moderna*:

I read in the music periodical *Il plettro* of Milan (30 July 1909) a letter from the illustrious Prof. Vanzo in which, rightly deploring the positive lack of good music for the mandolin and similar instruments (something which definitely contributes to the continuance of the instrument at a very low level which it really does not deserve) and deploring also the lack of good composers for plectrum instruments, he goes on to say 'however, I do not wish to forget amongst them the remarkable Munier of Florence, whom one can admire for many fine compositions'. It is with great pleasure that I associate myself with the illustrious Mᵒ Vanzo's next remark: 'And is Munier known and appreciated as fully as he deserves to be?'

Professor Munier, a serious and skilful composer of genius, and an excellent mandolinist perhaps without equal in the whole of Italy, has dedicated the whole of his active life to the purpose of raising and ennobling the mandolin and plectrum instruments in general, a purpose in which, to my mind, he has been completely successful, with his compositions in a profound and elegant style—with his complete method for mandolin, a conscientious and artistic work—with his pieces for mandolin, and, above all, his trios and quartets for mandolins, mandola, and liuto in a formal and elevated style. And truly, Munier is not known and appreciated as he deserves; and the fault lies especially with publishers who prefer certain other music which, it is my belief, only pushes the mandolin further down. I join therefore with Mᵒ Vanzo in praying for improvement in the mandolin repertoire, and in rendering justice to the worth of Prof. Munier, who, to our shame, is perhaps better known and appreciated abroad than in Italy. (*Musica moderna*, 31 Oct. 1909.)

On 6 October 1909, Munier performed before King Victor Emmanuel III at the ancient castle of Sommariva Perno, playing two of his own compositions (a Prelude in D major and *Mazurka da concerto* No. 1: 'A Lei! . . .', Op. 224) and receiving warm congratulations from the monarch.[19] By now Munier felt that the mandolin was finally becoming part of the classical musical world, academically and orchestrally, and, in an article published at the end of that year, he looked back with some satisfaction on his career:

What follows is not just my opinion, but an absolute conviction, and events will shortly bear me out: the complete and rational study of mandolin and guitar will be accepted into conservatoires and musical institutes, alongside the other instruments of indisputable worth; and the orchestra (which already has such a wealth

[19] Munier (1909: 4).

of instruments) will welcome into its midst the entire plectrum quartet as an effective new colour. The improvement made in so short a space of time in the art of the mandolin is impressive enough, and gives a formal assurance of ever-increasing progress . . . I pride myself on setting a good example, because I have fought for more than thirty years and have never grown tired. And I have had disillusions, enough almost to discourage even me! (Munier 1909: 4.)

Sadly, Munier was not to live long enough to attain his goal. In the autumn of 1910 he made a European tour, visiting Marseilles, Antwerp, and Toutralle (Switzerland), where, on 18 November, he conducted an orchestra of forty male and female mandolinists and also performed his 'Love Song', Op. 275, to tremendous applause from the audience in the hall, which 'was crowded with important artistic and literary personalities of the highest rank.'[20] He returned to Florence, but in early February suffered a sudden stroke which deprived him of the power of speech and paralysed the entire right-hand side of his body. He died on 10 February 1911, leaving behind a total of some three hundred and fifty works for mandolin.[21]

The Reale *circolo* mandolinisti Regina Margherita continued to be one of the most highly respected mandolin orchestras in Italy throughout the 1890s. Bianchi, Graziani-Walter, Matini, and Munier were its central members and also its leading composers, with their music published by the reputable firms of Bratti, Venturini, Forlivesi, and Maurri.[22] Although a rival Circolo Italia was founded in December 1893, with Adolfo Sarcoli as director and Agostino Pisani as secretary,[23] it never reached the extremely high standards of the original Reale *circolo*. Amongst the concerts given in Florence by the Reale circolo was one in November 1894, to celebrate the birthday of its patron, Queen Margherita. Matini directed the orchestra, and the programme included 'Due cuori, colloquio d'amore' by Munier; 'Fior di siepe: notturno' by Matini; 'Nebel: serenata caratteristica' by Bianchi; and 'Mestizia' for mandola and orchestra by Giarritiello, in an arrangement by Munier, who also performed the solo part.[24] A year later, on 27 November 1895 at the Teatro Salvini, Munier, Bianchi, and Bizzari were the mandolin soloists, but the concert also included a cellist, pianist, and baritone.[25] The composers included Munier, Carlo Graziani-Walter, and Matini, who also directed.

---

[20] *Il concerto* (15 Jan. 1911: 1).   [21] *Il plettro* (28 Feb. 1911: 1) and *Moderne Musik* (20 Apr. 1911: 3).
[22] *Il mandolino* (15 Aug. 1893: 4).
[23] *Il mandolino* (15 Dec. 1893: 4). In this ref., Sarcoli's Christian name is given as Alfredo but, as I have never come across a player with this name, I have assumed that it was actually Adolfo Sarcoli.
[24] *Il mandolino* (15 Jan. 1895: 4).   [25] *Il mandolino* (30 Dec. 1895: 4).

Matini seems to have ceased conducting the orchestra shortly after this, because on 10 February 1896 it gave a performance under Bianchi,[26] and at its 138th concert on 31 May 1897 at the Teatro Salvini, in the presence of the king and queen and the royal court, the new leader was Graziani-Walter, who also arranged and/or composed all the music. Their programme on that occasion included a grand fantasia on Bellini's *Norma*, another on Puccini's *La Bohème*, and Graziani-Walter's own *Suite villageoise*.[27] The orchestra maintained its close association with Munier, being involved with him in the running of the first national mandolin and guitar school and, in January 1905, sharing a concert in the Sala filarmonica with his quartet.[28] Amongst the orchestra's associates was Enrico Marucelli, who trained as a double-bass player at the Reale istituto musicale and often played with the Reale circolo on this instrument.[29] He became interested in the mandolin and later emigrated to London. Agostino Pisani, a founder member of the Circolo Italia, also reviewed many of the Reale circolo's concerts for *Il mandolino* and proved to be a perceptive mandolin journalist. He is most notable for writing *Manuale teorico pratico del mandolinista* (published in 1898 by Ulrico Hoepli of Milan),[30] a small but remarkable book that intelligently discusses the origins, history, technique, and manufacture of Milanese, Roman, and Neapolitan mandolins, and also contains the earliest known bibliography of mandolin literature.

Milan

After his success at the Genoa concourse at the age of 17, Leopoldo Francia was hailed as Milan's leading mandolinist. Although he had played the Milanese mandolin in the orchestra at Genoa, his solo performances were given on the more popular four-course instrument, in his case a four-octave mandolin built for him by the Neapolitan maker Umberto Ceccherini.[31] He often conducted the Milan *circolo*, giving a concert with it on 20 September 1892 that included a work especially composed for the occasion and dedicated to Francia—a Lyric Symphony by Bazzini.[32] Antonio Bazzini was the head of the Milan conservatoire (where Mascagni and Puccini were amongst his students), and was probably the most important Italian chamber music composer of his

[26] *Il mandolino* (15 Apr. 1896: 4).   [27] Adelstein (1905: 10).
[28] *Il mandolino* (30 Apr. 1905: 4).   [29] *Il mandolino* (30 Mar. 1898: 4).
[30] *Il mandolino* (15 Oct. 1898: 4). This book was reissued by the same publisher in 1913.
[31] *Banjo World* (Oct. 1896: 167).
[32] *Banjo World* (Dec. 1896: 21). I have not yet been able to locate a copy of this work.

generation, playing a great part in the revival of the nation's instrumental tradition. Although the mandolin was not formally accepted into the conservatoire, Francia was presumably permitted to study it there by Bazzini, because
he subsequently remarked that 'I am myself an example of what can be done
with it [the mandolin] at the Milan Conservatoire'.[33] Amongst Francia's many
successes in Italy was a command performance before Queen Margherita, but
in 1894 he chose to leave his native city and settle in London, where he was
to spend most of the next decade as that city's leading player.

After Francia's departure (and Armanini's death in 1895), Angelo Alfieri
took over the role of premier player, directing the Milan *circolo* and giving
solo performances on his Milanese mandolin. Alfieri was the first Italian mandolinist whose playing can still be heard today, since he made dozens of recordings on cylinders and discs for the Gramophone and Pathé companies, the
earliest being a performance of his own composition 'D'amor passagero', issued
in July 1899 (Gramophone 2805).[34] We even know the circumstances in which
some early recordings were made. In 1901, a new system of recording on to
hard wax tablets had been developed by Emile Berliner, making it possible for
the first time to produce almost limitless numbers of copies from a single
master. The following spring, Fred Gaisberg of the Gramophone Company
took this new equipment to Milan, installed it at Spatz's Hotel, and began to
record musicians, amongst them the great *verismo* tenor Enrico Caruso, who
sang ten arias for the company on 11 April 1902 and promptly became the
first internationally famous recording artist.[35] More importantly for us, Alfieri
also made recordings there:

> Mr. F. W. Gaisberg, Record Manager of the Gramophone Company has just returned
> from Milan, where he made records of the celebrated Italian mandolinist, Angelo
> Alfieri. 'Histoire d'un Pierrot Serenata' is an especially pretty and effective record,
> as also is that of 'La Mandoline' (Thomé). He (Signor Alfieri) plays his own
> Concertos on a Milanese Mandoline. (*Banjo World*, May 1902: 109.)

Alfieri's discography includes several original mandolin compositions, such as
his own 'Serenata lombarda' and 'Changez la dame: polka', and the serenade

---

[33] *BMG* (Dec. 1904: 36–7).

[34] I am indebted to Neil Gladd for providing me with a list of Alfieri's recordings.

[35] Gaisberg (1946: 47–8). Caruso subsequently made hundreds of recordings (mostly in the USA), including the
following accompanied by Bianculli on the mandolin: New York (7 Jan. 1915), 'Perché?' (Pennino), Victor-Matrix
C 15568, 'A luna' (Varelli), Victor-Matrix B 15571–1 (destroyed); New York (20 Mar. 1916), 'Santa Lucia' (Cottrau),
Victor-Matrix C 17344; Camden (11 July 1918), 'Maria, mari' (di Capua), Victor-Matrix C 22127–1/2/3 (three versions, all destroyed).

from the pantomime *Histoire d'un Pierrot* (1893) by Pasquale Antonio Cataldo Mario Costa; many others are arrangements of melodies from popular operas, such as the siciliana from Mascagni's *Cavalleria rusticana* and 'Casta diva' from Bellini's *Norma*. Alfieri's reputation remained high throughout the 1900s. In 1901 he was described as 'this concert artist of indisputable worth . . . directing with loving artistry the Circolo lombardo'[36] and he seems increasingly to have devoted himself to working with orchestras. On 14–15 September 1907, at a competition in Vicenza, he directed a *circolo* from Busto Arsizio (near Milan) in a performance of Domenico De Giovanni's Symphony in G,[37] and in 1911 it was noted that he was the director of several mandolin societies, but was still available to instruct other *circoli* in Milan or the provinces.[38]

Milan dominated music publishing in Italy, and it is not surprising to find that mandolinists from all the country sent their works there, especially to Ricordi, which had become one of the world's largest printed-music businesses. At least two mandolin magazines were also published in Milan during this period. The first number of *Il plettro* was issued on 15 March 1906, and it appeared fortnightly until 1914, after which it became a monthly journal. *Il mandolinista italiano* first appeared as a monthly publication (before 1913), but seems to have been retitled *Mandolinista italiano* in June 1915, after which it was published fortnightly by A. Monzino & figli.[39] The Monzino firm, located at via Rastrelli 10, was now making quartet instruments on the Lombardian system, as well as excellent Milanese mandolins. One of its most distinctive innovations was the arcichitarra (invented in about 1890 and also known as the chitarrone moderna), a large instrument tuned like a conventional double bass, plucked with the fingers of the right hand, and intended to reinforce the bass-line in mandolin orchestras. It was used by many Milanese *circoli*, but its lack of volume (more noticeable in orchestras that used steel-strung Neapolitan instruments) prevented its universal adoption.[40]

Rome

Although Mascagni, Leoncavallo, and Puccini are nowadays credited with the development of *verismo* opera, several other Italian composers active during

---

[36] *Vita mandolinistica* (5 Jan. 1901: 2).   [37] *L'Estudiantina* (1 Nov. 1907: 3).
[38] *Il plettro* (28 Feb. 1911: 1).   [39] Pisani (1913: 131–2) and private research by Tetsuro Kudo.
[40] Ranieri (1925: 1994) and Pisani (1913: 143). Monzino also made guitars, violins, violas, and cellos. See also the App.

the 1890s also achieved great success with strong, dramatic works on contemporary, realistic themes. Many of them were associated with Naples, but Nicola Spinelli, who scored a great triumph with *A basso porto*, lived in Rome. First performed in Cologne in 1894, this popular three-act opera dealt with aspects of contemporary Neapolitan life, and used mandolin and guitar in several scenes, including a beautiful serenade in Act II, 'Mare d'argento' (a sinister version of this serenade, with all the plucked instruments tuned a semitone higher, returns to accompany the murder which ends the opera), and the Prelude and Intermezzo from Act III (Ex. 5). Silvio Ranieri said that in this opera Spinelli 'wrote some truly wonderful pages for solo mandolin',[41] and Samuel Adelstein, who attended the first performance in Rome (on 11 March 1895 at the Teatro Costanzi, in the presence of the King and Queen of Italy), noted that 'The most effective and taking number was the mandolin solo written especially for the opera by the composer and performed by the celebrated mandolinist of Rome, Sig. G. B. Maldura, accompanied by the orchestra. It was received with great success, several encores being demanded.' (Adelstein 1905: 7.)

Maldura was famous as a performer, but his enduring legacy to mandolinists was his work with Luigi Embergher during the 1890s, which resulted in the creation of the Classical Quartet; two mandolins, a mandoliola (tuned like a viola, and usually called a tenor mandola in English), and a mandoloncello (tuned like a cello, and also known as a mandocello), conceived as a family of Roman instruments and built in exact proportion to one another. This group of instruments, first heard in Rome in 1897 and displayed internationally at the Turin exhibition of 1898,[42] duplicated the ranges of the classical string quartet and allowed mandolinists, once they had familiarized themselves with the alto and bass clefs, to perform chamber music written for bowed strings with no need for any modification of the original parts. To differentiate between this new form of quartet and the traditional arrangement of two mandolins, octave mandola, and either liuto or guitar, the latter type was normally referred to as the Romantic Quartet. The Romantic Quartet (usually with guitar, since the liuto was a comparatively rare instrument) was an ideal vehicle for bringing the flavour of Italian folk-music into the concert-hall, and it always remained more popular than the Classical Quartet. However, many musicians rightly pointed out that the Embergher–Maldura instruments were better suited to

---

[41] Ranieri (1925: 1992).   [42] Janssens (1982: 25) and *Mandoline* (15 May 1904: 23).

Ex. 5. Spinelli: Intermezzo from *A basso porto*, bars 51–8

the interpretation of the string quartet repertoire, and possessed a homo-
geneous texture throughout their range, whereas viola parts did not always sit
well on the octave mandola, and the guitar was an intruder into the mandolin
family:

> *Classical Plectrum Quartet—Embergher System* . . . The chief value of this arrange-
> ment lies in the tuning of the instruments in fifths and the use of the same clefs
> as the string quartet: the two mandolins in the violin clef, the mandoliola in the
> viola clef, the mandoloncello in the bass clef. This classical plectrum quartet per-
> mits the playing of all classical music written for string instruments, making new
> musical effects possible. New treasures of classical music have enriched the reper-
> toire of the above-named plectrum instruments.
>
> There are various quartets for plectrum instruments and a still greater number
> for two mandolins, mandola and guitar. Others are arranged for two mandolins,
> mandola, and the Neapolitan lute with five double strings, thus resembling the clas-
> sical quartet of Embergher. But the value of neither of these quartets equals that
> of the Embergher. The first mentioned adds the guitar and, as sustained notes and
> the tremolo cannot be obtained on it, the character of the classical quartet is changed,
> the pizzicato of the guitar altering its whole nature. The second quartet resembles the
> classical quartet more but has some defects. To play classical music with this
> quartet, special arrangements would be necessary. This makes a large repertoire
> impossible; besides there is no acoustic, polyphonic scale having the same tones
> from the highest note of the mandolin to the lowest note of the lute.[43]
>
> The Embergher quartet is a happy solution to all these difficulties, and we hope
> to see many artists and amateurs manifesting an interest for it, which is even now
> being quite widely used; we hope they will found plectrum quartets on this sys-
> tem for the studying of classical music. On the success of his wonderful discov-
> ery we extend our heartiest congratulations to Meister Embergher in Rome.
> (*Mandoline*, 15 May 1904: 23.)

Embergher employed numerous apprentices in his workshop, each of whom
concentrated on a small part of the overall manufacture, while he oversaw
production. One of them, Domenico Cerrone, began working there at the age
of eight, and showed such talent that Embergher decided to train the boy as
his successor. Embergher made several types of mandolin (a student instrument, four types of orchestral mandolin, and three concert models), all of
which were sold in Rome at his shop in via Leccosa 1–2.[44] According to

---

[43] The string lengths of the instruments of the Embergher quartet, unlike all previous quartets, were in exact
proportion to their pitches.
[44] Janssens (1982: 29) and *Mandoline* (15 Apr. 1904).

Ranieri, Embergher was also the creator of the *terzini*, a small orchestral mandolin that used the same notation as a standard instrument, but produced notes a minor third higher.[45] However, it was his Roman concert mandolins that won him an international reputation, with many of the world's finest soloists considering them to be the perfected form of the instrument. Chief amongst these virtuosi was Silvio Ranieri, who gave his first concert in his native Rome in 1897 at the age of 15, to huge public acclamation,[46] after which he began to tour throughout Europe. Louis Quievreux, a Belgian journalist who became a close friend, later spoke of Ranieri's desire to elevate the mandolin:

> Why had he selected the mandolin? A secret and patriotic sentiment told him that he could ennoble it by turning it into a concert instrument. To this end, he undertook to make himself known to the world. He was applauded in the principal cities of Europe, in Russia, in England, in France, in Holland, and in Belgium, where he settled permanently in 1901. (Quievreux 1956: 2.)

Although Ranieri spent the remainder of his life based in Brussels (where we shall hear much more of him later), he retained close connections with Rome and with Embergher. He always performed on Embergher mandolins, which he likened to Stradivarius violins in their perfection[47] and, during the First World War, acquired a particularly splendid instrument from the maker himself:

> Early in 1915, he made a concert tour of Italy which was, in reality, a propaganda tour for Belgium. The [German] occupying force realized this and, when the virtuoso returned home, he was arrested. A council of war sentenced him to two years in prison. This imprisonment scarcely troubled Ranieri, since an immense joy had overwhelmed him in Rome. Some days before his first recital he had admired, at the premises of the luthier Embergher, a superbly carved mandolin bearing the label 'Gold Medal. Paris, 1900'. He tried it and found it superior to all others that he knew. He wished to buy it. 'Not for sale!' said Embergher, who however consented to let him use it for the recital.
>
> It came as no surprise to Ranieri to see, at the end of his concert, a tearful Embergher rush towards him with outstretched arms: 'I won't sell it to you! I will give it to you!' (Quievreux 1956: 2.)

Ranieri's brilliance was universally acknowledged. Munier called him 'an extraordinary performer',[48] and the dozens of reviews that appeared in

---

[45] Ranieri (1925: 1993). [46] Quievreux (1956: 2), although *Mandoline* (15 June 1904: 33) says that he was 16.
[47] Ranieri (1925: 1993). [48] Munier (1909: 4).

mandolin journals are full of superlatives, noting the perfect marriage between artist and instrument, as in this account of a concert given by Ranieri in Leipzig on 29 November 1903:

> Much praise is also due to the artist Embergher in Rome who has constructed an instrument of wondrous beauty for Ranieri. We are sure that Ranieri will not be offended if we ascribe a part of his great triumphs to the excellence of his wonderful instrument. The instruments of Embergher are unequalled, not only the richness and fullness of tone are remarkable but the intonation is also perfect. (*Mandoline*, 15 Apr. 1904: 21–2.)

Although Embergher's superb instruments placed his reputation far above that of any other mandolin-maker in Rome, Giovanni De Santis also continued to work with Maldura, making fine instruments that obtained distinctions at many international exhibitions and were used by the Italian royal court.[49] Giuseppe Branzoli remained Rome's leading authority on the mandolin. His *Metodo teòrico-pratico per mandolino lombardo distribuito in 98 lezioni* was published in Florence in 1906,[50] and on 15 January 1907 the first issue of a new monthly journal, *Il mandolino romano*, appeared. Edited by Branzoli, it continued after his death in 1909, eventually ceasing publication in 1911.[51]

Mario Bacci was an important Roman arranger of mandolin music, many of his orchestrations and transcriptions being published by Ditta Maurri of Florence.[52] Isidolo Angelo Figliolini was a highly respected performer in Rome, but remained little known outside of the city. Giuseppe Cesolari began his musical career as an apprentice in a lutherie in Rome, until an impresario offered him work as a member of a group of mandolinists and guitarists. He toured Europe, performing Neapolitan songs and accompanying the famous Italian soprano Lina Cavalieri, before founding a mandolin and guitar workshop in Paris, which he relocated in Mans in 1898.[53] One of Rome's leading orchestral directors was Giuglio Tartaglia, who in 1904 conducted a very large ensemble at a state occasion:

> During the visit of President Loubet [of France] in Rome the well-known mandolinist Prof. Cav.r Giuglio Tartaglia gave a mandolin, mandola, and guitar concert in which 150 players took part, he himself directing it in his usual perfect style. A great crowd visited the so-called 'Monte Pincio' the scene of the concert; the vast audience can be measured from the fact that more than 12,000 free tickets were

[49] Vannes (1951).   [50] *Dizionario biografico degli italiani.*   [51] From private research by Tetsuro Kudo.
[52] *Le Plectre* (1 Jan. 1914: 4).   [53] *Le Plectre* (July 1992: 6).

issued. The pavilion specially erected for the orchestra was tastefully decorated, and with its orange-coloured chinese lanterns had the appearance of a fantastic flower covered arbor. Among the players were several ladies. (*Mandoline*, 15 June 1904: 34.)

At about the same time that Ranieri was settling in Belgium, Mario Maciocchi emigrated from Rome to Paris, having first been to that city while directing two mandolin orchestras at the Universal Exposition of 1900.[54] His subsequent influence on Paris was to be almost as great as that of Ranieri on Brussels.

Naples

Although Naples had not been able to send a *circolo* to represent the city at the Genoa concourse, the Calace brothers founded one shortly afterwards, the Circolo mandolinistico Calace, which gave its inaugural concert during June 1893, playing music by Bériot and Vieuxtemps (with Nicola and Raffaele as soloists on the mandolin and the liuto respectively).[55] Nicola was the group's musical director for several years, but in 1901, apparently after an argument with Raffaele, he emigrated to the USA, where he continued making mandolins (under the pseudonym Nicola Turturro) until his death in 1924.[56] With Raffaele as director and Francesco Della Rosa as its most prominent orchestral member,[57] the *circolo* remained the focal point for the mandolin in Naples until the First World War.

Amongst the instruments manufactured by the firm of Calace was the mandolira, a mandolin with standard Neapolitan tuning but a lyre-shaped body, designed by the brothers in the mid-1890s and kept in production for many years. Its chief advantage was the ease with which all twenty frets could be reached by the left-hand fingers, but this hybrid instrument aroused little interest outside Naples. However, mandoliras were regularly used by the *circolo*, whose unusual instrumentation also included mandolins, liuti, harps, piano, and harmonium. At a concert given in Naples early in 1905, this ensemble scored a great success with a performance that included extracts from *Thaïs* by Massenet and two new compositions ('Notturno' 'Minuetto Pompadour') by Raffaele Calace: 'The originality of this little ensemble lies precisely in

---

[54] *La Mandoline* (1981: 41).   [55] *Il mandolino* (30 June 1893: 4).

[56] *Dizionario biografico degli italiani*, with additional information from Arena Anna ved. Calace, in a letter to me, Jan. 1992. After 1901, the labels inside Calace instruments no longer read 'Fratelli Calace', but 'Prof. R. Calace'.

[57] *Il mandolino* (30 Mar. 1895: 4) and Adelstein (1905: 12).

the perfect fusion of the diverse voices. The interesting voice of the liuto, grave and singing at the same time, blends with the light, purring tremolo of the mandolins, mandoliras, harps, etc., in completely new ways.' (*Musica moderna*, Apr. 1905: 7.)

Raffaele Calace was the editor and proprietor of *Musica moderna*, which commenced publication in January 1905 (initially appearing monthly, then fortnightly) and continued until 1910, when it was forced to close owing to his increased activity as a concert artist and composer. Whereas most of the journals quoted in this chapter were intended to appeal only to players of fretted instruments, *Musica moderna* displayed a broad range of musical and literary interests that placed it amongst the most important Neapolitan artistic publications of its day. Amongst its collaborators were Alessandro Longo (the first scholar to catalogue the complete keyboard sonatas of Domenico Scarlatti), Paulo Serrao (a leading composer of operas and church music, and Raffaele's former composition teacher), Leopoldo Mugnone (a composer and conductor who gave the first performance of *Cavalleria rusticana*), and many of the most prominent poets and painters in Naples. The journal argued passionately on behalf of Wagnerian opera and of new music (such as the symphonies of Mahler, which were then unfamiliar to Neapolitan audiences), and championed the revival of instrumental composition in Italy.

This breadth of artistic understanding lends a particular authority to the series of extended articles on the mandolin and liuto that Calace published in *Musica moderna* during 1908, since they were written from the perspective of an experienced, knowledgeable musician with wide-ranging tastes, not a specialist concerned only with plucked stringed instruments. Like Munier, he was convinced that the mandolin and liuto ought to be incorporated into the symphony orchestra, not to replace any of the existing instruments but to augment them:

Formerly, the mandolin appeared in the orchestra, and I say this with certainty: there will come a day when it will take a permanent position there. In fact this delicate instrument, so useful in all harmonic rhythm, is necessary in the orchestra, not as a central characteristic, but as one ingredient on the musical palette. Do we not hear the tambourine, the castanets, the tam-tam, and, since Strauss, has not the xylophone been introduced? Naturally, all these instruments serve only to provide an opportune touch or an accentuation, seeing that, compared with the four bowed strings and the woodwind, they have only a secondary function; but each knows well the importance of its caress to the musical phrase as a whole. That touch ... is sometimes the happiest part of a whole composition. Consequently, to add the mandolin and the liuto is to enrich the orchestra with new effects, or else to pair together, for example, the mandolin and flute, or a liuto melody with little bursts of mandolin commenting on the woodwind, or after an orchestral crescendo leave isolated a melody on mandolin or liuto; or accentuate an oboe melody with the mandolin playing staccato notes and certainly you will get the most novel results and miraculous effects ... I conclude by asserting, without any fear of disappointment, that the mandolin and the liuto are classical instruments, and today, when everyone is breathless to discover the means of obtaining new effects, they will be tested artistically, and carried into the orchestra. They will be the founts of glory and advantage to those who have the initiative to use them ... When recently at our San Carlo, Mozart's *Don Giovanni* was performed, everyone noted that the performance of the opera was passing with a certain indifference, and the public were only excited and started to applaud when came the famous serenade, accompanied by the liuto, as Mascagni [the conductor] had desired. (Calace 1908*a*: 4.)

Calace believed that only two things prevented the mandolin's universal acceptance by serious musicians: the poor construction of most instruments, and the unsystematic and inadequate approach to technique shown by many teachers and players. These points were raised in *Musica moderna* in 1906, in an unsigned article (clearly written by Calace, or at his behest) which pointed out that commercial considerations were forcing many makers to produce mandolins and guitars at impossibly low prices, with inevitable results:

They are being forced to construct their instruments not with art, reasoning, and attention to detail paramount, but concerned only with finding the best means of making an instrument for 6 or 7 lire. Just think. A worker, adopting such a means of production, has to make four or five instruments each day; think of how little scrupulous attention to detail he can give ...

These makers of money boxes in the shape of mandolins have, up until now, had a fair wind in their sails because entrepreneurs would buy their mandolins to sell abroad at a good price, with a ribbon tied around them, as mementoes of Italy, as drawing-room decorations. And in many of the drawing-rooms of London, Paris, and Brussels one sees these mandolins hanging from the wall, no one taking care of them, or playing them, with everyone convinced that they are *souvenirs of Naples*, and not musical instruments.

And this deluge of pseudo-mandolins has produced another, greater disaster: a veritable blizzard of pseudo-teachers ... who give credibility to instruments that really only merit a priest to administer the last rites to them ... These teachers-by-ear have given rise to the belief that the mandolin cannot attain anything more than they themselves can attain. But, one after another, makers and players have become dissatisfied, and the time has now come for those who have studied with love and intelligence, and who are concerned with art, and not only with employment. The firm of Raffaele Calace has obtained world-wide success. There, art is the only consideration, and the mandolins it builds merit serious consideration. Its instruments are not playthings; and the few true maestri use only mandolins from the Calace firm, although its prices are ten times those of the others mentioned earlier. (*Musica moderna*, 31 Oct. 1906: 4.)

Calace neatly combined artistic aspirations with business interests by offering a course of free lessons to anyone who purchased an instrument from his workshop at via Chiaia 207. The lessons were given by Nicola Romano and Francesco Della Rosa, former professional violinists (Romano had played in the San Carlo and Covent Garden orchestras) who became two of Naples' leading mandolin performers and teachers.[58]

As Calace's opus numbers are (approximately) in chronological sequence, we can use them to form an accurate picture of his compositional career. By early 1905, when he wrote the 'Minuetto Pompadour', Op. 32,[59] he had published fewer than three dozen pieces for the mandolin. During the next few years he composed only a handful more, but completed his greatest technical work, the six-volume *Metodo per mandolino* (Opp. 37–42), which explored the instrument's technique more thoroughly even than Munier's tutor.[60] From about 1910 onwards (the year when he closed *Musica moderna*), he began to concentrate on composition to a far greater extent, becoming not only more prolific, but also more profound and imaginative. His mature style developed beyond the easy melodies and simplistic forms in which Italian instrumental music had been constrained for so long, and he started to produce a stream of memorable, accomplished works that have since come to form an essential part of the repertoire of the classical mandolin.

Central to his output was a series of eighteen unaccompanied preludes, ten for mandolin and eight for liuto, which he began writing about 1910. These were the most advanced set of pieces that had then been composed for the instruments, and the best of them are a perfect marriage of musical thought and extreme technical demands. Several have been favourite solo items amongst

---

[58] *Musica moderna* (30 Nov. 1906: 4).   [59] *Musica moderna* (Apr. 1905: 7).

[60] Vol. ii of the method was pub. in June 1907 (*Musica moderna*, 1–15 June 1907), as was 'Douce souvenir', Op. 33; vol. iii appeared in Oct. 1908 (*Musica moderna*, Oct. 1908).

Ex. 6. Calace: Prelude No. 2, closing bars

virtuosi ever since, in particular Prelude No. 2 in D minor, Op. 49 (Ex. 6),[61] dedicated to the Greek virtuoso Demetrius C. Dounis. After a striking chordal opening, much of this prelude takes the form of a brooding cadenza, with slow, haunting tremolo melodies (held over staccato accompaniments) alternating with rapid arpeggio sequences, before concluding with a powerful

[61] Composed *c.*1911.

Allegro in the tonic major. Many of the preludes composed around this time, such as No. 3 in B minor, Op. 63, and No. 5 in D major, Op. 74, have a similarly free form, with melodic fragments (usually presented in duo style) interrupted by extended scale passages and bravura flourishes, followed by a fast, rhythmic closing section. Calace demonstrated a sophistication of compositional skill and instrumental technique throughout these eighteen preludes that has seldom been equalled in the unaccompanied mandolin repertoire, and the principal reason why many of them are so rarely heard today is that only a handful of players can perform them.

Calace wrote numerous concert pieces for mandolin and piano (many of which also exist in versions with guitar accompaniment, and in trio or quartet form) during these years, in a variety of styles. Some were short, typically popular Neapolitan items, for example the 'Rapsodia napoletana', Op. 66, and the Tarantella, Op. 18. Others were extended classical compositions, such as the *Gran duetto* Opp. 70–2 (Marziale–Largo–Rondo scherzoso) for mandolin and liuto, premièred by Ernesto Rocco (mandolin) and the composer (liuto) at an artistic evening given by Mme la Marquise Acquaviva de' Medici in Naples late in 1913, and performed again by Calace in Marseille early in 1914, this time with Laurent Fantauzzi on the mandolin.[62] Like many Italian composers of his generation, he was fascinated by the almost forgotten legacy of Baroque and Renaissance music that was then being revived by Italian scholars, and pieces such as the simple, stately 'Pavana', Op. 54, and the lively 'Saltarello', Op. 79, reflect that interest. He also composed numerous ensemble works for mandolin, mostly using the Romantic Quartet (with liuto), and pieces for solo guitar.

A man of extraordinary energy, Calace was also an active performer. For many years he directed his own Quartetto classico a plettro (Illustration 12 shows the members of this quartet in about 1900), which, at a concert given on 26 February 1912, included his daughter Maria on the first mandolin, his son Giuseppe on the tenor mandola, and Raffaele himself on the liuto.[63] At another concert, given at the Calace family house on 8 May 1909, Raffaele performed pieces by Beethoven, Moskowski, and Grieg on the mandolira (accompanied on the piano by another son, Vincenzo, who studied with Busoni and later became a distinguished concert performer and vice-principal of the

---

[62] *Le Plectre* (1 Jan. 1914: 4). *Musica moderna* (30 Nov. 1909) notes that Mme la Marquise Acquaviva de' Medici was herself a fine concert mandolinist.

[63] Details from a concert programme, provided by Arena Anna ved. Calace.

Illustration 12. A rare, damaged photograph of the Calace Quartet, *c.*1900. From left: Raffaele, Maria, and Nicola; the identity of the fourth player is unknown (photograph courtesy of the Calace family).

Milan conservatoire), and the Ninth Concerto by Charles de Bériot on the liuto.[64] He also directed the full plectrum orchestra, which gave a grand concert in the sala Maddaloni on 16 April 1910, performing original mandolin music by Beethoven and Calace. Calace played the mandolira and liuto, with an orchestra consisting of mandolins, mandolire, liuti, harps, pianoforte, harmonium, and timpani.[65] Such concerts were given several times a year in Naples.

As well as these performances, Calace made regular tours of Europe, combining his recitals with business commitments:

Our Editor Professor Raffaele Calace, proprietor of the noted and reputable house of music that bears his name, the editor of *Musica moderna*, the worthy liutist whose name is so well known throughout the musical world, has left for his annual solo tour abroad. He has undertaken the trip partly for commercial reasons

[64] *Musica moderna* (31 May 1909).   [65] *Musica moderna* (31 Mar. 1910).

(meetings with various correspondents and agents for his firm), and partly because he has been invited to give concerts in the capital cities of Austria, Saxony, and Prussia.

Calace is following this itinerary: Rome, Bologna, Venice, Trieste, Vienna, Munich, Nuremberg, Dresden, Leipzig, Berlin, Hamburg, Bremen, Liège, Brussels, Paris, Mericourt, Basle, Zurich, Lucerne, Interlaken, Milan, Genoa, and then returning to Naples.

On his trip, Raffaele Calace will be occupied not only with dealings with agents for his new mandolin, which is so popular among intelligent players, but with showing in practice his great gifts, playing in concerts, and summoning the citizens of the great cities of Austria, Germany, and France. Good luck and good wishes! (*Musica moderna*, 1–15 June 1907: 1.)

The new mandolin was the 'Mandolino Calace '900 brevettato', designed by Raffaele as the ideal concert instrument. The model shown in Illustration 13 has only nineteen frets, but some were made with extended fingerboards, necessary when playing Calace's own compositions, which required up to twenty-seven frets. Calace believed, now that concert instruments and well-trained players were becoming widely available, that there was no longer any valid artistic reason why the mandolin should not be given a regular place in the orchestra. He took heart from the example of Mahler, whose symphonies had recently begun to include the mandolin:

It is a fact that composers and masters of music, searching for the beautiful and the new, and wishing to complete the musical palette, have read with great interest how I have counselled and predicted a great triumph for plectrum instruments. These most delicate instruments, so strongly picturesque, are today beginning to be studied with true understanding by distinguished musicians. Meanwhile, the great maestro Gustav Mahler, former director of the Imperial Theatre in Vienna, has written a Seventh Symphony, augmenting the orchestra with the addition of the mandolin and other instruments. When this symphony was superbly performed under the composer's baton at the Imperial Theatre in Prague, it received the approval of all the intelligentsia. The critics almost unanimously praised the beautiful initiative, and called Mahler an innovator of genius. Naturally there was the odd puritan with the odd objection; but these were no more than isolated voices ... Gustav Mahler has, therefore, put the mandolin into the orchestra. Certainly this is not a new state of affairs, as I have written before that Mozart required the instrument for his famous serenade. Mahler however gives it a post in the orchestra; he declares it in short necessary on a level with the brass, the woodwind etc., a part of the full instrumentation of the orchestra, enriched by a new element.

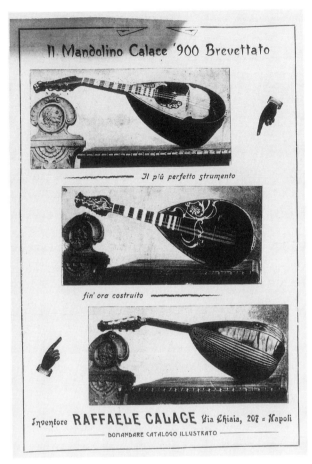

Illustration 13. An advertisement for the 'Mandolino Calace '900 brevettato' (from *Musica moderna*, 30 Nov. 1906).

It is beyond question that the maestro Gustav Mahler has made a great step forward for the mandolin, but I wish that his attention had been attracted to the entire quartet. Did he know of their existence? Certainly not. Otherwise he would have used them in his symphony.

One wishes that an Italian maestro might make a similar initiative; it would, I repeat with conviction, produce a marvellous effect. (Calace 1908*d*: 1–2.)

Although Calace's versatile genius placed him far above any other Neapolitan mandolinist of the period, the city housed many other fine makers, players, teachers, and composers. Salsedo, De Meglio, and Ceccherini all continued to make good instruments, but next to Calace, the most important of the hundreds of mandolin-makers in Naples were the members of the Vinaccia family (who had split into two or more competing businesses by the turn of the century). The firm of F. Vinaccia was manufacturing instruments during the early part of the century, and Giuseppe and Achille Vinaccia were also active makers,[66] but the most significant luthier was Gaetano Vinaccia of rua Catalana 96. He had a fine international reputation, supplying many of Europe's leading plectrum orchestras—in Cremona, Turin, Genoa, Brussels, Lausanne, Geneva, Vienna, and Boulogne-sur-Mer—as well as famous soloists such as Ernesto Rocco, who provided this testimonial: 'I am happy to tell you that the mandolin which you have made for me, and which serves me in all my concerts, has always given me complete satisfaction, for amplitude of sound, sweetness in high positions, and for its clear, vibrant sound.' The Rocco concert mandolin (Gaetano Vinaccia's finest instrument) retailed in France at 75 f. just before World War I.[67]

Ernesto Rocco was perhaps the most brilliant mandolinist that Naples ever produced, with a technique that surpassed even that of his close colleague Calace. He seems to have been universally admired by his contemporaries: Ranieri dedicated his D major Concerto to Rocco; Calace gave the first performance of his *Gran duetto*, Opp. 70–2, together with Rocco; and Munier said that 'simply to read one of his programmes gives an idea of the *tour de force* he produces at his concerts.'[68] When Rocco made a tour of Italy in 1906, the review in *Bollettina musicale* (a Venetian periodical) of his first concert was fulsome in its praise:

> Ernesto Rocco is a young Neapolitan who has brought the study of the mandolin to perfection, drawing from this instrument, which is strummed and maltreated by many, splendid effects of sonority and sweet melody. In his foreign concerts, the press unanimously praised and applauded the young concertist, and there are remarkable articles in the *Berliner Tagenblatt*, *The Times*, *Novóie Vremia*, *Pester Loyd*, etc. (Quoted in *Il plettro*, 15 Mar. 1906: 1.)

Later on that tour, he played in Bologna, again with great success:

> Finally, that Paganini of the mandolin, Signor Ernest Rocco, has given a recital at the Eleanora Duse Theatre, and achieved a triumph by the elegance and vigour of his playing. His programme included an Andante and Fugue by Bach, a concerto by Paganini, Tartini's 'Trillo del Diavolo,' a Fantasia on 'Carmen,' and melodies by Bazzini and Grieg. (*BMG*, June 1906: 144.)

---

[66] Vannes (1951).   [67] *L'Estudiantina* (15 May 1914: 3).
[68] *Le Plectre* (1 Jan. 1914: 4) and Munier (1909: 4).

Rocco's output as a composer was modest, but he produced at least one remarkable work, the Serenade in G minor, Op. 1, for unaccompanied mandolin (Ex. 7).[69] This piece extends the technical possibilities of the solo mandolin beyond anything found even in the preludes of Calace: right- and left-hand pizzicato across the strings, four-part chords made using the left thumb, duo-style passages with pizzicato, and a four-octave chromatic flourish descending from *a''''* all support and embellish a beautifully simple central melody. Although Rocco did not possess Calace's depth of compositional thought, his use of the mandolin is strikingly imaginative and original, and the piece remains a perfect (though immensely difficult) miniature.

Calace and Rocco chose to spend their lives in Naples, but many other fine players went abroad. Poor housing and a low standard of living (wages were often no more than 6*d*. a day)[70] persisted throughout the south, and emigration became an increasingly attractive option for those with marketable skills. By 1913, there were officially 5,557,746 Italians living abroad, and the true figure was probably much higher.[71] Given the enormous popularity of the mandolin in Europe and the USA, it is scarcely surprising that many Neapolitans with a talent for the instrument were tempted to travel abroad.

Giuseppe Silvestri still divided his time between Paris and his native city. Salvatore Leonardi, who was born in Catania (Sicily), grew up in Naples, where he studied the violin at the conservatoire and the mandolin with an uncle. After winning mandolin contests in Florence and Rome, he began to tour the world, teaching in Egypt, Malta, and London before settling in Paris at the turn of the century.[72] Two of his tarantellas, 'La bella sorrentina' and 'Souvenir de Naples', are attractive, typically Neapolitan pieces for mandolin (with guitar or piano accompaniment), while his fantasia for unaccompanied mandolin, 'Angeli e demoni', is a graphic (though not particularly serious) musical depiction of the battle between good and evil. Another prominent player was Bernardo De Pace, who studied the violin and the mandolin under Francesco Della Rosa, won an international mandolin competition at the age of 13, and travelled as a soloist to Paris, Berlin, and St Petersburg before settling in England and later emigrating to the USA. Vittorio Monti, also born

---

[69] Dedicated 'To my energetic impresario in Moscow, A. Schmit, in memory of sixty-four concerts in four months, in Russia and Asia'.

[70] A fortieth part of £1 sterling, and barely one tenth of the sum that a worker could expect to earn daily from working in a factory in London or Paris.

[71] Wallace (1917: 145).   [72] Bone (1972: 210).

Ex. 7. Rocco: Serenade, bars 1–21

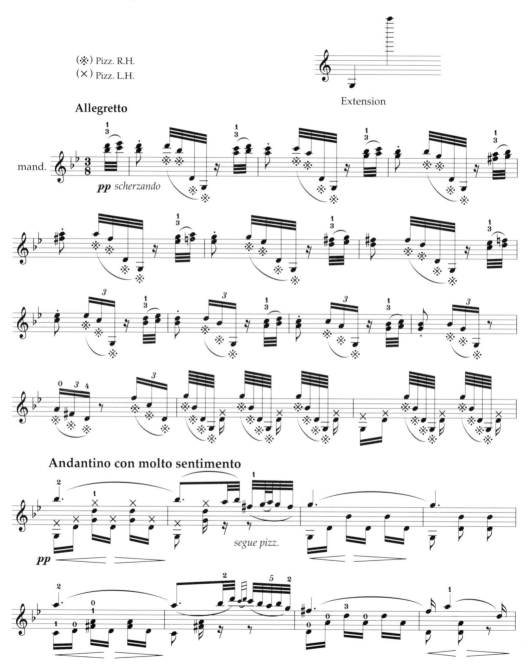

in Naples, was little known there but, after arriving in Paris just after 1900, he had a significant effect on mandolin life in his adopted city.

The mandolin appeared frequently in Neapolitan opera, especially in the new wave of works that dealt with contemporary society and its problems. In *Santa Lucia* (first performed in Berlin in 1892), Pietro Antonio Tasca portrayed the lives of Neapolitan fishermen, and featured the mandolin in the prelude and in a serenade in Act I.[73] Umberto Giordano used the mandolin in several operas, including *Il voto* (1892). The instrument's most successful appearance in an opera about Naples was probably in *I gioielli della Madonna* (first performed in Berlin in 1911) by Ermanno Wolf-Ferrari, a Venetian composer. The opera is set amongst the Camorrists of Naples, and in Act II a lively waltz-like serenade, 'Aprila o bella, la fenestrella', is accompanied by mandolins and guitars. The mandolin also appears in one of his earlier operas, *Le donne curiose* (1903).

Other Italian Cities

Turin had become an influential centre for the mandolin, owing mainly to the success of *Il mandolino*, which was widely disseminated throughout Italy and through which numerous competitions for composition and performance were organized. On 22–3 May 1897, for example, it held a competition in Turin for amateur soloists from any Italian region. Contestants were each required to perform two pieces, one to be received eight days beforehand, and the other to be sight-read after five minutes' examination; there were separate divisions for men and women, and also for mandola players and guitarists. At the same time, the journal held its Fourth Grand International Competition for new compositions; contestants were required to submit a small sinfonia for Romantic Quartet, or an intermezzo for mandolin trio (first mandolin, second mandolin or octave mandola, and guitar).[74] By 1910, the journal was organizing its Ninth Grand International Contest, this time requesting a sinfonia, composed in the classical style for a small mandolin orchestra (*orchestrina mandolinistica*) and not more than 250 bars in length.[75] The winning pieces were subsequently published in the journal.

Giovanni Navone was one of the leading performers in Turin. He founded a mandolin quartet in October 1893 and gave a prominent solo mandolin

---

[73] Zimmern (1906: 251) and Bone (1972: 356). His first name was often given as Pierantonio.
[74] *Il mandolino* (30 Apr. 1897: 4).   [75] *Il mandolino* (15 Nov. 1910: 4).

recital at the Teatro Gerbino on 12 March 1894, with a programme that included the *Faust* Fantasia by Sarasate and the 'Moto perpetuo' and 'Le streghe'
by Paganini.[76] There were at least two orchestras: the Circolo mandolinistico
torinese, directed by B. Monsello, which had begun performing by 1892, and
the Associazione mandolinistica, directed by Luigi Todo, which was founded
in 1896.[77] In 1911, the Quartetto Burdisso (led by Mº Burdisso), which had
recently won a competition in Cremona, gave a concert in Turin that included the overture to *Zampa* by Hérold, Munier's Second Quartet in D, Sarasate's
Variations on *Faust*, and the String Quartet Op. 1 No. 3 attributed to Haydn.[78]
The most internationally celebrated player to hail from the city, however, was
Maria Scivittaro (née Margherita Boccadoro), who won first prize at an international competition held in Turin in 1898, when she was just seven years old;
she then began to tour South America and Europe before settling in Paris in
1911.

Many of the major towns in the north had their own mandolin orchestras.
The leading figure in Genoa was C. A. Bracco, director of the mandolin section of the Club musicale genovese.[79] Amongst his achievements as a composer was the winning of two gold medals: one for his sinfonia, *I mandolini
a congresso*, at the Sixth Grand Competition held by *Il mandolino*, and another for his short piece 'Notte stellata' at the Third Grand Competition.[80]
During the mid-1890s, the Circolo dilettanti mandolinisti in Bergamo was
directed by Attilio Tarenghi.[81] In Modena, Primo Silvestri was the principal
figure, directing the Circolo mandolinistico Silvestri. In Verona, the Circolo
Margherita (which was founded in 1890 and won a silver medal at the Genoa
concourse in 1892) combined with another group on 1 March 1897 to form
the Club mandolinistico Veronese, led by Regolo Romani. This club ran an
independent school for those wishing to learn the mandolin, and had given
about a hundred concerts by 1904.[82] In Trieste (under Austrian rule until 1918),
the Club mandolinistico was led by Giovanni Battista Marzuttini.[83]

At first sight, Venice appeared to have a particularly close association with
the instrument. Images of mandolin-playing gondoliers abounded throughout
Europe, as did mandolin compositions with titles such as 'Serenata veneziana'

[76] *Il mandolino* (30 Oct. 1893: 4 and 30 Mar. 1894: 4). His death was announced in *Il mandolino*, 15 June 1907: 4.
[77] *Il mandolino* (30 Dec. 1892: 4, and 15 Feb. 1896: 4).   [78] *Il mandolino* (15 June 1911: 4).
[79] *Il mandolino* (15 Feb. 1905: 4) records that Bracco had died on 22 Jan. 1905. Bone (1972: 56) incorrectly
gives this date as 1903.
[80] *Il mandolino* (15 June 1895: 4).   [81] *Il mandolino* (15 Jan. 1896: 4).
[82] *Mandoline* (15 Aug. 1904: 54).   [83] Janssens (1982: 113).

and 'In gondola'. However, organized mandolin orchestras were virtually unknown there, and the instrument seems to have been played almost solely for the benefit of tourists. Leopoldo Francia made this clear when an interviewer asked him (with admirable forthrightness) why the mandolin was so badly played in Venice:

> Because there it is simply an artificial cult for the foreigners. The mandolin is played by night on the Grand Canal in order to obtain lire from the English. It is comparatively well studied in Genoa. I am myself an example of what can be done with it at the Milan Conservatoire . . . all over the north of Italy it is somewhat exotic. The South is the home of the mandolin, the part where the playing is indigenous, natural, and excellent. (*BMG*, Dec. 1904: 36–7.)

Exotic though it may have been in the north, there were many cities where it was superbly played, above all in Cremona. The Circolo mandolinisti-mandoliniste di Cremona, founded in 1896 and directed by G. F. Poli, totally dominated national and international competitions during the early 1900s. The *circolo* was organized into three groups, who usually shared concert performances. The Classical Plectrum Quartet (two mandolins, tenor mandola, and mandoloncello) performed entire classical string quartets and original works for mandolin, such as Munier's quartets (the scores of which the composer presented to the *circolo*). The Plectrum Orchestra had about twenty-five members, and contained a wide range of plectrum instruments—piccolo mandolin (in F), first and second mandolins (Lombardian and Neapolitan), mandolas (Lombardian and Neapolitan), Neapolitan lutes, mandoloncellos, guitars, and pizzicato basses—and its repertoire included Mozart symphonies and works by Ponchielli, Verdi, Donizetti, Rossini, Hérold, and Weber, arranged by Poli. Lastly, a flute, harmonium, trumpet, trombone, viola, violoncello, double bass, harp, glockenspiel, two clarinets, two horns, ocarinas, kettledrums, and cymbals were added to the Plectrum Orchestra to form the Grand Orchestra, which was used principally to play whole acts of operas. Articles about the *circolo* emphasized that most of its seventy members were either from noble families or else were well-educated professionals:

> 25 of the number are ladies of distinction . . . It is of importance to state that all members are amateurs, many of them having arrived at the age of discretion (lawyers, doctors, engineers, bookkeepers, merchants, etc.) who, by their common interest in art, are united in warm, ideal friendship. The social features are a great source of attraction for the members and their families. (*Mandoline*, 1 Oct. 1904: 2–4.)

The successes of this *circolo* included victories at competitions in Trento (1904), where four hundred mandolinists took part; Vicenza (1907), where it performed Poli's transcriptions of the overture to Mozart's *Magic Flute* and the sinfonia from Verdi's *Oberto*; Turin (1911), where it competed against orchestras from Italy, France, Belgium, and Switzerland; Como (1906), where it won with a performance of Beethoven's overture to *Prometheus*; and Monaco (1906), where it played Munier's Quartet in C Major to a jury that included the composer himself.[84] This description of the *circolo*'s success at the Trento competition on 19 June 1904 is typical of the rapturous reception it received at its concerts:

> The mandolin players, ladies and gentlemen, of Cremona, directed by G. J. Poli, had chosen a selection from Act IV of *Mefistofele*. The beautiful, difficult music of Boito was interpreted so well, the reception of some parts was so enthusiastic that one could imagine oneself at a complete symphony concert. Endless cheering rewarded the players. An encore was demanded; however, the *Hymn of Trento* was given instead, amid bursts of applause. Ladies stood up in the boxes and threw flowers to the players, who were quite overwhelmed by their stormy reception. (*Mandoline*, 15 July 1904: 42.)

In Bologna, there was at least one *circolo* in existence before 1892, and a new group was formed in September 1893.[85] Also, the mandolin journal *Il concerto* began publishing fortnightly there in January 1897. *Il concerto* consisted mainly of simple mandolin and guitar duets, but occasionally included more substantial compositions, such as the Concerto in G Major by Figliolini, a virtuoso showpiece (with guitar accompaniment) which appeared in the issue of 15 February 1911, dedicated to 'the famous maestro Carlo Munier', who had died only days earlier. The most famous soloist from the city was Carolina Grimaldi, whom both Ranieri and Francia regarded as being amongst the leading Italian performers. On Sunday 26 October 1895 she gave a concert with the Circolo mandolinistico Felsineo (an orchestra of 'young and exceptional women'), at which she performed music by Bériot and Wieniawski, as well as 'Le Cygne' by Saint-Saëns.[86] In 1911, she enjoyed another great success in her home town.[87] When Giuseppe Sgallari visited Bologna in 1906, he took part in a concert given by the thirty-five members of the mandolin club there, the

---

[84] *Il mandolino* (15 July 1904: 4; 30 Dec. 1907: 4; 15 Sept. 1911: 4; and 15 June 1906: 4) and *L'Estudiantina* (15 Aug. 1907: 6).

[85] *Il mandolino* (15 June 1895: 4).   [86] *Il mandolino* (15 Nov. 1895: 4).

[87] *Il concerto* (30 Feb. 1911: 1).

SIGNOR G. SGALLARI.

Illustration 14. Giuseppe Sgallari, *c.*1904 (from *BMG*, May 1904: 116). Photograph courtesy of the British Library.

programme including operatic excerpts from works by Wagner, Bellini, Gounod, and Verdi, as well as a potpourri from Ponchielli's *Gioconda*.[88]

Giuseppe Sgallari (Illustration 14) was born at Spilambarto, near Bologna, but first achieved success in Lerici (a coastal town near La Spezia), where he directed a mandolin orchestra, La giovane Lerici.[89] Although he had no formal conservatoire training, he spent eight years in his native town studying harmony and counterpoint under the Master of the Orchestra of the Government Warships, after which *Il mandolino* began publishing his light compositions. These proved to be popular enough at the time for him to begin an international career as performer, teacher, orchestral director, and composer, and we shall encounter him again both in Brussels and in London.

Throughout central and southern Italy, there were many other fine makers and players besides those listed here. In Sicily, for example, the instruments made by Salvatore Indelicato of Catania remain highly regarded today, as do those of his son Giuseppe. However, with the exception of Rome and Naples,

---

[88] *BMG* (June 1906: 144).   [89] *Il mandolino* (30 July 1894: 4).

there was little documentation of mandolin activity in these parts of Italy; the mandolin was an integral part of popular musical culture absorbed from birth, rather than an instrument to be formally studied. While Munier, Calace, Ranieri, and their contemporaries were performing sophisticated classical music in the concert-halls of Europe, for most Italians the mandolin remained the instrument of simple songs and serenades, such as in this description by a reporter of an evening in Siena:

> I was about to ascend to the Cathedral square when I was arrested by the tones of another mandolin—but such a one, and played exquisitely. Discreetly peering about, I saw in my immediate vicinity one of those tower-shaped corners you see in Italian houses. From an upper open window, behind green curtains, came soft light, and imagination might picture some lovely Marcaline or Lucia there breathlessly listening to the strains meant for her. In the shadow of the opposite side stood a man, apparently of some distinction in appearance, and he it was who was serenading the unseen dame hidden by the green curtains. Was it a lover to his lass, or a peccant to some too compliant wife?
>
> All else in the street was silent as the grave, except the sound of my own footsteps. No one else seemed to be occupying themselves with this voice of love and its hearer; for he made his mandolin breathe the sweetest, tenderest pleadings—now cooing and low as the voice of a man in the very ear of his mate as he begs for fresh complaisance, now fast and furious as the passion of the player expressing itself in a shower of semiquavers. How long the serenade lasted I know not. I heard my fill of this masterly manipulation, and then ascended to the Cathedral square. (*BMG*, Sept. 1906: 179.)

3.2 *The Heyday of the Mandolin in Europe*

The years roughly corresponding to the *belle époque* in France, the Wilhelmine Reich in Germany, and the late Victorian and Edwardian periods in Britain were also the time when the mandolin's popularity reached its zenith in Europe. Millions of instruments were bought, tens of thousands of original compositions and arrangements were published, and, by the beginning of the twentieth century, the mandolin had become one of the most widely played musical instruments in many of Europe's major cities. Most of this activity consisted of inexpert players performing fashionable but undemanding music for the amusement of themselves and their immediate circle of family and friends, and is of more interest as a social rather than a musical phenomenon. However, there were many towns and cities where serious musicians (usually gathered around an Italian virtuoso) dedicated themselves to the instrument and attained artistic standards as high as those we have already observed in Naples, Rome, Florence, and Milan.

Britain

The growing interest in fretted instruments in Britain led Clifford Essex (together with the banjoist Alfred Davies Cammeyer, with whom he ran a music studio in Piccadilly, London) to produce a specialist periodical, the *Banjo World*, which first appeared in November 1893 and was devoted to the banjo, mandolin, and guitar. Other fretted-instrument-manufacturers also produced their own journals, most notably Barnes & Mullins, who began publishing the *'Jo* in 1894 (changing its name in 1896 to the *Troubadour*), S. J. Dallas, who produced *Dallas' Musical Monthly and Advertiser* (1908–14), and John Alvey Turner, who published a monthly journal, *Keynotes* (1907–14). The news and advice contained in each of these periodicals (particularly about choice of instruments) naturally tends to reflect the commercial interests of its publisher, but, taken collectively, they provide us with an enormous amount of information about the mandolin.

At the start of this period, G. B. Marchisio was an important figure in London, teaching at Trinity College of Music, composing for the instrument (about 200 pieces, including a concerto), and directing Signor Marchisio's Orchestra of Mandolines and Guitars.[90] Signor Guerra, from Italy, settled in the capital and became a popular teacher and performer whose concerts included a mandolin and liuto recital at the Steinway Hall on 25 June 1894, 'to an appreciative and refined audience.'[91] Carlo D'Amato was also resident in the city at this time, teaching at his West Brompton studio, where weekly rehearsals were held for his Mandoline and Guitar Ladies' Band.[92]

However, when Leopoldo Francia arrived in 1894, he rapidly became London's most prominent mandolinist. His Ladies' Mandoline and Guitar Band (composed mainly of members of the titled aristocracy) regularly performed under

---

[90] *Banjo World* (Sept. 1894: 88) and Bone (1972: 221–2). An advertisement for Trinity College of Music in the *Musical Times* (1 Jan. 1899: 8) lists Marchisio as 'Professor of Mandoline', but he was already teaching there well before then. Until 1900 in Britain, the most common spelling of the instrument's name was the French 'mandoline'; after 1900, the final 'e' was often dropped, probably owing to the increasingly strong American influence in British fretted instrument literature, reflected in such journals as *BMG*.

[91] *Banjo World* (July 1894: 70).   [92] *Banjo World* (Jan. 1894: 32).

his direction at such prestigious venues as the Prince's Hall in Piccadilly, and the (small) Queen's Hall, Langham Place, where this concert took place on 22 March 1898:

> Signor Francia gave a masterly display of his superb technique and brilliant command over the instrument . . . it is long since a more ravishing performance has been heard than Signor Francia's delicate and tender interpretation of Mr. Elgar's 'Salut d'Amour'. He duly brought out the wailing pathos of Grieg's 'Elégie in A Minor', and fairly carried the audience with him in his startling and consummate rendering of Bazzini's 'Witches' Dance'. For this he was loudly encored, and obliged with an unaccompanied and very complicated solo. Later, his new and taking composition, 'Lo Zingaro', was vociferously demanded . . . The Ladies' Guitar and Mandoline Band played with delightful verve, steady time, and beautiful gradations of light and shade. Whilst their performance reflects the greatest credit on their painstaking conductor, Signor Francia, it also redounds to the individual credit of each lady whose skill assists so excellent a combination. The overture to 'Mirella' went admirably, as did the concluding 'Serenade' by Clementi . . . perhaps the *chef-d'oeuvre* was the characteristic Fantasia from the pen of Signor Francia, in which a duet was charmingly elicited from the mandoline of Lady Clayton and the mandola of Mrs. Slade, whilst the orchestra attacked the coda with a vivacity which was rewarded by prolonged applause. (*Banjo World*, Apr. 1898: 58.)

Like most professional mandolinists in Britain, Francia earned his living mainly through teaching, and performing in music-halls and variety theatres (such as London's Lyric Theatre, where he was engaged for a season in 1896).[93] Although audiences at such venues expected to be amused rather than edified, it was not uncommon for music-halls to feature acts which nowadays would be considered high art rather than popular entertainment. Many musicians of standing appeared there—Leoncavallo, for example, conducted numerous performances of a shortened version of Pagliacci—and when Anna Pavlova and the Russian Imperial Ballet first came to England in 1910, they were engaged at the Palace Theatre, a year before their first appearance at the Royal Opera House.[94] In such theatres, Francia usually played a repertoire based around his own light compositions, and often performed duo style unaccompanied pieces (his *Virtuoso School for the Mandolin*, written in 1896, contains the earliest examples of duo style I have yet found). However, his best works were

---

[93] *Banjo World* (Jan. 1896: 22).

[94] *The Oxford Companion to Music* (1970: 667) and Hynes (1968: 340). Non-English readers should note the important distinction between a concert-hall (where serious music was performed) and the music-hall (any theatre offering vaudeville-style entertainment).

more substantial, and were good enough to interest serious composers, as he revealed in this interview:

> Sir Arthur Sullivan had a long conversation with me. He carefully read the score of my 'Characteristica Fantasia,' and was very complimentary about the way in which the parts were allotted to the instruments. He then asked me to minutely explain the compass and capabilities of the mandoline and mandola. I told him how I always had the mandola tuned like a viola, and of the fine effects I derived from this novel method of treating this fine instrument. Sir Arthur Sullivan much admired the latter instrument, and told me he should most certainly compose for the mandoline and possibly a duet for mandoline and mandola. (*Banjo World*, Mar. 1899: 74.)

Sadly, Sullivan died a year later, apparently without having composed the piece, but other prominent composers did write for the mandolin. William Henry Squire, one of the most acclaimed cellists and light-music composers of his generation, composed eight simple but attractive pieces (with piano accompaniment), including the beautiful 'La calma del mare', in the years around 1892; these were written 'expressly for Miss Florrie Pierpoint', a young mandolinist whom he was then courting. Percy Grainger, the celebrated Australian composer who lived in London from 1900 to 1914, composed *Father and Daughter* (based on a Faroe Island ballad) for five men's voices, double chorus, strings, brass, percussion, and a mandolin and guitar band; at its first performance, forty mandolins and guitars took part. Charles Villiers Stanford included mandolins and guitars in Claudio's serenade in Act II of his opera *Much Ado about Nothing* (first performed at Covent Garden, 30 May 1901). The mandolinists on that occasion were the Misses Kay-Clifford, a trio of sisters who usually performed in variety theatres and at garden parties. They were also engaged by the Royal Opera House for two seasons of performances of Verdi's *Otello*.[95]

Most mandolin music then being published in Britain was written by specialist composers, and little of it merits serious attention. Besides Francia (who composed over 500 works for the instrument), one of the better composers was Angelo Mascheroni, who came to London from Bergamo and published several attractive pieces for mandolin and piano during the 1890s.[96] Clara Ross (later Ross-Ricci) composed prolifically for the mandolin; perhaps her best piece was a 'Sicilienne' in A minor, published (like most of her output) by

---

[95] *BMG* (June 1904: 132).   [96] Bone (1972: 225).

John Alvey Turner, and dedicated to her own orchestra, Miss Clara Ross'
Ladies Mandoline & Guitar Band.

During the mid-1890s, two celebrated Spaniards spent extended periods in
London. Between 1895 and 1897, Señor Zerega conducted a mandolin and
guitar band, and also led the Zerega Spanish Troubadours, all of whom appar-
ently used Italian instruments.[97] Manuel Lopez, a former student at the Madrid
conservatoire, played at the Promenade concerts in 1893–4 and returned to
Britain in 1895, performing a repertoire that included pieces by Paganini and
Sarasate, Bazzini's 'Witches' Dance' and the overture to Rossini's William Tell.
In an interview, he spoke of his preference for the bandurria:

> It [the bandurria] has twelve strings, whilst the mandoline has only eight. It is
> tuned in fourths. Ah, but it has depth, power, brilliancy. The sounds it yields are
> full and strong. You shut your eyes and you hear an entire orchestra. You open
> your eyes and see you are listening to a bandurria . . . (*Banjo World*, Nov. 1896: 3.)

However, the most significant players were almost all Italians. Enrico
Marucelli, a Florentine mandolinist, spent the latter part of the 1890s in London
before returning to his native city in 1901. He published compositions under
the name of E. M. Celli, and conducted a Ladies Mandolin and Guitar Band
(comprising sixty ladies of rank and title) whose numerous concerts included
one at the Royal Albert Hall in 1901.[98] Edouardo Mezzacapo, who was based in
Paris, also conducted this band during periodic visits to London in the early
1900s. Jean Pietrapertosa moved from Paris to London in 1900, teaching from
a studio at 50 York Street, Portman Square, and giving numerous recitals,
including one at the Steinway Hall in 1901; he subsequently returned to Paris.[99]

In 1903, Giuseppe Sgallari arrived in London from Brussels, making his first
public appearance at a concert in Kensington Town Hall on 7 May.[100] His
arrival coincided with a dispute between Cammeyer and Clifford Essex, which
prompted the latter to start up a business in his own name and a new magazine, *BMG*, for which Sgallari acted as mandolin specialist until his return to
Italy in 1906. Sgallari taught technique and the art of orchestral arrangement
for mandolins, and also led Li gondolieri, a troupe of players, singers, and
dancers who dressed in Italian national costume (green silk blouses, white
flannel trousers, and red sash) and performed a repertoire that included

---

[97] *Banjo World* (July–Aug. 1895: 81; and Feb. 1896: 39).
[98] Bone (1972: 224). R. Maurri of Florence publishes several of his compositions.
[99] *Banjo World* (July 1900: 143).   [100] *Banjo World* (June 1903: 125).

Neapolitan songs, and medleys from *Rigoletto*, *The Barber of Seville*, and *La Bohème*, all played from memory.[101] Like many Italians, he stressed the importance of an advanced right-hand technique, something most British players lacked:

> The national fault is that the English play the mandolin as though it were a violin ... Of your crack players nearly all began on the violin, and finding they were not Joachims or Ysayes, turned their own genuine abilities towards the mandolin, adapting their experience with the violin. This causes them to mar the tone ... The genius of the mandolin lies in the right hand, and wrong technique absolutely prevents justice being done to the mandolin. (*BMG*, May 1904: 116.)

The 'crack players' whom Sgallari mentioned were mostly students of one of the leading Italian soloists. Walter M. Vaughan studied with Francia, and also played in Francia's quartet during the late 1890s (as did Marchisio).[102] A. F. Cramer studied with various Italian professors before starting to teach in Manchester; he performed a mandolin obbligato for the celebrated soprano Adelina Patti at the Albert Hall in 1892, and played the mandolin part in *Otello* at Covent Garden in 1895.[103] Another member of the *Otello* stage band was Ethel Beningfield, who accompanied the great Italian tenor Francesco Tamagno (the original interpreter of the title role). She rarely played original mandolin music at her recitals, preferring to borrow from the violin repertoire, especially the preludes of Wieniawski.[104] Lizzie Keevil was a student of Francia whose repertoire ranged from unaccompanied solos by Francia to Hungarian Dances by Brahms. Like her teacher, she thought that the mandolin was very roughly played in Venice, attributing this to the local custom of using an extremely long plectrum, resulting in a scratchy tone.[105] Frederick Winslow, by contrast, was a self-taught mandolinist (although he knew Francia and Sgallari personally) who formed the Swindon Mandolin Quartet in 1905; its many appearances included performances at the Steinway and Grotian halls in London.[106]

One of the best young British players was Lillie Selden, whose repertoire included the violin concertos of Beethoven, Mendelssohn, and Bruch. She studied at the Guildhall School of Music and was one of the first mandolinists to be awarded the diploma AGSM, in 1906.[107] During this period, the academic

---

[101] *Mandoline & Guitar* (Oct. 1906: 7); *BMG* (Jan. 1906: 52); and *Mandoline* (15 May 1904: 28).
[102] *Banjo World* (Dec. 1897: 221).   [103] *Banjo World* (Sept.–Oct. 1895: 92; Nov.–Dec. 1895: 11).
[104] *Banjo World* (Jan. 1899: 37).   [105] *BMG* (July 1904: 148–9).   [106] *BMG* (Aug. 1959: 277).
[107] *BMG* (Aug. 1908: 164). Additional information from past annual prospectuses, held at the Guildhall School of Music.

status of the mandolin varied greatly in London, from one institution to another. Neither the Royal College of Music nor the Royal Academy of Music (the two most prestigious institutions) accepted the instrument, but several other colleges did. Marchisio taught at Trinity College of Music. The London College of Music held examinations for the instrument. The Guildhall School of Music had offered mandolin tuition since 1891, and when Madame Fiammetta Waldahoff, an Italian, was appointed as a teacher there in 1897, it became a popular instrument. The school ran a mandolin and guitar orchestra, annual mandolin prizes were awarded, and Waldahoff continued to teach there until at least 1916.[108]

Waldahoff was influential in founding the British Guild of Mandolinists and Guitarists, which held its inaugural meeting on 9 June 1906 and dedicated itself to the advancement of the mandolin, mandola, liuto, and guitar. The guild, modelled on a similar American organization, published its own magazine, The *Mandoline & Guitar*, which began in October 1906 before combining with The *Music Students' Magazine* in January 1907 to become the *Minstrel*.[109] Although the guild was short-lived, it did attempt to raise artistic standards amongst mandolinists and guitarists, in particular by excluding banjoists from their ranks. Unlike those of continental Europe, most British fretted-instrument orchestras comprised a mixture of banjos, mandolins, and guitars, an arrangement that suited the commercial interests of large manufacturing houses, but was disastrous when any attempt was made to play sophisticated or subtle music. Although banjos are capable of far greater expressivity than is often realized, in banjo, mandolin, and guitar (BMG) orchestras they totally dominated the other instruments, (especially from the second decade of the twentieth century onwards, when the orchestral banjo began to be played with a plectrum on all-wire strings, replacing the earlier, more subtle, finger-style technique on gut strings), producing a forceful tone that drowned out the more fragile, sensitive sounds of mandolin and guitar. Such BMG orchestras doubtless gave enormous pleasure to those who played in them, but they also contributed to the low artistic standard of most mandolin ensemble playing in Britain.

Thankfully, there were some orchestras which adhered to the Italian instrumentation and excluded banjos. The Polytechnic Mandolin and Guitar Orchestra, founded in 1891, continued to give concerts under the direction of B. M.

---

[108] The Guildhall School of Music has a gap in its records after 1916; by 1924, when records recommence, neither Waldahoff nor the mandolin features in the prospectus.

[109] *Mandoline & Guitar* (Oct. 1906: 6) and *Music Students' Magazine* (Aug. 1906: 105–6, 119).

Illustration 15. The Polytechnic Mandolin and Guitar Orchestra outside the Crystal Palace, 1903. This photograph was taken on the afternoon of the concert, when a third of the orchestra's members (mostly men) were at work. The evening concert featured 190 performers (from *BMG*, Feb. 1904: 78).

Jenkins. It performed at London's most prestigious venues, including the Queen's Hall, the Royal Albert Hall, and the Crystal Palace, where, on 30 June 1897, it included seventy-five first mandolins, twenty-five second mandolins, three mandolas, ten guitars, two bass guitars, a liuto, a liola, and a double bass guitar (tuned an octave lower than an ordinary guitar).[110] On 12 September 1903 it played to an audience of 2,000 at Earl's Court, and shortly afterwards it gave a concert at the Crystal Palace with 190 members (Illustration 15).[111]

The finest orchestra that Britain produced was undoubtedly the Luton Mandolin Band, founded in 1890 and directed by Philip J. Bone, who had studied with Marchisio at Trinity College of Music, and later with Ranieri.[112]

[110] *Banjo World* (Aug. 1897: 165–6).   [111] *BMG* (Feb. 1904: 78).
[112] A letter dated Feb. 24 1988, from Richard Valery of Cranz & Co. to Barry Pratt, mentions that Bone was a pupil of Ranieri.

He amassed a group of talented and dedicated musicians, and trained the Luton Band to the point where it could compete with the best European orchestras. On 29–31 May 1909, it took part in its first international competition in Boulogne, where 650 mandolinists represented orchestras from Italy, Monaco, Belgium, France, Algeria, and Switzerland before a jury that included the renowned organist Alexandre Guilmant. Bone was astounded at the high standard of performance:

> solid English players have no idea of the subtle nuances of expression, the mellow liquid, rippling tone, the power and grandeur of the fortissimos, and the masterly execution of such mandolin bands as those from Cremona, Lausanne, and Lille ... It must be understood that their instrumentation, particularly in the tenor and bass, is as far in advance of the English instrumentation as is their playing. They include instruments unknown to English bands—the guitaron, a double bass guitar of marvellous vibrating and sustaining power, far superior in such bands than the ordinary double bass, and also several each of lutes, tenor and bass mandolas, and liolas (double bass mandolins). The guitar sections are also particularly strong and pleasing, the effect being equal to several good harps ... The quartets were limited to 1st and 2nd mandolins, mandola, and guitar, and in the 'honours' section such music as Beethoven's Quartet no. 8, Haydn's Quartet in D major, 'Poet and Peasant' [Suppé] and 'Semiramide' [Rossini] overtures were perfectly performed. (Bone 1909: 171.)

Inspired by these performances, the Luton Mandolin Band succeeded in emulating the standards of the best Continental orchestras, as this review of their performance of an original overture for mandolin orchestra by (Bracco) (given on 9 December 1910 at Kensington Town Hall) makes clear:

> It was the first performance of this work in England, and that it should be full of the effects which are most suitably rendered by plectral instruments was not a matter of surprise, but it was more noticeable that there were the instruments and the players to produce them. It was no great number of performers all playing the same part, with one or two Mandolas and Guitars hidden and unheard in the background, such as we were familiar with only a year or so ago. There were only about twenty in all, but each seemed to play with the conviction that on her or his individual work the success of the whole lay ... we have heard from nothing of its kind here in London before. (*Keynotes*, Jan. 1911: 127.)

The Luton Band continued for many years under Bone's direction, achieving one of its best results on 26 May 1912 in Paris, when it won second prize.[113] However, Bone's lasting contribution to the mandolin was his book *The Guitar and Mandolin*, first published in 1914. This work, a collection of 'biographies of celebrated players and composers' has been much maligned (especially by guitarists) for its many inaccuracies and the disproportionate amount of space it devotes to major composers with only a peripheral connection to plucked instruments. However, Bone's biographies of late nineteenth-century and early twentieth-century mandolinists are extremely well informed, and the book remains a splendid pioneering venture, one that has influenced all subsequent mandolin scholarship.

Fine Italian players continued to arrive in Britain. Bernardo De Pace came to England in 1900, playing with the Blackpool Winter Gardens' Orchestra for three seasons, and spending another seven touring variety theatres across the country with his brother, Nicola, as a mandolin and guitar duo, before emigrating to the USA.[114] In 1906, Leopoldo Matini visited London, teaching in Maida Vale and giving a recital with his mandolin and guitar trio at the Bechstein Hall on 10 May, where he eschewed original mandolin music in favour of violin compositions by Sarasate (the 'Jotá de San Fermin' and 'Romanza Andaluza'), Beethoven, and Bazzini:

> Perhaps the finest performance of the afternoon was Signor Matini's rendition of the 'Witches' Dance' [Bazzini]. The possibilities of this piece as a mandolin solo must be heard to be believed, and it was presented with all the sparkle and verve that such a composition demands. Signor Matini's technique is magnificent, albeit his tremolo passages do not convey that impression of sustained tone combined with cantabile and sostenuto effects that we expect from the Italian School of Mandoline players … (*Music Students' Magazine*, June 1906: 43.)

In 1909, Benedetto Persichini came to the capital, creating a sensation with his extraordinary technique. He used special tunings to play six- and seven-note chords, and performed on an Embergher mandolin with a very narrow fingerboard, which permitted him to finger intricate passages with extreme rapidity. John Anson first heard Persichini play at the Manchester Hippodrome:

> He was the first turn on the 'bill', an unknown Italian mandolinist. He walked on to the huge stage, sat on a lone chair before an ordinary drop scene and began to play to the vast audience before him. No Francia stage magic to get the audience on his side, only his beautiful instrument and a great faith in his ability to play it well.

---

[113] *BMG* (July 1912: 146).   [114] Bone (1972: 262).

What did he play? A tune we all know well, 'Carnival of Venice'—but those variations! The audience were interested and, as variation followed variation, they sat spellbound. Another front-rank artist had arrived! He certainly put that audience in a good humour by his wonderful playing of the Paganini variations of a well-known tune—and he made a profound impression on me . . . Persichini was a very likeable person but temperamental and excitable. He must have been the despair of some of his landladies. He actually slept with his beloved mandolin at his bedside and thought nothing of trying out some tune that had entered his head at a time when most people were fast asleep. (Anson 1954*a*: 292–3.)

Far below the elevated heights of these concert artists, the mandolin was being studied by tens (probably hundreds) of thousands of people who enjoyed music-making at a simpler level. The advertisement and news pages of mandolin journals reveal that almost every town in the south-east of England had at least one mandolin teacher and orchestra, and that in many other parts of Britain (principally in and around large cities such as Manchester, Leeds, and Birmingham) the instrument was enormously popular, especially with young women. While the average standard of performance was probably not very high, this was an age when a thirst for self-improvement coexisted with an appetite for innocent entertainment; learning to play the mandolin was an agreeable and inexpensive way to satisfy both these desires.

The general popularity of the mandolin increased throughout the 1890s, and reached its peak in the early years of the twentieth century. In particular, the Italian Exhibition at Earl's Court in 1904 captured the popular imagination:

One part was *Venice by Night*. . . . Here one may listen to Neapolitan melodies on mandolines and guitars amidst a scene which actually reproduces the characteristics of the 'City of the Islands'. . . . Embarking at the gondola wharf, one is eventually steered into the Grand Canal, where the Giacomo Gianni Troupe, of Venice, render Venetian serenades from a moored barge. The Masianello Concert and Tarantelle Party perform on the Grand Piazza. (*Banjo World*, June 1904: 114.)

By 1906, the mandolin vogue was at its height:

It is becoming very fashionable to be able to play the banjo, the mandoline, or the guitar, and in Society pretty girls are learning these instruments, and young men are practising them in view of the coming summer . . . There is everything to be said for learning one or other of these instruments because the task is not a difficult one . . . a mandoline . . . can easily be carried from place to place. (*Weekly Dispatch*, quoted in *Music Students' Magazine*, June 1906: 55.)

Illustration 16. A family of flat-back mandolins made by Clifford Essex (advertised in *BMG*, Dec. 1910: p. iii).

Many people chose to study the mandolin at private music schools. In London, the largest of these was the Victoria Park Academy of Music which, since 1886, had been running classes in violin, piano, singing, and mandolin, at five shillings a term. It also published the *Music Students' Magazine*, which was devoted to these interests.[115] The prices of instruments varied enormously, with the best Italian mandolins costing several weeks' wages for the average working man. British instruments, such as the flat-back family of mandolins shown in Illustration 16, were somewhat cheaper and, although lacking the aesthetic appeal of good Italian models, were well made and accurately fretted. However, what caused many musicians to regard the mandolin as an inferior instrument was the large number of poorly constructed models being bought and played. Many of these were the sort of cheap Italian instruments that Calace had complained about, shoddily made and incapable of being played in tune. Others were German, and could be sold only because of their low price:

[115] *Banjo World* (Sept. 1901: 162).

One often sees the mandoline amongst a lot of toys exhibited in shop windows. Such mandolines are nearly always German-made instruments, and probably the association of the mandoline with the toys is due to the fact that they are almost invariably made in the same workshop, which is but a poor recommendation. If this is not the explanation then it is due to the mandoline's comparative cheapness in manufacture. Nevertheless, it is a pity such a sweetly pretty instrument should be thus cheapened in the public mind. (*Banjo World*, July 1898: 114.)

Poor manufacture led to low musical expectations and, although virtuoso players demonstrated to audiences just what the instrument could achieve, the average standard of mandolin playing in Britain never rose beyond a basic level. This can be seen from the response of the editor of the *Minstrel*, who, when a piece by Romano (from Naples) arrived at his office in 1907, could only lament that Italian players and composers had reached standards still undreamed of in Britain:

From Messrs. Forlivesi & Co., of Florence, we have received a *Capriccio fantastico* for Mandoline and Piano, by N. Romano. This piece would be a revelation to the average English mandolinist, as showing the kind of music published for and played by Italian mandolinists. The opening unaccompanied cadenza alone runs into eight lines before a series of rushing demisemiquaver passages ushers in a *cantabile espress.* of a few short bars, which rapidly develops an ornate and fanciful form, extending through a repetition of the opening demisemiquavers and leading to the introduction of a gavotte, which in turn gives place to a mazurka, followed by a valse. This rapid alteration of various rhythms would be strange to our accepted traditions, especially as the tempo is constantly interrupted by short rallentando passages. The finale includes some very effective left-hand pizzicato and a closing presto that would 'bring down the house'. If such music was published in England for the mandoline, players would not have to resort to violin pieces when making up a programme of mandoline music, and the instrument would be respected by the musician as one possessing possibilities that are at present unknown among even the best of English players. (*Minstrel*, March 1907: 68.)

France

During the 1890s, Jules and Madeleine Cottin were two of the leading mandolinists in Paris. Jules, who had already published a tutor for the instrument in 1891 (a second edition appeared in 1902), later wrote a series of detailed studies about the mandolin and guitar for *Paris soleil*; his sister Madeleine also

QUATUOR MEZZACAPO.

A mon cher Ami et Collègue le Professeur Samuel Adelstein,
Edouard Mezzacapo,
Paris.

Illustration 17. The Quatuor Mezzacapo during the 1890s. Note the added bass strings on the guitar, enabling it to provide fuller harmonic support for the mandolins (from Adelstein 1905: 18).

published a method. Jules and his guitarist brother Alfred were popular musical performers, as *L'Art musical* noted: 'The virtuosity of these two is well known, and their performing abilities are appreciated at home and abroad.'[116] Jean Pietrapertosa was another highly respected performer and teacher, as was Edouardo Mezzacapo (Illustration 17), an Italian whom Adelstein regarded as 'the only one of the prominent Parisian mandolinists who uses and adopts the true Italian system of the [plectrum] mechanism in his original compositions. His music is considered among the best of European writers for the mandolin.' (Adelstein 1905: 18–19.)

Although the mandolin was widely played in and around Paris, the city's first regular journal did not appear until 15 December 1905, when Mario

[116] *L'Art musical* (Jan. 1893: 3).

Maciocchi—a prominent performer, prolific composer, and shrewd business-man—edited and published (under the pseudonym of M. de Rome) the first issue of *L'Estudiantina*, a fortnightly magazine intended for mandolinists and guitarists. Subtitled *Courrier des sociétés mandolinistiques*, the journal includ-ed a new piece for *Estudiantina* (a mandolin and guitar ensemble) in each issue, and immediately set up international competitions for composition and performance. The most popular forms of serious amateur music-making in France—*Harmonies* and *Fanfares* (brass bands) and *Orphéons* (choral soci-eties)—had long been organized into regular competitive events that often involved groups from other European countries, with famous composers act-ing as patrons, and prominent musicians taking part in the judging. When the first international competition held by *L'Estudiantina* took place in Monaco in June 1906, it was run along similar lines; groups from Italy, Spain, Switzerland, and France took part, the patrons included Massenet and Saint-Saëns, and Munier was a member of the jury.[117] Before long, international music compe-titions organized by French towns (such as the one held in Avignon on 12–13 May 1907) began to include a section for *Estudiantinas*, something that the journal strongly supported.[118]

The winning composition in the first competition for new works for *Estudiantina* was *Roman de Pierrot* by Ugo Pizzi. Pizzi, born in Cesena near Rimini, had spent his career as an orchestral violinist in Rome and Aix-les-Bains, before becoming violin professor at the National School of Music in Chambéry (in south-east France) in 1885. There, he founded and directed the forty-strong Estudiantina chambérienne and began composing for this new medium. *Roman de Pierrot* is a simple but appealing fantasia in five move-ments—'Introduction', 'Entrée de Pierrot', 'Sérénade à la lune', 'Désespoir de Pierrot' (Ex. 8), and 'Ronde des petits Pierrots' (with tambourine)—whose programmatic layout and occasional musical quirks made it a very popular work with *Estudiantinas* during the next few years. Another of his pieces, *Christmas: Fantasie originale*—which began with an imitation of the chimes of a distant clock and required players to double on toy trumpet, toy drum, rattle, and a bleating toy 'mouton' for one movement—won the second com-petition and enjoyed a similar success with amateur players.[119]

[117] *L'Estudiantina* (15 July 1906: 2).   [118] *L'Estudiantina* (1 Feb. 1907: 2).
[119] *L'Estudiantina* (15 Oct. 1906: 6; 1 Feb. 1907: 2). The edn. of 15 Oct. and 1 Nov. 1906 included the whole of *Roman de Pierrot*, the fourth movement of which is reproduced in Ex. 8. *Christmas* appeared in the issues of 1 and 15 Feb. 1908. Photo of Pizzi in *L'Estudiantina*, 15 Oct. 1906: 6.

Ex. 8. Pizzi: *Le Roman de Pierrot*, 4th movement: 'Désespoir de Pierrot'

Ex. 8 (Continued)

Ex. 8 (Continued)

There was a clear distinction made in France between an *Estudiantina* and a mandolin orchestra: the former consisted only of mandolins, mandolas, and guitars (Pizzi's unusual additions were for humorous effect), whereas the latter often incorporated bowed and wind instruments, and full percussion. Léon Cailleux (the founder and director of the Estudiantina de Paris) argued that, although the orchestra had greater musical possibilities, it was difficult and expensive to bring one together regularly for rehearsals, and he pointed out the advantages of the smaller, simpler grouping, where the instruments were well balanced and only a few players were needed to play all the parts: 'The difference between the two is the same as that which exists between a brilliant evening out on the town, and a modest and calm evening in with the family.' (*L'Estudiantina*, 1 Mar. 1907: 3.)

In a later article, Cailleux suggested that the portability of the *Estudiantina*, and the traditional alfresco associations of mandolins and guitars, should give rise to a new category of music:

There is chamber music, why not have garden music? One invites, in winter, friends to a musical event in a salon; why not invite them, in summer, to a musical event taking place in the garden? And in default of a garden there is always the countryside. Like chamber music, garden music has a repertoire already: everything written for Estudiantina, mandolin duets, songs with guitar accompaniment etc. One can find it for all tastes and all forces ... And, besides, what could be more aristocratic than a garden party? Because, however modestly one organized the thing, it would always be a garden party, in the proper sense of the word. (*L'Estudiantina*, 1 Mar. 1908: 3.)

Of the dozens of *Estudiantinas* in and around Paris, several names regularly recurred in journals. In 1900, the Estudiantina Lombarde de Paris performed a programme of classical transcriptions at the Paris Opéra; later, in the autumn of 1907, Mezzacapo became their director.[120] In the years around 1908, the Estudiantina de Paris (led by Cailleux) was giving regular concerts, as were the Sérénade du XIe, the Estudiantina Parisienne (founded in 1892), the Cercle Mandoliniste (directed by Edgar Bara), and La Stella (Saint-Maur), this latter ensemble being directed by Vittorio Monti.[121] On 30 April 1910, another group bearing the name V. Monti—composed of top-notch mandolinists and guitarists—gave its first concert at the Salle Berlioz, performing a programme that included 'Czardas' by Monti, who also directed.[122] This famous virtuoso showpiece has long been a favourite encore item with violinists, who generally believe it to be an original work for their instrument; however, it appears to have been one of many mandolin compositions written by Monti before World War I. Amongst his other works are a mandolin method, Op. 245, numerous pieces for *Estudiantina*, and an opera-pantomime, *Noël de Pierrot* (1900), which includes an obbligato mandolin part in the orchestration. He was also one of the collaborators on a new journal for mandolinists and guitarists, *Le Médiator*, published fortnightly in Paris between 1910 and 1913; his colleagues included Pizzi, Munier, the Cottins, the luthier Lucien Gélas, and the guitarist Miguel Llobet.

While the very best groups, such as Monti's, were run on a professional basis with highly skilled performers, most were strictly amateur, giving a few concerts each year but existing mainly for the enjoyment of their own members. A typical advertisement of the time, proposing to set up a new *Estudiantina*, detailed how such a group might be run; it would meet each Friday evening at 8.30, devoting the first half-hour to *solfège* and the remaining one and a half hours to mandolin and guitar tuition and the playing of ensemble pieces, all for a monthly contribution of half a franc from each member.[123]

On 26 November 1905, the Fédération des Estudiantinas was founded in Paris, under the patronage of Théodore Dubois (a composer of operas and church music, and director of the Paris Conservatoire) and Jules Massenet, with the Cottin brothers amongst its most prominent members.[124] *L'Estudiantina*, which wanted the mandolin ensemble to be accepted as a valid

[120] Saint-Clivier (1960/81: 23) and *L'Estudiantina* (1 Nov. 1907: 6).   [121] *Le Plectre* (1 Dec. 1908: 4).
[122] Saint-Clivier (1960/81: 23).   [123] *L'Estudiantina* (15 Oct. 1907: 3).
[124] *L'Estudiantina* (15 Dec. 1905: 6); *Le Plectre* (1 Dec. 1908: 4).

form of music-making on a par with *Harmonies* and *Fanfares*, disapproved of the separatist tendencies of the Fédération, but what began as a tactical difference soon became a long-running and ill-tempered dispute; consequently, there were few references (other than derogatory ones) to either the Fédération or the Cottins in the pages of *L'Estudiantina*.

Most of the best mandolin-makers were based in Mirecourt, but there were several in Paris. The Spanish mandolinist Manuel Sarrablo y Clavero, who directed an *Estudiantina* in Paris for many years, created a range of Sarrablo mandolins and guitars, made by the firm of Thibouville Lamy (of Paris and Mirecourt), one of France's leading musical-instrument-manufacturers.[125] Giuseppe Cesolari founded a workshop in Paris during the 1890s, although he soon moved it to Mans. And G. Parmentier, who had founded a fretted-instrument business in the Boulevard Haussmann in 1892, made a wide range of mandolins, from student models right up to the Pietrapertosa mandolin, which had a concert-length fingerboard and retailed at 500f.[126]

Of the numerous composers of mandolin music in Paris, the most significant were probably Maciocchi, Mezzacapo, and Monti. Edgar Bara, who often played the mandolin at the Opéra, wrote some attractive pieces for *Estudiantina* and a mandolin method (1902), and Alexander Georges composed several works for mandolin orchestra, including 'Fête à Florence'.[127] Gervais Bernard Salvayre, who principally composed operas, ballets, and church music, also wrote a number of light pieces for mandolin and piano; and Paul Antonin Vidal used mandolins and guitars in his lyric drama *Guernica* (1895).[128] The instrument also occasionally appeared in new works for the opera-house, notably in *Chérubin* by Massenet (produced in Monte Carlo, 1904, and Paris, 1905); a serenade in this opera requires 'a minimum of six excellent mandolinists and six expert guitarists'. We should also note that Maria Scivitarro, the Torinese virtuoso, settled in Paris in 1911 after marrying Jules Scivittaro, a violinist (and winner of the Prix de Rome in 1883). She temporarily abandoned her musical career at about this time, working in a hospital during World War I.

One of the most significant artistic revolutions of the twentieth century took place in Paris from about 1907 onwards and, although it might initially seem quite unconnected to our topic, was indirectly influenced by the

---

[125] Bone (1972: 310).   [126] *L'Estudiantina* (15 Sept. 1906: 6).

[127] Sleeve notes to 'Piquanteries', *Quintettes de Mandolines de Paris* (1990, EPM, FDC 1106); Bone (1972: 136).

[128] Bone (1972: 307–8, 362).

mandolin in several ways. Pablo Picasso, Georges Braque, and Juan Gris had begun experimenting with the style known as Cubism, no longer realistically representing objects upon the canvas but abstracting the images instead. Mandolins and guitars turn up frequently in their paintings for several reasons. Firstly, both instruments were popular with the clientele of the cafés in which these painters relaxed, and the artists soon realized that the distinctive geometric shapes of the mandolin and guitar could allow for considerable transformation without total loss of recognition. Secondly, as the artists broke with the past in style, they nostalgically looked to traditional subjects for content, especially to the *commedia dell'arte* and to the art and lifestyle of the classical south. Pierrot and Harlequin frequently appear in their works, and mandolin and guitar serenades are also a recurring theme.

There was a third reason too. The nineteenth-century landscape painter Jean-Baptiste-Camille Corot had, during his later years (*c.*1860–5), produced several strikingly advanced and impressionistic atelier portraits. Many of these depict a young woman in Italian costume, holding a mandolin and sitting silently in an attic, contemplating an easel on which sits a landscape by Corot himself, and clearly represent an attempt by the ageing artist to recapture the joy of his earlier life in Italy. Few of his figure paintings had been publicly exhibited before 1909, when a large bequest was made to the Louvre. This hitherto unknown aspect of Corot's work had a great effect upon the Cubists, and many of their subsequent canvases reflect his influence: Gris produced a cubist version of Corot's *Dreamer with a Mandolin* in his *Woman with a Mandolin* (1916), mandolins appear in several of Picasso's works, and Braque later created a pastiche work *Souvenir of Corot: Woman with a Mandolin* (1922–3) in which, enigmatically, the mandolin had become a guitar.[129]

One man, Laurent Fantauzzi (Illustration 18), totally dominated the mandolin scene in Marseilles, throughout this period and beyond. Born in the Neapolitan province of Atina, Fantauzzi was resident in Marseilles for his entire adult life, giving innumerable performances in the city (for example, two successful concerts at the Brasserie Noailles, in April 1895 and on 6 January 1896) and was soon acknowledged as a top-flight virtuoso.[130] A highly respected teacher, he also ran a shop at 8, rue de Jeune-Anacharsis, catering for mandolinists and guitarists. Amongst his close associates was the luthier Lucien Raymond Olivier Gélas, who built mandolins in his workshop in

---

[129] Clarke (1991: 104, 143).   [130] *Il mandolino* (30 Apr. 1895: 4; 15 Jan. 1896: 4).

LAURENT FANTAUZZI

Illustration 18. Laurent Fantauzzi (from frontispiece of his *École de la mandoline*, 1910).

Marseilles (and also at Mirecourt and Mattaincourt), which were later sold by Fantauzzi, with his personal guarantee. These instruments had a revolutionary design feature to increase the volume of sound—the 'double table d'harmonie' or second soundboard, parallel to the first—and were extremely popular with French orchestras, many of whom used exclusively Gélas mandolins.

On 1 November 1903, the first edition of *Le Plectre* appeared, published by Fantauzzi, who was also the artistic director. This was France's first periodical aimed especially at mandolinists and guitarists and, although *L'Estudiantina* subsequently became more widely known, *Le Plectre* remained one of the most important of all mandolin journals. Fantauzzi also wrote a two-volume *École de la mandoline* (with a foreword by Massenet), the first part of which was published in 1910.[131] It is estimated that about fifty mandolin methods

---

[131] *Il mandolino* (30 Dec. 1910: 4).

were published in France during the first decade of the twentieth century, several selling more than 100,000 copies; Fantauzzi's was perhaps the best, and also probably the most commercially successful.[132] Amongst his numerous compositions, 'Crépuscule' for solo mandolin is one of the most interesting; subtitled 'sextuor pour mandoline seule', it requires the eight strings to be tuned $g - b\flat - d' - f' - a' - a' - e'' - e''$, allowing the performer to play six-note chords on four courses. Although Fantauzzi was based in Marseilles, he often embarked on concert tours, playing at prestigious venues such as the Salle Berlioz in Paris, where he appeared with the Cercle mandoliniste de Paris (directed by Bara) in the spring of 1907, playing the Ninth Violin Concerto by Bériot, 'Czardas' by Monti, 'Ballade polonaise' by Vieuxtemps, and 'Love Song' by Munier.[133]

Besides Paris and Marseilles, the mandolin was also particularly popular in Strasbourg, and in Boulogne-sur-Mer, where the numerous groups included La Sévillana (an *Estudiantina* comprising sixty young girls) and the Société des Ocariens et Mandolinistes.[134] In Angers, mandolins and guitars were often used to play religious music in church, and both instruments were also popular in Algeria (then a French possession), where a concourse was held between 19 and 21 April 1908, with Fantauzzi on the jury; as usual at this time, the Circolo mandolinisti di Cremona won the *Estudiantina* section, while the Cremona Quartetto a plettro took the quartet prize with a performance of Munier's First Quartet in G major.[135]

The leading French instrument-makers were Gélas in Marseilles and Louis Gérôme who, at the beginning of the century was employing about twenty workers at his premises in Mirecourt.[136] Many French players preferred these instruments to Italian imports, but mandolins by Monzino, Vinaccia, Embergher, and Calace were highly prized. As regards music, it is curious to note that, although several items from the eighteenth century were known—some of Beethoven's mandolin pieces were in print, as was a set of Gervasio duets, and a writer in *L'Estudiantina* in 1906 discussed 'the excellent principles contained in Fouchetti's [1771] tutor'—mandolinists do not seem to have comprehended the extent or significance of this early repertoire.[137] Music composed before

[132] *La Mandoline* (1981: 40).   [133] *L'Estudiantina* (1 May 1907: 6).   [134] *L'Estudiantina* (15 Apr. 1907: 3).
[135] *L'Estudiantina* (15 Apr. 1908: 3; 15 May 1908: 4).   [136] *Le Plectre* (no. 0, 1992: 9).
[137] Barry Pratt possesses P. J. Bone's copy of Beethoven's Adagio for mandolin (pub. Breitkopf & Härtel, Leipzig), which is marked 'Bought of Richard Harrison, 1894'; *Mandoline* (14 Mar. 1904) has an advertisement on the back cover listing 'G. Ricordi & Co, Musikverlag, Leipzig. 105545 G. B. Gervasi 6 Duetti all'antica für 2 Mandolinen'; *L'Estudiantina* (1 March 1906: 2) mentions the Fouchetti tutor, first pub. 1771.

1800 was very rarely heard at mandolin recitals, and any piece more than thirty years old would almost certainly have been a transcription of a work for violin, usually by Bériot or Vieuxtemps.

Although France had numerous fine exponents, and composers such as Massenet and Saint-Saëns championed its cause, many musicians remained suspicious of the mandolin. The reasons were accurately summarized in an article in *L'Estudiantina*:

> Some years ago the mandolin was gradually introduced to the general public. At first it was played by high society, and these were the days of glory and money for the master mandolinists. But it descended the social scale and now clerks, labourers, dressmakers, and milliners play the mandolin.
>
> This popularity of a musical instrument with the public—and we do not rebuke them—is due to the ease with which it can be learned, as everyone knows how to place their fingers on the fingerboard at the spot indicated in the tutor books. Therefore we have a great number of amateurs who play, usually worse rather than better, an instrument which is considered to be a simple musical distraction, and not an instrument capable of stronger musical impressions. This has resulted in a host of pieces pretending to be music; and a woeful taste in playing popular melodies ...The trouble lies, above all, in the first place that the mandolin is not considered as an instrument of music; in the second place that the study is incomplete; and in the third place that those who study the instruments are not sufficiently the musicians that they pretend to be. One could therefore say that the mandolin has been popularized, but that it has not made musical progress through the very fault of mandolinists themselves. (Deblaive 1906: 2.)

Belgium

In Antwerp, Romain Van den Bosch was leading numerous ensembles during the 1890s and 1900s, including one of the country's best *Estudiantinas*, La Napolitaine (founded 1904); Cesar and Florimond Costers were two other important figures in that city, both as performers, teachers, and composers. In Brussels, the instrument only started to attain a significant popularity from 1897 onwards with the arrival of Giuseppe Sgallari, who began teaching amongst the English community there and also conducted a mandolin orchestra, La Mandolinata. H. Gerard, the president of this orchestra, recounted Sgallari's contribution: 'Since the residence among us of Signor Sgallari the mandolin has acquired a very important position in musical festivals ... We were known

Illustration 19. Silvio Ranieri with his quartet. Left to right: Degreef (tenor mandola), Ranieri (mandolin 1), De Breemaeker (mandocello), Tamburini (mandolin 2). (Photograph courtesy of Henri Gamblin.)

to none and yet we ventured to appear at *la Grande Harmonie*, the most select and the most critical society in Brussels.' (*BMG*, Nov. 1903: 27.)

The orchestra performed three of Sgallari's own light compositions at this concert—'Columbina', 'Défilé des Marionettes', and 'Argentina'—meeting with great success. For several years, Sgallari was the leading mandolinist in Brussels, and his move to London in 1903 was undoubtedly connected with the decision by Silvio Ranieri (Illustrations 8 and 19) to settle in the same city two years earlier. As well as possessing a prodigious technique, Ranieri was a highly cultivated musician who immediately set about raising artistic standards amongst mandolinists in Brussels, and Sgallari's reputation there must rapidly have paled into insignificance with serious musicians. Ranieri later described what he first encountered in Brussels:

When I settled in Belgium in 1901, the mandolin was in a primitive state. Amateurs used it to play waltzes, polkas, and popular romances, as in Italy. I brought together some enthusiasts and taught them, until they in their turn began to give lessons. The Belgian Mandolin School was faithful [to this teaching]. In Valenciennes (1911), and Paris (1912), the international concourse put the Brussels mandolinists in first place. Our quartet took the first prize and the gold medal in Milan (1920), and the same honours at Boulogne-sur-Mer (1923). (Quoted in Quievreux 1956: 2.)

From 1901 until his death in 1956, Ranieri remained the undisputed master of the mandolin in Belgium. In the period leading up to World War I, he made frequent European tours, continually receiving extremely positive reviews:

The mandolinist Silvio Ranieri has returned to Belgium after a triumphant artistic tour of Germany. Lack of space prevents us from publishing in full the reviews of different journals, all recognizing in M. Ranieri the greatest virtuoso of the mandolin. A glance at the titles of the pieces performed in the different concerts, with orchestral accompaniment, will give our readers some idea of the great worth of this young artist:

Concerto in D minor	Paganini
Concerto in G major	Bériot
Ballade et Polonaise	Vieuxtemps
Fugue in G minor	Bach
Romance	Beethoven
Danse des elfes	Popper
Concerto in D minor	Vieuxtemps

(*L'Estudiantina*, 30 Dec. 1905: 6.)

The tireless concert mandolinist Silvio Ranieri adds ever more to the long list of his successes. On Friday 16 March, at the Société Royale d'Harmonie in Antwerp, he performed a suite and fugue by Bach, and the 'Fantasia appassionata' by Vieuxtemps, which he interpreted with all his customary mastery. Here is the review which appeared in the Antwerp *Nouveau précurseur*: 'M. Silvio Ranieri, mandolinist, has been rightly applauded for his great virtuosity; rarely have we heard this instrument, currently rather fashionable in music-halls, played with more artistry.' (*L'Estudiantina*, 1 Apr. 1906: 6.)

This ecstatic report of his appearance at a festival held by the Cercle des Dames Mandolinistes de St-Ghislain in Belgium on 16 April 1906 was not at all unusual:

The Society hosted, for the second time, maestro Silvio Ranieri of Rome, soloist at the Royal Theatre in Berlin. He arrived directly from London, having travelled through the night. Silvio Ranieri! . . . As soon as that beautiful thoughtful head appeared on the platform, the entire hall was given over to delirious enthusiasm. One sensed the virtuoso, the artist of the very highest order, the star. One sensed that here was one of those privileged beings who have the gift to charm kings, and who hold souls enslaved through their playing. Add to this a modesty equal to the merit, and we can understand why Ranieri spreads delirium and receives ovations ceaselessly. We also understand why the German press in general, and Berliners in particular—whose severity in these matters is beyond question—have conferred on him the title of *The Paganini of the Mandolin*.

Ranieri played the Second Concerto (D minor) by Wieniawski; *Zigeunerweizen* by Sarasate and the 'Ronde des lutins' by Bazzini, as showpieces. He pursues a single goal in his artistic career: he wishes to elevate the mandolin to the level of the violin. He has succeeded in this so well that Leipzig—that most knowledgeable of musical cities—guards him jealously for several weeks each winter, and he attracts a crowd at Verviers for between four and six recitals a year. As for the St-Ghislainois, as one they pray for him to come frequently to train them in perfection. (*L'Estudiantina*, 15 May 1906: 6.)

Ranieri's output as a composer was slight, but included some important items. His most successful pieces were 'Souvenir de Varsovie' for mandolin and piano (still popular with performers today) and 'Canto d'Estate' (awarded a gold medal by *Mandoline: Internationales Musik-Journal* in its competition for new solo works in 1904), a 'sextet for solo mandolin' using a scordatura tuning. In 1906, the piece for *Estudiantina* which he submitted for a competition organized by *L'Estudiantina* had to be eliminated on the grounds that it was too difficult; it was awarded a special prize instead.[138] Ranieri produced an extremely comprehensive four-volume tutor for the instrument (published in 1910 by Cranz & Co.) and also wrote a Concerto in D Major (Ex. 9) for mandolin with piano accompaniment. Written in a traditional, mid-nineteenth-century style and dedicated to Ernesto Rocco, this work makes formidable technical demands on the soloist; although the outer movements are perhaps musically less satisfying than the central slow movement, it remains an important composition, demonstrating that the mandolin is capable of performing music that would stretch the technique of even the finest violin soloist to its limit.

---

[138] *L'Estudiantina* (1 June 1906: 3).

Ex. 9. Ranieri: Concerto in D Major, 1st movement, 1st mandolin entry

Ex. 9 (Continued)

Germany and Austria

As with other European countries, German interest in the mandolin was initially stimulated by Italian virtuosi. In Berlin, for example, Achille Coronati continued to teach, later being succeeded by his pupil Reinhold Vorpahl. Michele Fasano of Naples was another prominent performer and teacher, one of whose students, Carl Henze, became director of the Berliner Mandolinen und-Lautenorchester. Similar figures could be found in most of the principal German cities at the turn of the century.[139] Although a specialist periodical, *Die Mandoline*, had appeared in Munich as early as 1895,[140] the most internationally significant journal, *Mandoline: Internationales Musik-Journal*, did not begin publication until 14 March 1904 in Leipzig. Each issue appeared in German, French, and English, and featured reports, articles, and advertisements from across Europe. At the outset, the journal stated its objectives:

> Not very long ago but little attention was paid to the mandolin, but today it is quite in vogue and we are certain that all who are interested in this instrument, players and manufacturers will welcome with pleasure a magazine devoted to its interests . . . Compared with other instruments the number of great artists who have chosen the mandolin to express their emotions is very small, but as their number increases it is also necessary to improve its construction. In many factories the mandolin manufactured is far from perfect. (*Mandoline*, 14 Mar. 1904: 1–2.)

In its first year, the journal ran a competition for new compositions, and published some excellent articles about the mandolin in Italy, acknowledging that that country was far ahead of Germany in its development of the instrument. Reviewing a concert given by the 'Società di beneficenza italiana' in Leipzig, it noted:

> The next number on the programme was 'Capriccio spagnolo' by Munier for mandolin and piano, rendered by Messrs. Scalzo and Sacerdoti. The composition appears to us to be one of the best original concert pieces for the mandolin. The pronounced Spanish melody, and the quick tempo are very pleasing; although the composition presents difficulties (runs, passages of accords etc.) which can be mastered easily only by a very skilful player, its effect is truly grand. The young virtuoso played the composition with a brilliancy that astonished older artists. . . .

[139] Janssens (1982: 113). Wölki (1984: 16–17) lists players in many other German towns. Although a few pioneers were reviving interest in music for the Renaissance and Baroque lute, the *Lauten* used in many German orchestras at this time were not really lutes at all, but guitars with lute-shaped bodies, a design that enjoyed a considerable vogue in Germany during the early part of the century.
[140] Wölki (1979: 9). Elsewhere (1984: 15), Wölki gives the date as 1894.

Before closing we wish to state that the public manifest great interest in the mandolin and we hope that the intelligent German public will not be satisfied simply by hearing mandolin and guitar playing; we hope they will begin to study it diligently and with perseverance. In Italy, America and France there are celebrated teachers of these instruments, but in Germany their number is limited. On hearing a foreign mandolin virtuoso a German audience is always astonished that such beautiful effects can be produced by this instrument, but the Italian, French and American public have become accustomed to its beauty. (*Mandoline*, 14 Mar. 1904: 6.)

Naturally enough, *Mandoline* frequently reviewed concerts in Leipzig, including many given by the Harmonie mandolin and guitar club, directed by Otto Schick. With forty-eight members (said to include twenty-one first mandolins, six second mandolins, three mandolas, sixteen guitars, and three basses), this was the largest such orchestra in Germany, and had developed from the guitar club founded by Schick in 1877.[141] Mandolin playing remained a strictly amateur affair in the country, but developed a large and enthusiastic (mainly middle-class) following. By the time that the first issue of *Die moderne Hausmusik* (a journal that attempted to unite all German-speaking plucked-instrument societies in Germany, Austria, and Switzerland) was published in Pforzheim on 15 January 1913, it was estimated that there were two hundred mandolin and guitar clubs in northern Germany alone.[142]

We have already noted the generally poor quality of factory-built German mandolins, but happily there were exceptions, as *Mandoline* pointed out in a piece devoted to the town of Markneukirchen (Saxony), where craftsmen built (and still build) good instruments using traditional skills:

Since the time of the Thirty Years War, when the art of violin manufacture was introduced by Bohemians, the little town has become well-known ... Originally it was noted for its manufacture of violins but other branches, such as the manufacture of bows, strings, lutes, wood and brass instruments have been added, and today almost all instruments are made there. It is of special interest to us that the Neapolitan, Roman, and Milanese mandolins are made there; the Russian national instruments, the balalaikas and domras; the northern lutes and the Spanish bandurrias, the banjos and the Romanian copcas and tamboritzas (tambourins), the guitars exported to all parts of the world, and the Turkish mandolins destined for the harems. (*Mandoline*, 15 June 1904: 35.)

---

[141] *Mandoline* (15 Apr. 1904: 13–14). The arithmetic is clearly awry here.   [142] Wölki (1984: 18).

Alongside this Italianate music-making, another, distinctly Germanic, style was evolving. Ever since the country's unification in 1871 (and the rapid industrialization that followed), there had been a growing nostalgia amongst idealistic middle-class youths for the days when the country had consisted of small principalities, with the *Volk* united in rural contentment behind the old aristocracy. Modern bourgeois culture, especially when it contained foreign influences, came to be regarded as effete and undynamic by many of the young, who increasingly took inspiration not from their parents' generation, but from a romanticized view of Germany's distant past. In music, this ideology took the form of a passionate reawakening of interest in national folk-music.

The *Jugendbewegung* (Youth Movement) originated in 1897, amongst *Gymnasium* (grammar-school) hiking groups in the Berlin suburb of Steglitz.[143] It idealized the virtues of rustic simplicity and the vagabond life, encouraging teenage boys and young men (not girls) to get away from the mechanization of the city and from parental authority, and rediscover Nature by hiking through the countryside, camping in barns and cooking around campfires. The aim of its musical section, the *Jugendmusikbewegung*, was to educate through the cultivation of folksong, singing, and playing the *Klampfe* (guitar); by 1901, these groups had become known as *Wandervögel* (keen hikers, lit. hiking birds). Although the *Klampfe* was initially their preferred instrument, the mandolin (which they regarded as a relative of the lute and of German ancestry) was also popular, provoking mixed reactions amongst middle-class players:

> The *Wandervögel* (hiking birds) enthusiastically took up the mandolin and *Klampfe* (colloquial for guitar) but not now to play Italian serenades, but rather to carry on German folk music traditions. In mandolin clubs at large, this development was on the one hand welcomed, because it meant expansion, but on the other, because of the predominantly bourgeois attitudes of these groups . . . the folksy string-picking of the young was felt to be an incursion by primitives. (Wölki 1984: 18.)

The movement quickly spread throughout Germany and into Austria, where the mandolin had hitherto been regarded primarily as an Italian instrument. In Vienna, one of the first societies had been the Circolo mandolinistico, founded in 1895 and directed by a succession of Italian conductors; this orchestra later amalgamated with the Vereinigung der Mandolinenfreunde. Other orchestras included Estudiantina (founded 1902), Vindobona (1903), and the Deutscher

---

[143] I am indebted to Keith Harris and Frau Gerda Wölki for many of the details concerning the *Jugendbewegung*.

Mandolinenkreis (1904), in addition to which there were many smaller societies and quartets giving regular concerts.[144]

While the popularity of such ensembles, which Gustav Mahler probably heard many times in the coffee-houses of Vienna during his years as director of the Vienna Court Opera, was doubtless one of the influences that persuaded him to include the mandolin in his later symphonies, the nostalgic, naturalistic philosophy of the *Wandervögel* (sentiments reflected in many of Mahler's songs), and the shared love of German folksong, must surely have been the overriding factors. His Seventh and Eighth symphonies (1905 and 1910) and *Das Lied von der Erde* (1908) each include at least one mandolin in their orchestration (the Eighth had four at its first performance), although the instrument is always used very sparingly, usually as part of the percussion, only occasionally being given a melodic phrase of its own. This fragmentary usage of the instrument has influenced many composers since, probably the first being one of Mahler's Viennese admirers, Anton Webern, who incorporated the mandolin into his brief, epigrammatic *Five Pieces*, Op. 10 (1911–13); in the third piece, the instrument provides a shimmering tremolo backdrop to the main theme, while it begins the fourth piece with a solo six-note phrase. Hans Pfitzner also used the instrument in his most successful opera, *Palestrina* (1917), as did Franz Lehár in *Die Lustige Witwe* (1905).

Elsewhere in Europe

Considerations of space preclude an exhaustive inventory of mandolin activity during this period. Britain, France, Belgium, Germany, and Austria were the most significant countries (although even they have necessarily been represented by one or two major cities in this section), but the instrument was so popular throughout Europe that its dissemination in a dozen other countries could usefully have been studied in detail here. However, before we move on, we should briefly take stock of developments elsewhere.

Switzerland possessed some of the best players and orchestras outside Italy, a virtue ascribed to its nearness to the home of the mandolin. Amongst the journals published there was the German-language *Moderne Musik* (Zurich, 1911–14), a monthly periodical devoted to the mandolin, guitar, and lute. Of the many fine ensembles, perhaps the most acclaimed was La Choralia of

---

[144] Nederost (1921: 14).

Lausanne, which received this review after a concert given on 18 June 1908, in the Jardin du Cercle de l'Art: 'We have long known of the artistic worth of this brilliant *estudiantina*, and we are happy to state that each of its concerts is a new triumph . . .'. (*L'Estudiantina*, 1 July 1908: 6.)

The earliest known ensemble in Denmark was Mrs Bang's Mandolin Orchestra, formed in 1903. Simon Julius Petersen founded the Copenhagen Mandolin Club in 1907, while his daughter, Frida Petersen, became a pioneer for the instrument in Denmark, being one of the country's first professional mandolinists, teachers, and conductors. The first mandolin-maker on a large scale was Peder Stochholm, who made instruments with a Milanese shape, a flat belly, and Neapolitan stringing that became very popular in Denmark. Finally, Alberto Bracony (a former pupil of Munier) settled in Denmark in 1915, with an international career as teacher, conductor, and chamber musician already behind him, and founded the Bracony Mandolin Trio.[145] Bulgaria's first orchestra was formed in Sofia in 1906, with twenty-five performers playing mainly Bulgarian songs and dances.[146]

In Spain, zarzuelas often included set pieces with bandurrias and guitars, such as the polka in *Los cocineros* by Joaquin Valverde. A number of chamber ensembles, similar to Italian mandolin quartets, also flourished. Baldomero Cateura, author of a method for the bandurria, formed a quartet (and later a quintet) of bandurrias, guitars, and lutes, while Angel Barrios, a noted flamenco guitarist who did much to popularize the bandurria, founded the Trio Iberia in 1900, comprising bandurria, guitar, and a bass lute.[147]

Although the bouzouki (an instrument combining elements of the Italian mandolin and the Turkish saz) had become the characteristic fretted instrument of urban Greece by the end of the nineteenth century, the Neapolitan mandolin was also widely played there during this period. The first mandolin orchestra was founded on the island of Zákinthos in 1901, and there were soon many others throughout Greece, mostly performing pieces from the Italian repertoire. The Mandolinata orchestra of Athens made a concert tour of New York, Chicago, and Boston in about 1911,[148] while that city's

---

[145] Müller (1991) provides an excellent summary of the mandolin's history in Denmark. Bracony was one of the first musicians to introduce Embergher mandolins into the country. These instruments have remained the preferred choice of many Danish concert performers to this day.

[146] *CMSA Newsletter* (Feb. 1992: 5).

[147] Bone (1972: 17, 77, 360). Bone does not explain exactly what he means by a lute or bass lute in this context, but I presume that the instrument was a large bass bandurria.

[148] Wölki (1984: 17).

most famous soloist was Demetrius C. Dounis (to whom Calace dedicated his Prelude No. 2, Op. 49). Zarh M. Bickford, who played the piano accompaniment for Dounis on his first American tour, called him 'a wonderful mandolinist', and noted that, unusually, he kept his right-hand little finger motionless on the scratchplate at all times 'as though it was glued to the instrument!'.[149] Dounis was undoubtedly a brilliant soloist and, although the reviewer from *Le Plectre* (who was an orchestral viola player) had some criticisms, he ultimately had to concede that his technique was faultless:

> Concert mandolinists in general ought to be suspicious of certain works which, to connoisseurs of music, compromise the real worth of the instrument . . . for example: Romance in F by Beethoven, 'Ronde des lutins' by Bazzini, Paganini concertos etc., which I heard performed last Saturday in the salle des Agriculteurs. These works are not of a musical style sympathetic to the instrument, and they highlight its weaknesses! The enforced comparison is to the detriment of the mandolin.
>
> Leave this genre of composition to the violin for which they were conceived and created, and since the violin literature offers us a vast field of research, gather the ones, know how to gather the ones just as beautiful and noble as those mentioned above, but which are suited to the mandolin . . . Now that I have written what I believe to be the truth I swear that the *Rondo capriccioso* and *Airs bohémiens* of Sarasate permitted this likeable performer to take his revenge in a manner dazzling to my eyes, by performing perfectly (including the *Sérénade* by Drdla) these pieces of the highest difficulty. The public acclaimed him unreservedly, and certainly Dounis can chalk it up as a success to his credit. (*Le Plectre,* 1 December 1912: 4.)

The mandolin was, by now, one of the most widely played instruments in Europe, mainly amongst dilettantes, but also amongst serious musicians. In the next section, we shall see that its popularity was by no means confined to that continent, and that its appeal had now become world-wide.

3.3 *The USA and Elsewhere*

The USA

As the USA possessed what was by now the world's largest community of Italian immigrants, the mandolin's increasing popularity there is unsurprising.

[149] *BMG* (June 1956: 217).

Amongst the most prominent Italians were Carlo Curti, author of *Curti's Complete Method for the Mandolin* (New York, 1896), and Vincent Léon, a former member of Curti's student group. More significant was Giuseppe Pettine, born in Isernia (Italy), who began to study the mandolin at the age of nine and moved with his family to Providence, Rhode Island, three years later. Pettine was soon touring America as a concert mandolinist, and became an important teacher; his influence in Providence continues to the present day, and his six-volume mandolin method is one of the most comprehensive works yet published in his adopted country. Amongst his compositions are the *Concerto patetico* (with piano accompaniment) and 'Murmuring Brook', a short unaccompanied duo-style piece still popular with performers. Calace dedicated his Concerto No. 1, Op. 113, to Pettine.

However, the Italian community at this time was scarcely integrated into mainstream American culture, and the mandolin achieved widespread popularity there only with the emergence of a generation of indigenous players, who took their inspiration from Italy but developed their own distinctive style. We have already encountered Samuel Adelstein, who visited Florence, Naples, and Rome in 1890, seeking tuition from the leading players there. On his return, he gave a major public recital in the Metropolitan Hall in his native San Francisco in February 1891, accompanied by pipe-organ. He gave the first-ever mandolin recitals in Portland, Oregon (1892), and Sitka, Alaska (1893), and in 1894 left on a world concert tour that included the Hawaiian Islands and the Far East.[150] Later, in 1908, he formed the Adelstein Mandolin Orchestra, composed of teachers and students from the San Francisco area.[151]

Valentin Abt studied the violin in Pittsburg and taught himself to play the mandolin, rapidly acquiring a virtuoso technique. In 1900 he moved to New York and, between concert tours, taught advanced students from his Carnegie Hall studio. His concert repertoire was a mixture of romantic works for violin and his own compositions, of which the Impromptu (1897, Ex. 10)[152] was the most notable. This remarkably advanced piece for unaccompanied mandolin includes passages in duo, trio, and quartet style and a variety of left-hand pizzicato effects (some of which had to be written on two separate staves), and it inspired other American players to compose works exploring the solo possibilities of the instrument, at a time when European mandolinists had

---

[150] Adelstein (1905: 13–16).   [151] *Le Plectre* (Dec. 1908: 4).
[152] Bone (1972: 1) states that Abt died in a mental institution in 1923, but Neil Gladd has established that he was still alive there in 1940.

Ex. 10. Abt: Impromptu, bars 1–16

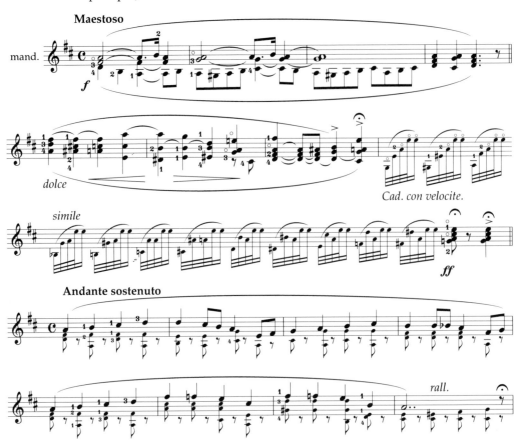

barely considered such techniques. In about 1908, Abt also formed the first American classical plectrum quartet—two mandolins, tenor mandola, and mandocello—with Zarh Myron Bickford playing the second mandolin.

Bickford (born Myron, he adopted the astrological name Zarh in about 1915) was a professional violinist and pianist with a keen interest in fretted instruments who studied mandolin with Abt, and also excelled as a guitarist and banjoist. Based in Springfield, Massachusetts, he was one of the founding members of the American Guild of Banjoists, Mandolinists, and Guitarists in 1902, and later twice became its president. The four-volume *Bickford Mandolin Method* (New York, 1920) was one of the most successful tutors of the period, while his impressive compositional output included many substantial and intelligently written pieces for plectrum ensembles (as well as many literary

Illustration 20. Samuel Siegel (from *Banjo World*, Aug. 1899: 151).

works devoted to astrology and other esoteric subjects). Aubrey Stauffer, from Denver, Colorado, left some 300 solo compositions and transcriptions that testify to a truly astonishing technique. Sadly, many of the former seem unacceptably crude and unsubtle to modern ears, while the latter (arrangements for unaccompanied mandolin of such large-scale works as the 'Halleluiah Chorus' from Handel's *Messiah*) often appear lamentably misguided. In Stauffer's defence, it should be remembered that he was performing in an era before amplification and primarily to boisterous vaudeville (not sedate classical) audiences. One of his better solo compositions is the graphically descriptive piece 'Storm at Sea' (1902).

One performer who moved from the vaudeville circuit to the concert-hall was Samuel Siegel (Illustration 20), born in Des Moines, Iowa. Unlike most of his contemporaries, Siegel began his musical studies on the mandolin rather than the violin, and believed that this gave him an advantage:

The majority of leading mandolinists of today began as violinists. I believe I am the only one who has never played the violin. To this I attribute the fact that I understand the right hand far better than some great players. They think that because the left hand is of such paramount importance on the violin, a sufficiency of dogged practice with the plectrum will make them expert mandolinists. Knowledge of the capabilities of the left hand enables them to do something, but the plectrum is far more difficult to manipulate than the bow of the violinist. Certainly it is possible for anyone, by a great deal of practice, to gain sufficient technique, but no amount of mere practice will atone for lack of study of tone qualities. (Siegel 1900: 38.)

Siegel lacked a formal training and did not read music well, but he was nevertheless a remarkable musician who saw that the future of the mandolin depended on the development of an original repertoire, rather than on violin transcriptions. He composed many fine pieces (which were notated for him), including a fantasia on 'Nearer my God to Thee' and a 'Witches' Dance', the latter becoming a popular showcase item for experienced players. During the 1890s, he performed mainly in vaudeville and, by the end of the decade, was widely regarded as the best American performer:

Samuel Siegel . . . probably enjoys the unique and proud distinction of being the recipient of more laudatory press comments than any other living mandoline soloist . . . Owing to the extraordinary inducements held forth, like a number of other first-class artists, Mr. Siegel entered the ranks of vaudeville, playing in all the principal cities in the United States and England, including two engagements at the Palace Theatre, London, being the first mandoline soloist from America to appear before a London audience . . . Mr. Siegel is an indefatigable worker, possessed of natural musical ability, and his playing represents what may be accomplished by earnest devotion to the true principles of music, artistically applied. This is what distinguishes his work from the mechanical efforts of many other soloists. Undoubtedly this will be his final season in vaudeville, as arrangements have been made for an extended concert tour, under the management of Mr. Arling Shaeffer of Chicago. While Mr. Siegel is meeting with unbounded success, both popular and financial, being featured on all programmes as 'America's Greatest Mandoline Virtuoso,' 'Direct from his successes at the Palace Theatre and St. James's Hall, London,' 'The King of the Mandoline,' etc., etc., he does not feel he is now doing himself justice. The fine effects he is capable of producing, exquisite phrasing, delicate tone colouring and marvellous technique, is hardly appreciated by the average vaudeville audience, which necessitates rendering a programme catering to the popular taste. As a composer, his works are well known, and the best in mandoline music. (*Banjo World*, May 1900: 102.)

The purity of Siegel's tone was remarked upon as frequently as his virtuosity. Many years later, when Siegel was staying at the Savoy Hotel in London, the editor of *BMG* visited him and was astonished by what he witnessed:

> I wish every mandolinist in this country could hear what I heard a day or two ago. The mandolin has often been described as tinkling, or tinny, or wiry, and indeed it sometimes is when in the hands of an incompetent player . . . I can truthfully say that never before have I heard a mandolin played with such a mellow and velvety quality of tone. As a matter of fact, tone has always been Mr. Siegel's principal object when studying and playing the mandolin. (*BMG*, May 1923: 100.)

In 1900, Siegel became the first mandolinist to record on Emile Berliner's newly invented disc system (although W. C. Townsend had recorded a few light pieces on Edison cylinders the previous year).[153] 'Nearer my God to Thee', the first of several dozen recordings he made during the next few years, was performed in a solo version that displayed his technique to the full:

> Finally our most absorbing conference was wound up by Mr. Siegel giving an absolutely masterly account of his fantasia on 'Nearer, my God to Thee,' in which chords are in some passages given with the rapidity with which other players execute a scale, and it was small cause for surprise to learn that this is the performer's favourite. (*Banjo World*, Aug. 1899: 152.)

Of the numerous American soloists, two others were particularly noteworthy. Seth Weeks (the only black virtuoso I know of during this period) had begun to study the mandolin in about 1886 and, by the turn of the century, had acquired a technique and a reputation to rival Siegel's, touring the USA, Canada, and Britain to huge popular and critical acclaim. He made several recordings for Edison's Phonograph in 1900, and his many compositions included solos in duo style and a Mandolin Concerto, Op. 7 (1900), with piano accompaniment.[154] William Place Jun., born in Providence, where he became a pupil of Pettine, reputedly surpassed his teacher in both tone and technique; his concert programmes were mainly based on violin repertoire, supplemented with works by Calace and Munier.

As in Europe, a few dozen professionals were supported by a huge number

---

[153] I am indebted to Neil Gladd for details of these early sound recordings.
[154] *Banjo World* (Dec. 1900: 20).

of middle-class amateur mandolinists, who used the instrument for simple, recreational music-making: waltzes, sentimental parlour songs, college songs, light classical music, and marches, as well as vaudeville-style ragtime and cake-walks. During the late nineteenth century, the secular, amateur musical life of America took place almost entirely in club rooms and parlours, small spaces where the mandolin could be heard to best advantage: 'It is claimed that in the parlor the mandolin and guitar, played by experts, produce a soft and desirable music, which makes a pretty effect, and it is for this reason that they are being used to such an extent in private residences.' (*Musical America*, repr. in *Cadenza*, Jan.–Feb. 1899: 9.)

The instrument's popularity was greatest in the fashion-conscious eastern cities of Boston, Washington, DC, and Philadelphia, and also New York, where its vogue in the 1890s was such that shop-girls started to carry mandolin cases in public, to give the impression that they were really Society ladies.[155] Almost every college had its own mandolin club, as did most sporting and bicycling organizations. Nor was its popularity entirely confined to these eastern cities. Clarence L. Partee noted that, as early as 1888, Kansas City already had a hundred mandolin clubs and orchestras, 'mainly social organisations number-ing from five to thirty-five members each, and their principal function was the entertaining of friends and the serenading of lady-loves &c.'[156] In 1902, the same writer reported:

Suffice it to say that every city in the United States now has its leading mandolin soloists and teachers, numbering in some cases a dozen or more in each city. Many towns of 10,000 population or less have at least one mandolin teacher of good standing, who occupies a position of prominence in the musical community, sim-ilar to the leading local violinist or pianist . . .

As an instrument for the home, in the parlor or drawing-room, accompanied by the guitar or piano, the mandolin is delightful and furnishes artistic and pleasing entertainment. Its portability, handy size and adaptability for use at formal and in-formal gatherings of all sorts make the mandolin one of the most effective and use-ful of musical instruments for young men to take up, as well as the young and

---

[155] *New York World* (quoted in *Banjo World*, Mar. 1894: 39) carried this eavesdropping of a conversation between two shop-girls, criticizing a third: 'She is such a fraud. She clerks in a store down town, and doesn't want peo-ple to know that she is a shop girl. So she carries that ever-lasting mandoline back and forth to convey the impres-sion that she is a society girl out for a music lesson. I have known of her little dodge for more than a year, and I am tired of it. I wish she would carry a tennis racket or a poodle for a change. The mandoline case is very con-venient though, for another girl told me that she carries her lunch, her overshoes, a comb and brush, and lots of things in it. It is not honest though, and I feel contempt for her.'

[156] *BMG* (Dec. 1912: 43).

middle-aged of both sexes. As a means of amusement, recreation, and also for serious study and for laying the foundation for a musical education, the study of this instrument is unsurpassed; its mastery is an accomplishment which may well be striven for by the modern young man or woman, and when attained is a never-failing source of pleasure. In that respect the mandolin stands to-day without a rival. (Partee, 1902: 19, 41.)

Of the dozens of American journals devoted to fretted instruments (none were exclusively for mandolin), two were of particular importance: the *Cadenza* (1894–1924, New York and Boston), published by Partee, who was also largely responsible for the founding of the American Guild of Banjoists, Mandolinists, and Guitarists in 1902;[157] and the *Crescendo* (1908–33, Boston), edited and published by Herbert Forest Odell, who had studied the mandolin in Paris with Pietrapertosa in 1895.[158] Both sought to elevate the instrument above the 'trashy' level of popular taste, and by the turn of the century Partee was asserting the view commonly held in the USA: that American players, thanks to their development of duo-style technique, were now far ahead of their European colleagues in performance and composition:

The chief defects of the foreign methods of writing are found in the lack of originality so often displayed and, in the case of mandolin compositions, often a total absence of effect or the development of a fitting climax; the use of too many repeated notes, over-use of the tremolo, the almost continual employment of single note passages, even in solos, and the lack of variety shown by the preponderance of rapid single note passages or sustained tones on single strings, are characteristic of both French and Italian schools of mandolin playing, and show at once just where they are deficient . . . Our journalism of the present day, our large manufacturing establishments, and the work of our best composers all show a higher accomplishment than any other nationality has been able to demonstrate up to the present time. (Partee 1901: 5–6.)

While Partee correctly identified the inadequacies of much European mandolin music, he was presumably unfamiliar with the better Italian composers—such as Munier, Calace, Maciocchi, Fantauzzi, Ranieri, Francia, and Monti—to whose mature output such criticisms rarely applied. It is undeniably true however

---

[157] The *Cadenza* began in 1894 as a journal appearing every two months (New York). It was briefly pub. in Kansas, *c*.1899, but in 1900 returned to New York as a monthly periodical. In 1908, it transferred to Walter Jacobs of Boston and continued monthly. In 1924, two journals were merged into *Jacobs' Orchestra Monthly and The Cadenza*, which continued until *c*.1943. The Library of Congress in Washington, DC, possesses a full run of both *Cadenza* and *Crescendo*.

[158] Wölki (1984: 17). Many other journals are listed in *BMG* (Jan. 1916: 11) and Wölki (1979*a*: 22).

that duo-style playing became (amongst the best performers) an established part of American technique several years before Europeans began to use it in a systematic way.[159] When Munier published his *Il nuovo stile dei duetti* in 1906, he mentioned that 'This new style of *Duets for Solo Mandolin*, already well-known and developed in America, is still unfamiliar in Italy',[160] while two years earlier the editor of *BMG* had lamented its rarity in Britain:

> I am surprised how little use is made in England of the duo style, and also in play-
> ing of full harmony on all four strings. This kind of mandolin work is very little
> known over here, the only exponent I have yet heard being Mr. Aubrey Stauffer,
> the celebrated American player. In his method of executing both an air and an
> accompaniment clearly on one instrument, he furnished me with the only exam-
> ple personally brought to my notice of a mandolin solo which really needs no
> accompaniment.... The full harmony style consists of giving the accompaniment
> on the mandolin in a series of full chords on all four strings.... Both these meth-
> ods open fields of mandolin development absolutely unperceived in Europe. (*BMG*
> Aug. 1904: 162.)

Around the turn of the century, demands started to be made in many countries for the study of a musical instrument to be included as part of the general education curriculum. In the USA, this led to the establishment in 1902
of the American Guild of Banjoists, Mandolinists, and Guitarists, formed
initially to obtain a government charter allowing them to act as an examin-
ing body.[161] The guild argued that fretted instruments were ideally suitable
for schoolchildren commencing music tuition, a contention that had the
full backing of USA manufacturers, who saw a huge potential for increased
sales.

Although American mandolin-manufacturing had been insignificant during
the 1880s, it grew rapidly over the next decade, partly because many of the
European imports were of poor quality (inaccurately fretted and prone to
joint-separation in conditions of rapidly changing humidity), and partly because
high import tariffs made foreign instruments less competitive. The largest
manufacturers of the 1890s, Lyon and Healy of Chicago, began to recruit
Italian and Spanish workmen and, by 1894, were making 7,000 mandolins

---

[159] As noted earlier, Francia had already published duo-style pieces in 1896, and presumably used the technique in unaccompanied solos during the 1890s without identifying it as a distinct style of playing. He later remarked that 'In America this method of playing has revolutionized the mandolin. It is not really novel, but now that it is recognized, it is never again likely to be dropped'. (*BMG*, Dec. 1904: 38.)

[160] *Il mandolino* (30 May 1906: 4).   [161] *Banjo World* (Apr. 1902: 82).

annually.[162] The highly respected firm of C. F. Martin & Co. (Nazareth, Pennsylvania, founded by Christian Friedrich Martin, an immigrant guitar-maker from Markneukirchen) added the instrument to its catalogue in 1896 (in 1902, its best model cost $100),[163] and several other makers followed suit at about the same time. In almost all cases, the standard Neapolitan round-back design was used as the template for these mandolins; only a few flat-back instruments were manufactured (in both the USA and Europe) during the 1890s, and they generally met with little success. A uniquely American innovation was the one-piece cast-aluminium mandolin, patented in 1896 by Neil Merrill of Oshkosh, Wisconsin. Whatever their faults, these round-back metal mandolins at least eliminated the problem of joint-separation, and were marketed in 1897 by the Aluminium Musical Instrument Company as 'the Wonder of the Age. For purity, sweetness and volume of tone THEY EXCELL ALL OTHERS. The bodies are made from Aluminium and the soundboard from selected spruce. They are practically indestructible. Used exclusively by Valentine Abt and many other noted artists.' (Advertisement in *Cadenza*, Sept.–Oct. 1897; quoted in Hambly 1977*a*: 402–4.)

The tone of aluminium mandolins is far more agreeable than one might expect, and they sold well for several years, but the most distinctive and successful innovation in American manufacture was yet to come. Orville Gibson, a maverick inventor from Chateaugay, New York, spent much of the 1890s adapting the principles of violin-manufacture to the mandolin, eventually taking out a patent on 1 February 1898 for a mandolin body with sides cut from a single piece of wood (rather than being bent) and carved top and back plates. In 1902, a consortium of businessmen provided the capital to establish a factory (making guitars as well as mandolins), which went into full production in Kalamazoo, Michigan, early the following year.[164]

Gibson designed two main types of mandolin which, with their carved tops, carved backs, and use of a bass bar, were quite unlike any previous flat-back

[162] *Banjo World* (Sept. 1896: 161) and Hambly (1977*a*: 12). Lyon and Healy made 12,000 banjos and 13,000 guitars in the same year. Much of Hambly's diss. (1977*a*) is concerned with the manufacture of mandolins in the USA during this period, and it contains a wealth of fascinating information, incl. details of instruments made from glass, ivory, tortoiseshells, and vegetable gourds.

[163] Longworth (1975: 79) and *Cadenza* (Mar.–Apr. 1898: 17). According to Partee (1912: 38), poorly constructed mandolins retailed for as little as $5 in 1912, but $25 was the minimum for a well-made instrument.

[164] Siminoff (1975: 5) and Hambly (1977*a*: 435–44). Orville Gibson was neither a stockholder nor a partner in the company, and seems quickly to have been excluded (or excluded himself) from its affairs. His latter years were dogged by ill health, and he died in St Lawrence State Hospital (a psychiatric centre), New York, on 21 Aug. 1918.

Illustration 21. A Gibson F-5 mandolin, serial no. 75329. Made in 1924, it incorporates f-holes rather than an oval soundhole, a feature introduced by Lloyd Loar in 1922. This instrument was resold in the early 1990s for $24,500 (photograph by Trip Savory, courtesy of Mandolin Central).

instrument. The A-series had symmetrical bodies, while the F-series (Illustration 21) incorporated a scroll on the bass side, an art-nouveau feature that also increased the size of the resonating chamber.[165] Various models appeared in both series (there was also an H-series of mandolas, a K-series of mandocellos, and a J-style mandobass), all of them (during Orville's lifetime), having either a round or an oval soundhole. The early models are nowadays considered rather primitive and of interest only to collectors but, from about 1909 onwards, instruments of a very high standard were produced, many of which are much sought after by professional performers today.

Ever since Gibson mandolins first appeared, arguments have persisted over whether they are superior or inferior to top-quality round-back instruments

[165] Some models in the A- and F-series were designated (for no discernible reason) 'Artist' and 'Florentine' models respectively.

(or, indeed, a species of gittern and not mandolins at all). Compared with an Embergher or Calace mandolin, a Gibson instrument has a larger resonating chamber, a longer fingerboard, and considerably more wood in its construction; the result is a deeper, more guitar-like tone, with a punchy, powerful attack, but fewer high harmonics and less brilliance. Many American players (especially those performing ragtime, dance tunes, and other non-classical music) regarded the Gibson as demonstrably superior, and immediately switched their allegiance to it. However, a great number of American classical players (and the vast majority of Europeans) thoroughly disliked it, considering it garish and wooden and finding that its long fingerboard made it impossible to play intricate, polyphonic Italian works. Walter Kaye Bauer, a leading player, composer, and arranger, who studied with Siegel and has taught many American mandolinists throughout this century (including James Tyler), was certainly unimpressed: 'My opinion has never changed. They were miniature lumber-yards painted up like prostitutes.' (Quoted in Hambly 1977*a*: 450.)

The Gibson company marketed its new instruments extremely aggressively. It established a network of teachers to sell its products to pupils, persuaded leading American players such as Bickford and Place (who had previously used round-back mandolins) to endorse a Gibson model, and also started a campaign of denigration against traditional Neapolitan instruments. Several manufacturers (including Lyon and Healy, Gibson's largest competitor) made round-back mandolins with alternate black and light brown ribs, a traditional German lute style. These markings were similar to those of the Colorado beetle, which had recently been devastating the nation's potato crop, and Gibson seized upon this visual resemblance, placing advertisements in which round-back instruments were described as 'potato bugs' or 'tater bugs', unwanted infestations to be swept away by the irresistible force of progress. Gibson catalogues from this period read, in places, almost like evangelical tracts, denouncing unbelievers and exhorting the faithful to spread the word; but, however intemperate they may seem today, they were highly successful in persuading hundreds of orchestras and thousands of smaller ensembles to equip themselves exclusively with Gibson instruments. By about 1910, the company was making approximately 3,500 instruments (mostly mandolins) annually; in 1917 an A-series model cost $27.50 and an F-4 retailed at $110.[166]

[166] Siminoff (1975: 15) gives the serial numbers for each year 1905–27, showing the average annual output rising from 2,500 in 1905 to 9,000 by 1927. While these figures do not differentiate between mandolins, guitars, harp, etc., all sources agree that the mandolin was Gibson's dominant product during the period 1909–20. The prices are taken from Gibson's *Catalog 'J'* (1917).

By the end of World War I, Gibson had attained a position of commercial pre-eminence in America which it has retained ever since although, in the classical field, the reputation of its instruments remains equivocal, revered and despised in roughly equal measure.

South America

Large numbers of Italians emigrated to Argentina towards the end of the nineteenth century and, when *Il mandolino* began publishing in 1892, it soon acquired an enthusiastic readership there. The journal often carried reports from Buenos Aires and in 1894 reported that its appearance in the capital had caused a small revolution amongst maestri and dilettanti alike.[167] The most notable teacher was Professor Pedro Ubertone, most of whose pupils came from distinguished families in the city's English colony. In 1897, he formed the Belgrano Ladies Mandoline Club (described by *Il mandolino* as 'the premier female mandolin club in the Argentine republic'), consisting of some twenty-five women under his direction. They made their début in the Salone teatro della società italiana in September of that year (dressed in elegant white uniforms and with their instruments decked out with ribbons) before a large, mainly English audience; the concert included 'a magnificent piece by Branzoli' and a concerto played by Ubertone.[168] In 1906, three of Ubertone's pupils (one male, two female) took professorship exams at the city's Istituto musicale G. Verdi, playing such pieces as the Seventh and Ninth concertos by Bériot and the *Fantasia Mazurka* No. 2 by Munier. By 1908, Ubertone had founded in Buenos Aires the Accademia Carlo Munier, incorporated to the Scuola nazionale in Florence, where Munier was director.[169]

Brazil, a former Portuguese colony, also experienced Italian immigration on a large scale. At first, mandolins were all imported from Italy but, from about 1900 onwards, round-back instruments (the *bandolim napolitano*) started to be made there. However, before long the *bandolim português* (a hybrid mandolin with Neapolitan tuning but the flat back and round body of a Portuguese guitar) had become the most popular form. This instrument subsequently became the standard Brazilian bandolim, still widely played today. Most of the printed music available to performers at this time was the same Italian repertoire currently popular throughout Europe, but the bandolim was also central

---

[167] *Il mandolino* (15 Mar. 1894: 4).   [168] *Il mandolino* (30 Apr. 1897: 4; 30 Sept. 1897: 4).
[169] *Il mandolino* (15 May 1906: 4) and *Musica moderna* (June 1908: 0).

to the street music of Rio de Janeiro (the *choro*), where European dance tunes were improvised upon and reinterpreted through distinctively Brazilian rhythms.[170]

Japan

Japan's almost total isolation from the rest of the world, which had begun in the seventeenth century, ended in 1853 when a naval expedition from the USA sailed into Edo Bay and forced the country to begin trading relations. From this point onwards Japan took a keen interest in the West, first in its industrial processes, but soon in its culture as well. Western-style singing lessons were introduced into schools and universities in 1880, and in 1890 the Tokyo Music School was founded. Foreign musicians were encouraged to come to Japan as teachers, and Western music became extremely fashionable among the wealthy.[171]

The first known mandolin performance in Japan was given by Totsuji Shikama, a Tokyo music teacher and a graduate of Ongaku-Torishirabe-Kakari (the country's first Western-style music school), who played *Yachiyo-shishi* in a concert on 26 September 1894, on a mandolin given to him by an Englishman a few months previously. Soon afterwards, the Western mandolin repertoire was introduced there by Samuel Adelstein, who gave his first concert at the Town Hall in Yokohama on 13 October 1894, to an audience that included many Japanese nobles. On the eve of his departure he played before the royal family, and was offered a position (which he declined) at the Tokyo Conservatoire.[172] Of the first generation of Japanese who studied the instrument, the most notable was Professor Kempachi Hiruma, who made several study trips to Europe, returned with a mandolin in 1901, published the first Japanese mandolin method in 1908, and began to give concerts on the instrument throughout the country.[173]

[170] I am indebted to Paulo de Sá for much of the information about Brazil.

[171] Busch (1972: 138) and Harich-Schneider (1973: 534).

[172] Adelstein (1905: 14–16). The *Japan Weekly Mail* (20 Oct. 1894: 4) noted that 'There can be but one opinion regarding the Concert given at the Public Hall on Saturday evening by Mr. Samuel Adelstein and several of our local amateurs. It was a great success. As a mandolin player Mr. Adelstein can hold his own with the best masters of the instrument, but he is incomparably a better musician, in the true sense of the term, when playing upon the lute. With the latter instrument he obtained the most delicate shades of expression mingled with broad almost 'cello-like effects... An instrumental sextette, comprising violin, viola, flute, 'cello, mandolin, and piano, concluded one of the most enjoyable concerts ever given in Yokohama. We hope Mr. Adelstein will see his way to give us another concert before long.'

[173] *JMU Review* (May 1991: 0). An earlier issue of *JMU Review* (Oct. 1979: 5) reported that Hiruma had brought a mandolin with him on his return from an earlier trip in 1891, but this has now been discounted.

Morishige Takei (a Japanese baron) visited Italy in 1911 to study the language, and became fascinated by the mandolin. After returning to Japan he became an influential figure in artistic life there, first as Chief Officer of the Board of Music, and then as Chief Officer of the Board of Ceremonies of the Imperial Household Agency. In 1916, he began publishing the monthly periodical *Mandolin and Guitar* (Tokyo) and in the same year founded a mandolin and guitar ensemble, the Orchestra Sinfonica Takei, together with the mandolin virtuoso and composer Tsunehiko Tanaka.[174] The most important European figure was Adolfo Sarcoli of Siena, a mandolinist and tenor (he had scored a great triumph in Puccini's *Tosca* in Milan in 1908), who moved to Japan in 1911 and became coach to the Keio Mandolin Club (Tokyo). Sarcoli was to spend most of the rest of his life in Japan, and trained many of the second generation of indigenous players.[175]

Elsewhere

During this period the mandolin was played in considerable numbers in virtually every country which Western culture had permeated. Cheap, robust, portable, and easy to play a simple tune upon, it was an ideal instrument for travellers. Fretted instrument orchestras were inexpensive to equip, and could be found in most of the African and Asian countries that were then colonized by European powers. When Adelstein visited Cairo (Egypt) in 1895, he attended a concert at the Continental Hotel on 28 January, during which Professor J. Pugliese and the orchestra Le Sphinx (consisting of twenty mandolins, one mandola, three guitars, and one double bass) performed the Concerto, Op. 104, by Bériot, an overture by Suppé, and extracts from *Cavalleria rusticana* by Mascagni.[176] The first BMG festival in South Africa took place at the Metropolitan Hall, Cape Town, on Friday 2 September 1898, and included a performance by Signor Prati of Munier's 'Mazurka di concerto'.[177] Photographs of colonial orchestras show that, although they were almost invariably led by a European, the members were usually indigenous people.

---

[174] *JMU Review* (Apr. 1979: 8–12). Until 1924, this orchestra was called the Sinfonia Orchestra Mandolini.
[175] *L'Estudiantina* (15 May 1908: 3); *Mandolinista italiano* (30 Nov. 1925: 1). The latter pub. features a photo of Sarcoli with his eleven-strong orchestra, taken in 1912.
[176] Adelstein (1905: 12–13).
[177] *Banjo World* (Nov. 1898: 13). Probably E. Prati, who later had a piece pub. by R. Maurri, Florence.

Finally, the first mandolin teacher in Australia appears to have been J. W. Greene, an Anglo-Australian living in Melbourne, who began playing in about 1880. In 1909 he was leading two orchestras, one of which—the Tambouraska—consisted entirely of mandolins and had been in existence since 1902.[178]

[178] *BMG* (Feb. 1909: 68–9).

4

1918–1945

4.1 *Germany, Austria, and the Emergence of a New Style*

The devastating experience of World War I greatly affected the German working class, many of whom felt that not only the economic and social fabric of their nation needed to be rebuilt, but also its traditional cultural identity. Numerous left-wing workers' organizations emerged, devoted to the 'proletarian' folk arts rather than 'bourgeois' culture (which was regarded as over-reliant on fashionable, superficial influences). Before the war, organized playing of plucked-string instruments had mostly involved the middle classes, but after 1918 the mandolin was increasingly adopted by socialists, who considered it a legitimate instrument of the *kleiner Mann* (the 'little man'). Two organizations existed to represent these two camps: the politically neutral Deutscher Mandolinen- und Gitarrenspieler-Bund (D.M.G.B.); and the Deutscher Arbeiter-MandolinistenBund (DAMB), which believed in a vigorous 'proletarian' culture as part of the overall fight for a socialist society.

The D.M.G.B. was founded in Leipzig on 6 December 1919, and subsequently published two monthly journals, the *Chronik der Volksmusik* (Leipzig, 1919–28) and *Das Mandolinen-Orchester* (Leipzig, 1927–35).[1] The aims of the D.M.G.B. were apolitical—to raise playing standards, gain academic recognition for the instrument, and foster relations with foreign mandolinists—and its membership covered a wide social spectrum. The DAMB was established in January 1923, and published the monthly journal *Freier Zupfer* (Magdeburg, 1922–33). Avowedly socialist in its aims, it was strongly critical of the D.M.G.B., arguing that neutrality in music was impossible, and that art could only be honestly 'proletarian' or decadently 'bourgeois'. For the DAMB, playing German folk-music was a means to raise the political consciousness of the

---

[1] Wölki (1979*b*: 13) and information supplied by Tetsuro Kudo.

working class, rather than nostalgic escapism (as it was for the middle-class *Wandervögel*, who continued their rural idylls throughout the 1920s). The DAMB commissioned new pieces to celebrate the workers' struggle (such as *Prometheus: Ein Tag aus dem Leben des Arbeiters*, a melodrama for mandolin orchestra and choir composed by Ferdinand Kollmaneck in 1928), and forged links with workers' mandolin unions in other European countries. The DAMB and D.M.G.B. each had many thousands of members during the 1920s, but the latter organization ultimately had a far more significant effect on mandolin history, and we shall concentrate primarily on it.[2]

During the 1920s, the repertoire of the D.M.G.B. consisted largely of mainstream classical works (transcribed for plucked instruments) and original pieces by specialist German mandolin composers. Initially, these were published mainly in quartet form, to be performed by either four soloists or full mandolin orchestra. At first, German orchestras consisted solely of guitars (or so-called 'lutes' tuned like guitars) and members of the mandolin family but, as the decade progressed, they were increasingly augmented with woodwind, double basses, and brass instruments, until they began to resemble plucked-string versions of standard orchestras. Two concert programmes of 1929 (from a festival in Neustadt at which a dozen German orchestras participated) give an idea of the wide variety of transcriptions then being performed: Hungarian Dances Nos. 5 and 6 by Brahms; a potpourri on *Il trovatore* and a fantasia on *La traviata* by Verdi; the Romance in F Major by Beethoven; an impromptu by Schubert; and *In a Persian Market* by Ketèlbey. Amongst specialist mandolin composers, the most frequently performed was Theodor Ritter.[3]

Every major city had its mandolin orchestras, and the leading players were now Germans rather than Italians. In Dortmund, Theodor Ritter was the most prominent mandolinist; his compositions (in particular his serenade 'Music by Night' and his settings of German folk-tunes) appeared on many concert programmes, and his Dortmund orchestra was a popular ensemble, making numerous gramophone recordings for Homocord and Electrola from 1928 onwards. Ritter and Carl Henze of Berlin were two of the most influential teachers of their generation, together establishing the Union of Federal Teachers in the D.M.G.B. in 1922.[4] But the most significant figure was Konrad Wölki (Illustration 22), who became director of the Berliner Lautengilde in 1923 and composed

---

[2] Wölki (1979*b*: 13–14). The political issues were addressed in two polemics written in the 1920s: an art. by Konrad Wölki, ' "Bürgerlich" oder "proletarisch" ' (*Das Mandolinen und Lautenspiel*, June 1928: 49); and an editorial, 'Proletarisch oder bürgerlich?' (*Freier Zupfer*, Aug. 1928: 1.)

[3] *Festschrift zum dritten Gautag* (Neustadt, 5–6 Oct. 1929: 6–7).　　　[4] Janssens (1982: 128).

Illustration 22. Konrad Wölki (photograph courtesy of Gerda Wölki).

a series of symphonic works for mandolin orchestra (with wind), commencing with the Overture No. 1 in A major, Op. 1 (1924), and including the popular Overture No. 2 in F# minor, Op. 2 (1925), and the *Sinfonischer Satz* in E minor, Op. 12 (1929). In 1928, his Overture No. 4 in B minor, Op. 7 (1927), was performed in the Philharmonic Concert Hall in Berlin by the district orchestra of the D.M.G.B., augmented by the wind section of the Berlin Philharmonic Orchestra.[5] Although written in a mid-nineteenth-century style, these early pieces by Wölki convincingly demonstrated the dramatic potential and range of colour available from an expanded mandolin orchestra, and many of them are still frequently performed today.

Despite all this activity, the academic status of the mandolin in Germany remained low, with most professional institutions refusing to recognize an amateur instrument. However, it was often used in mainstream concert music, and appeared in several notable German operas: *Violanta* (1916) and *Die tote*

---

[5] Wölki (1979*b*: 8).

Stadt (1920) by the Czechoslovakian-born composer Erich Korngold; *Das Nusch-Nuschi* (1922, for marionettes) by Paul Hindemith; and (briefly) *Die Dreigroschenoper* (1928) by Kurt Weill. Major radio stations were also being established during these years, and many D.M.G.B. orchestras became regular broadcasters, as well as frequently recording for various gramophone companies. Although they now primarily performed German music, and used mandolins made in Saxony (no longer relying on Italian imports), the members of the D.M.G.B. were not isolationist; in particular, in September 1928 in Berlin, they organized a major international congress of mandolinists and guitarists, which was attended by musicians from ten countries including Belgium, France, Holland, Italy, Japan, Yugoslavia, and Austria.

Like the Germans, the Austrians had had their cultural identity badly shaken by the events of World War I and the collapse of the Austro-Hungarian Empire in 1918. In Vienna, many ordinary city-dwellers sought spiritual uplift in music, and plucked-string instruments were a popular choice for performing folk-music, as well as transcriptions of classical music from the city's rich tradition. In November 1918, the Apolloneum society for national music education was founded in the city; the courses on offer included a lute class, taught by Josef Zuth, and a mandolin class given by Professor Karl Friedenthal of the Neues Wiener Konservatorium. The mandolin orchestra of the Apolloneum made its public début on 10 June 1919 and played frequently in the city thereafter, performing a mixture of popular classical pieces (such as transcriptions of works by Mozart and Offenbach) and traditional folk-music.[6]

Although the mandolin had been a common instrument in Vienna around 1800, it disappeared so completely during the mid-nineteenth century that when it became popular again in the 1890s, it was regarded as an Italian instrument and was only played in tremolo style. The Beethoven pieces and the serenade in Mozart's *Don Giovanni* were well known, but the existence of an extensive original classical repertoire was not even suspected. However, during the 1920s, several players became aware of a large manuscript collection of chamber music—quartets, trios, concertos, and sonatas for mandolin and bowed strings, composed during the Classical period—housed in Vienna's Gesellschaft der Musikfreunde.[7] Vinzenz Hladky, an orchestral cellist with an interest in the mandolin, founded the Wiener Mandolinen-Kammermusik Vereinigung (in which he played the mandocello) in 1926, to perform this

---

[6] Nederost (1921: 17–21).

[7] See Tyler and Sparks (1989: 39–41, 56–8, 99–103, 157) for detailed information on this coll. and the composers.

rediscovered music. One of his pupils, Maria Hinterberger, prepared performing editions of many of the works, and also played mandolin in the concerts, along with Leopoldine Freitag, another of Hladky's pupils. Hladky subsequently published many of the pieces, while Josef Zuth drew academic attention to the collection in a detailed article.[8] Besides demonstrating that the mandolin had a rich musical heritage, these works were important for another reason: they made little use of tremolo, relying predominantly on a single plucking technique and giving the instrument an entirely different character, akin to a soprano lute.

During the early 1920s, the Viennese composer Arnold Schoenberg was developing the system of twelve-note (dodecaphonic), atonal composition known as serialism. Because his uncompromisingly radical style made his compositions commercially unsuccessful, he supplemented his income by making arrangements of well-known melodies for the amateur market, two of which (both dating from 1921) are of particular interest to us: a Schubert serenade, arranged for clarinet, bassoon, mandolin, guitar, and string quartet; and the Neapolitan song 'Santa Lucia', arranged for mandolin, guitar, piano, and string trio.[9] Between 1920 and 1923, he composed his Serenade, Op. 24, the first major work to use dodecaphonic techniques; its unusual instrumentation—clarinet, bass clarinet, mandolin, guitar, violin, viola, and cello (and baritone for one movement)—was doubtless partly inspired by his earlier arrangements. Mahler's use of mandolin and guitar was undoubtedly another important influence, as was the availability of skilled players in Vienna, not to mention the traditional association of plucked instruments with the serenade (Schoenberg would have enjoyed outraging conservative Viennese music-lovers by presenting such advanced music in such a traditional form).

The Serenade has proved to be one of Schoenberg's most successful compositions, and remains a landmark in the mandolin's history. Many great composers had written for the instrument before, but they had (in general) either given it a solo role or else used it sparingly. Now, for the first time, it was incorporated into the whole of a work of major importance, not as an occasional soloist but as an equal partner in a primarily polyphonic composition, playing almost continuously and contributing to the whole. Schoenberg employed the mandolin's tremolo technique in a restrained and tasteful way, and was obviously pleased with the result, because he used the instrument several more

---

[8] See Zuth (1931). The Hladky edns., are still in print, pub. Heinrichshofen, Wilhelmshaven. Some pieces originally written for six-course mandolino were adapted by Hladky for the Neapolitan instrument.

[9] Huck (1990: 106).

times during the next decade (much of which he spent in Berlin); in the *Four Pieces* for mixed chorus, Op. 27 (1925), the Variations for Orchestra, Op. 31 (1926–8), and the operas *Von Heute auf morgen* (1929) and *Moses und Aron* (1930–2). Another Austrian composer, Ernst Krenek, also scored for mandolin in his opera *Karl V* (1938) and his *Kleine Symphonie*, Op. 58.

The coming to power of the Nazi Party in 1933 had a catastrophic effect on the arts in Germany, and soon also on Austria.[10] Most of the major composers in both countries were (in Nazi eyes) 'guilty' of being Jewish or of writing 'degenerate' music (usually both), and were forced to flee; Schoenberg, Hindemith, Korngold, and Weill were amongst the many leading musical figures who emigrated. Those who remained often had to modify their musical language to conform to Nazi ideology, imposed under the policy of *Gleichschaltung* (through which all culture was to be encompassed within the party, to ensure that it was truly Germanic and free of all foreign 'taint'). Even the apparently innocuous mandolin was not exempt. The DAMB and the *Wandervögel* were both immediately abolished, and in 1935 the D.M.G.B. was also forced to close, its membership being absorbed into the Reichsverbande für Volksmusik (RfV, Imperial Association for Music of the People). In May 1935, shortly before its closure, the D.M.G.B. had 16,508 members, organized in 928 local groups.[11] Fortunately for the mandolin, interference went no further:

> It was relatively easy to get out of the politicization, because the sounds of mandolins and guitars are hardly suited to demonstrations ... The approved playing lists of *Group VII—Mandolin and Guitar Societies* established by the RfV thus remained free from political trends. There were musical criteria, such as suppressing entertainment music and 'alien' (Italian) mandolin music ... In the short time before the beginning of the war, things turned out to be such that musical societies had less to do with 'officials' than with musical specialists of the RfV, young music scholars who approached their task in an open manner and who guaranteed the validity of this branch of music. (Wölki 1979*b*: 20.)[12]

---

[10] Although the *Anschluss* did not occur until 1938, Austrians feared and expected annexation from the moment Hitler took power.

[11] Wölki (1979*b*: 23). In 1938, 921 mandolin orchestras were listed within the 'Greater German Reich'. Wölki gives a detailed description of events during this period from the perspective of a senior D.M.G.B. member. Wölki was dismissed from the board of the D.M.G.B. in 1935, being replaced by a party member. Ritter and Ambrosius both had connections with the Nazi party during this period, as did many other prominent figures.

[12] Keith Harris informs me that Wölki, who had himself been ostracized by many Nazi sympathizers during the Third Reich, was being rather generous to former enemies when he wrote this passage. As early as 1933, it was not uncommon for Nazi thugs to interrupt rehearsals and beat up players of 'incorrect' music, and many orchestras had their instruments confiscated.

From 1933 onwards, German mandolin composers began to rethink their entire approach towards the instrument, partly through political necessity but also because of a growing awareness of the mandolin's classical traditions. An important influence was Hermann Ambrosius, a young orchestral composer who had studied with Hans Pfitzner. He was invited to compose a work for mandolin orchestra, to be performed at the D.M.G.B.'s last-ever concert, held in Cologne in September 1935, and responded with the beautiful Suite No. 6. Ambrosius scored this work for *Zupforchester* (plucked strings only, without the wind section) and wrote in an accessible neo-Baroque style, using traditional dance movements from a Baroque suite—Präludium, Menuett, Sarabande, Gavotte, Badinerie (with Musette)—and including several passages without tremolo. This was the first in a long series of compositions for plucked strings that Ambrosius produced throughout his life and, sixty years after its first performance, it remains a favourite with German *Zupforchester*.

At the same time, Wölki (who had become a teacher at the Sternsches Konservatorium in Berlin in 1934) had been researching further into the eighteenth-century mandolin repertoire, studying the various *méthodes de mandoline* published in Paris during the 1760s and 1770s and confirming that the classical mandolin had been played almost entirely without tremolo at that time. Inspired by Ambrosius's suite, he went a stage further and, in his own Suite No. 1 for *Zupforchester*, Op. 29 (1935)—Präludium, Courante, Sarabande, Gavotte, Gigue—dispensed with tremolo altogether. Many players regarded the technique as the very soul of the instrument and were outraged, protesting that a mandolin without tremolo was like a violin without a bow, but others welcomed a return to traditional classical methods. Wölki relented a little in his Suite No. 2, Op. 31 (1937, subtitled 'Music for simple leisure hours'), by sparingly reintroducing the tremolo, but a distinctive feature of German compositions for *Zupforchester* has remained the restrained use of this technique, which is employed only where specifically indicated. Wölki continued to explore the early repertoire and techniques, publishing the results in his three-volume *Deutsche Schule für Mandoline* (Berlin, 1939); as an appendix to the third volume, he included his short but important *Geschichte der Mandoline*, which outlines the evolution of the mandolin from the seventeenth century through to the twentieth.

In Vienna, mandolin activity remained centred around Hladky, who now began encouraging contemporary composers associated with the city to write for the instrument in a classical style, with restrained use of tremolo. The

Viennese-born Hans Gál began composing a series of pieces for mandolin, most of them written after his forced emigration to Edinburgh (where he became a lecturer at the university). These works include a Partita for mandolin and piano and a Divertimento for mandolin and harp. Alfred Uhl composed the delightful Spielmusik (1936) for mandolin and string trio, and also a Suite for mandolin orchestra. Of several works by Norbert Sprongl, the most frequently performed nowadays is the Duo for mandolin and guitar.[13] Maria Hinterberger was the soloist in the first performances of many of them.

Gál, Uhl, and Sprongl expressed themselves in a tonal idiom (often an advanced, dissonant, polyphonic language) and, although they also produced symphonies, operas, and major choral and chamber works, their output has subsequently been overshadowed by the revolutionary atonal music that Schoenberg, Webern, and their associates were producing at about the same time. Moreover, the cultural insularity of Germany and Austria during these years denied many of these composers an international platform. None the less, all of them composed original and attractive music, and many of their pieces for mandolin are still frequently performed today. As mandolinists are well aware, the artistic worth of their instrument has often been denigrated by musicians who find the incessant use of tremolo unacceptable and annoying, and mistakenly believe that the mandolin is invariably played in this way. To such people, these Viennese works—which take their inspiration from the eighteenth century but speak in a distinctly twentieth-century voice—will come as an agreeable surprise.

4.2 *Elsewhere in Continental Europe*

Italy

The Fascist government that ruled Italy between 1922 and 1943 fervently believed in modernizing the country, imposing an authoritarian work ethic that had serious consequences for popular musical life. In Rome and Naples, the streets were cleared of casual performers as part of the drive against begging and petty crime, thus ending a long tradition of outdoor music-making

---

[13] Many of these 20th-cent. works (and their 18th-cent. precursors) are still in print, pub. Heinrichshofen, Wilhelmshaven. I have not been able to establish exact dates for all the 20th-cent. works; some were written after World War II and are mentioned in Ch. 5.1.

by singers, guitarists, and mandolinists. Visitors regretted this sudden disappearance, one British travel writer noting sadly in Naples that:

> I heard much less singing in the streets, on my most recent visit. I used to have the feeling that all of Naples was an outdoor opera. Latterly, the spirit of modernity seems to have made Neapolitans ashamed of too many things which were formerly a great charm for her guests. No one can quarrel with the fine new pride which has so greatly decreased begging. But I was sorry when I heard Neapolitan friends of mine decry the 'troubadours' singing the world popular Neapolitan songs, on the ground that those men ought to be busy about something more in keeping with a modern world. In the daytime perhaps—or, doubtless. But if Naples doesn't encourage more of them to do singing (for a little extra recompense, which *surely* isn't 'begging') at night, she's going to rob her visitors of something very precious . . . It is an important part of the incalculably precious enchantment which is Italy. (Laughlin 1928: 11.)

Concert music was, however, given great support by the Fascists, who particularly encouraged works that were tonal, nationalist, and recalled Italy's glorious past. The best-known orchestral pieces from this period are probably those by Ottorino Respighi, many of whose compositions drew inspiration from Italian history, and used stylistic elements from earlier centuries. Two celebrated pieces, *Pini di Roma* (1924) and *Feste romane* (1928), include prominent passages for mandolin, the latter conjuring up scenes of joyful, alfresco music-making in the concert-hall at the very time that they were being forcibly discouraged in reality.

The mandolin was now much more rarely encountered outdoors, except in tourist locations, but it remained extremely popular with concert performers and serious amateurs (although it was still not officially recognized by the national conservatoires).[14] Raffaele Calace, by now the most venerated figure in the mandolin world, increasingly devoted himself to composition, producing about half of his entire output during the last fifteen years of his life. Works for unaccompanied mandolin include the Prelude No. 12, Op. 137 (written in the Gulf of Siam, Bangkok, on 10 March 1925), the Prelude No. 14, Op. 149 (1927), the 'Gran preludio', Op. 175 (April 1932), and his final composition, 'Silvia', Op. 187 (1933). Amongst his works for unaccompanied liuto were 'Souvenir de Shanghai', Op. 140 (25 February 1925), and the Prelude

---

[14] *Le Plectre* (1 July 1933: 4) noted that A. Vizzari, the director of the magazine *Il Plettro* in Milan, was still attempting to persuade the government to include the mandolin amongst the instruments taught in national conservatoires.

No. 13, Op. 148 (1927), while for solo guitar (an instrument he had occasionally composed for earlier in his career) he produced a series of works during the final three years of his life (Opp. 163, 166–73, 176–7, 179, 181, and 183).

Calace's large-scale compositions include three concertos with piano accompaniment—two for mandolin (Opp. 113 and 144)[15] and one for liuto (Op. 150)—excellent virtuoso showpieces which remain popular repertoire items with the few players who can perform them. Many of his most beautiful pieces were written for mandolin and piano (some also existing in versions with guitar accompaniment, or in quartet form): most were composed in the traditional Italian style, but with a highly ornamented mandolin part accompanied by richly chromatic harmonies (such as the *Mazurka da concerto*, Op. 126, written for Mario De Pietro); others make use of Spanish rhythms (especially the Bolero No. 2, Op. 161, and 'Danza spagnola', Op. 105). Of his works for mandolin ensemble, two of the most successful were the *Concerto a plettro*, Op. 155 (for Classical Quartet and guitar), a complex contrapuntal work built from numerous short dialogues between the four plectral instruments; and *Mattino d'autunno*, Op. 164 (1931, for Romantic Quartet), an impressionistic work of great lyricism and expressive power, enhanced by constantly shifting tempos and tonality, and with a recurring sequence of rapidly descending chromatic chords, evoking the falling of dead leaves. There appear to be only three works by Calace originally composed for full mandolin orchestra: *Impressionismo: momento lirico*, Op. 145, inspired by poems from World War I that describe the passage of a soldier's troubled soul from rebellion to passive fatalism; *Intermezzo: mesto pensiero*, Op. 146; and *Impressioni orientali*, Op. 132 (composed on board ship in February 1925, while returning to Italy after a tour of Japan), a wonderfully exciting and atmospheric piece, strongly influenced by Middle Eastern scales and drones, that creates an extraordinary range of timbre.

The Calace firm continued to dominate instrument-manufacture in Naples, with Raffaele's son Giuseppe eventually succeeding his father (the labels changed from 'Prof. R. Calace' to 'Comm. prof. Raffaele Calace & figlio' in 1922).[16] As well as world-famous fretted instruments, they made violins, which also had a fine reputation, and were used by two famous figures from opposite

[15] Concerto No. 2 was dedicated to 'Mussolini, Artisan of the new Italy, 1925'. This inscription was removed by the Calace family after the downfall of Fascism.

[16] According to the entry in *Dizionario biografico degli italiani*.

ends of the cultural spectrum; the celebrated concert soloist Fritz Kreisler, and the notorious Fascist dictator Benito Mussolini, who was a keen amateur violinist.[17] Raffaele remained an active performer on both mandolin and liuto until the very end of his life, making several recordings of his own works and giving concerts throughout Europe, as well as making an important trip to Japan in 1924–5. One of his pupils, Michele Fasano, later described the effect of his liuto playing: 'what the rest of us strove to do with the mandolin, he accomplished without effort on the liuto. His tone was the nearest approach to the human voice I ever heard and his instrument always sang, for he was the master of phrasing.' (Tyrell 1952–3: 51.)

Raffaele also trained his daughter Maria to virtuoso standard (she had started on a piccolo mandolin at the age of six), and she rapidly became one of the most successful soloists on the Continent. In 1926, for example, she gave a series of concerts at the Neuer Saal in the Hofburg, Vienna, and others at the Sala del Conservatorio Niccolò Paganini and the national theatre in Genoa, besides regular appearances in Naples. In 1929, Raffaele formed the Accademia mandolinistica napoletana, an orchestra of forty players led by Maria. In 1931, she recorded ten discs in Berlin (for the Polydor company), including Beethoven's Adagio in E♭ and several pieces by Raffaele; her father accompanied her on the liuto for some of these. After Raffaele's death (on 14 November 1934), Maria founded the Calace Plectrum Quartet and the Calace Plectrum Sextet (her brother Giuseppe played the octave mandola in both groups). Their concert programmes were mostly based around her late father's compositions.[18]

The only Italian maker to equal (and perhaps even surpass) the Calace family was Luigi Embergher of Rome, whose mandolins continued to be the favoured instruments of many leading soloists. On 16 February 1938, shortly after his 82nd birthday, he formally transferred his business to his favourite pupil, Domenico Cerrone, his 'sole and absolute successor.'[19] Several magazines remained in print: in Bologna, *Il concerto* appeared fortnightly until the end of 1934; in Milan, *Il mandolinista italiano* and *Il plettro* both continued until 1943; and the most important journal of all, *Il mandolino*, finally ceased publishing in Turin at the end of 1937, more than forty-five years after it had begun. There were active mandolin orchestras in most Italian cities, one of the most successful being the Circolo mandolinistico Regina Margherita

---

[17] Tyrell (1952–3: 51) and Trapani (1982: 169).
[18] Tyrell (1952–3: 107) and *Fretted Instrument News* (Nov.–Dec. 1952: 8).   [19] Mastroianni (1993: 6).

from Ferrara, which won first prizes at competitions in Como (1921), Rome (1922), Milan (1923), and Paris (1924).[20] A typical Italian programme from this period featured transcriptions of music by Verdi, Haydn, and Schubert, alongside original works by De Giovanni and the 'Serenata lombarda' by Alfieri.[21] However, political events inevitably led to Italy's increasing isolation within Europe during the 1930s, and mandolin life within the country gradually began to ossify. Little new music of high quality was written after the death of Calace, and orchestras and soloists increasingly came to rely on classical transcriptions, or on compositions written a generation earlier.

France

From 1922 onwards, Marseilles was the foremost French city for the study of the mandolin, thanks to Fantauzzi who established, at the city's Conservatoire National, a mandolin class that continued until 1940, a year before his death. This was the first time that the mandolin had been formally integrated into the French academic system, and its new status inspired players in Italy: 'Marseilles, the leading city for the mandolin in France, has set the example with this fine initiative to put the mandolin in its true place, at the same level as the other instruments of the orchestra. . . . And in Italy, the cradle of music? When?' (*Il mandolino*, 30 December 1922: 4.)

Competition for places on this course was severe, and the standards were high. Joseph Vitali seems to have been Fantauzzi's best pupil, passing the highest performance examinations at the conservatoire in 1928 and broadcasting regularly on the radio station PTT (including a recital in October 1930 when he performed 'Bizzarria' by Munier and 'Charmeuse' by Fantauzzi).[22] He was a member of the Quatuor Fantauzzi, a group of soloists from the Orchestre à Plectre de Marseille whose personnel (between 1930 and 1933) was Joseph Vitali and Gaspard Resecco, mandolins; Mlle Mary Garibaldi, mandola; and M. A. Peduto, mandoloncello. In 1933, at a competition in Narbonne, Vitali won the soloist's prize, the Quatuor Fantauzzi took the quartet prize, and the Orchestre à Plectre de Marseille won the orchestral prize with a performance that included Ranieri's transcription of the overture to Rossini's *Barber of Seville*.[23]

---

[20] *Il mandolino* (30 Dec. 1924: 4) gives a brief history and photo. [21] *Il mandolino* (15 Jan. 1929: 2–3).
[22] *Le Plectre* (1 Nov. 1930: 4).   [23] *Le Plectre* (1 July 1933: 2).

In Paris, Mario Maciocchi continued to publish *L'Estudiantina* until 1934, when the journal became *L'Orchestre à plectre* (1934–9), a name he also gave to his shop in the rue Saulnier. He was particularly devoted to mandolin orchestras, transcribing many popular classics for plucked strings, composing hundreds of light but well-written pieces (often with Spanish influences), and directing his own orchestra, whose many concerts included one given at Arènes de Lutèce in 1921, with 300 performers and an audience of 7,000.[24] His orchestral scores often expanded beyond the traditional four-part arrangements for *Estudiantina*, sometimes calling for two mandola sections, mandocellos as well as guitars, and divisi mandolins 1 and 2.

The leading soloist in Paris was Maria Scivittaro, who resumed her professional career in 1930, becoming mandolinist at the Opéra and giving frequent radio recitals. In 1933 she signed a recording contract with Pathé Frères, her discs recorded over the next few years including Munier's 'Capriccio spagnuolo', Marucelli's 'Capriccio zingaresco', Leonardi's 'Souvenir de Sicile' and 'Souvenir de Naples', and Bériot's *Scènes de ballet* (the last-named being made early in 1936).[25] She was also engaged by Gustave Charpentier as mandolin soloist for a recording of *Impressions d'Italie*, a work he had originally written in 1889 while resident at the Villa Medici, after winning the Prix de Rome. One of her most notable pupils was André Saint-Clivier, who trained as a violinist but took up the mandolin at the age of 16, becoming a soloist with the *Estudiantina* of the radio station PTT. Publio Conti (an Italian who had won the soloist's prize at the international competition in Boulogne in 1909) was another highly regarded player, whose many concerts included a major one in Paris in 1926.

Mandolin orchestras remained popular throughout France. In 1936, for example, four competitions were organized in the Paris region alone, with an International Concourse held in Marseilles on 16–17 May.[26] One of the best orchestras was Les Mandolinistes Roannaises, a seventy-five-strong group, exclusively female except for their conductor. Lastly, we should note François Menichetti, a military bandleader in the French Foreign Legion with an interest in plucked-string instruments. He composed more than a dozen works for mandolins during the 1920s, although he did not become an important figure amongst French mandolinists until after World War II.

---

[24] *La Mandoline* (1981: 41, 44).   [25] *L'Orchestre à plectre* (1 Feb. 1936: 1).
[26] *L'Orchestre à plectre* (1 Feb. 1936: 1).

Belgium

Silvio Ranieri remained one of the world's leading players, and mandolin life in Brussels was centred around him. A journalist friend, Louis Quievreux, later recalled the first time he heard Ranieri play:

> In the 1920s, there was a room called the Concerts Artistiques, rue Neuve.... It was here that I heard Silvio Ranieri for the first time. He used to be spoken about a great deal in Brussels. It was said that he was the world's greatest mandolin virtuoso. The mandolin—with four double strings tuned like a violin and plucked with a plectrum—was an unimportant instrument until Ranieri appeared, associated with Italian folklore, with simple Neapolitan serenades. My astonishment at hearing Ranieri play at the Concerts Artistiques was unimaginable. With an outrageous virtuosity, he transformed the irritating tremolo into cascades pleasing to the ear. A musicologist and a musician, he drew on a repertoire which offered the widest possibilities to the instrument which he had chosen to revive. (Quievreux 1956: 2.)

For many years, Ranieri was director of the mandolin section of La Grande Harmonie, the largest musical society in Brussels. In 1932 he became its overall director, conducting the main symphony orchestra as well as the mandolin orchestra. He was highly regarded in the city and, in February 1926, the society held a festival in the rue de Ruysbroeck to celebrate his twenty-fifth year in Brussels, commemorating the occasion by striking a bronze bust of Ranieri. He was also awarded the *Ordre de la Couronne* for services to Belgium.

Of Ranieri's many pupils, the most successful was Frans De Groodt from Antwerp, who had also studied the mandolin with Florimond Costers and the guitar with Emilio Pujol. De Groodt won the solo prize at a competition in Milan in 1920 (the jury included Raffaele Calace, who subsequently dedicated his Prelude No. 10, Op. 112, to the Belgian), and he eventually succeeded Ranieri as his country's leading soloist. Ranieri's mandolin quartet (in which De Groodt played the tenor mandola) was one of Europe's leading ensembles, taking the gold medal in Milan and another at Boulogne-sur-Mer (1923).[27] The international concert success of Andrés Segovia also encouraged Ranieri to study the guitar. He taught both instruments during the 1930s, and compiled a valuable two-volume guitar tutor.

---

[27] Janssens (1982: 45–7) and Quievreux (1956: 2).

Elsewhere

Switzerland had a reputation for producing fine mandolin orchestras, above all Lausanne. In 1937, when the city's population was about 80,000, it had four thriving *orchestres à plectre* of which the best, Le Plectre, was reputed to be as good as the leading Italian ensembles.[28] In Zurich in 1936, it was noted that five *orchestres à plectre* had recently given broadcasts on Radio-Suisse, while in Geneva, the Orchestre Mandolinata was publishing a quarterly journal.[29] Other journals included *Mandolinismo* (Luchsingen, 1921–32) and *Moderne Volksmusik* (Zurich, 1921–?).

The leading figures in Holland were Joh. B Kok and H. Smits (or Smith) Jun. Kok was originally a professional violinist but later specialized in the guitar and mandolin, playing both instruments for many years with the Amsterdam Concertgebouw Orchestra. In 1930, he founded the Radio Mandolin Orchestra, which made over 150 broadcasts from Hilversum, and he edited the monthly journal *Het ned. mandoline orkest* (Alphen, 1926–30). He was also a prolific composer of music for *Estudiantina* and full mandolin orchestra. Smits, from Rotterdam, had a high reputation as a virtuoso. He had founded a mandolin orchestra, Ons Streven, in his native city in 1911, and between 1919 and 1939 edited a monthly (later bi-monthly) journal, *De mandoline-gids* (Hilversum).[30]

In Denmark, the inexpensive and portable mandolin became an important part of working-class culture, popular with members of the Danish Social Democratic Youth (DSU, founded 1920) and the Danish Rambling Association (founded 1930). The DSU in particular pursued a vehemently anti-militaristic programme, and adopted the slogan 'Don't listen to brass bands—you must have string music.' Mandolins were occasionally even used to provide the music at its public gatherings, but were better suited to the home or the countryside.[31] The mandolin remained an integral part of ordinary music-making in other Scandinavian countries, and also in many parts of Eastern Europe. Finally, we should not close without noting the use of mandolins in two movements of Sergei Prokofiev's most celebrated ballet, *Romeo and Juliet* (1938).

---

[28] *L'Orchestre à plectre* (1 May 1937: 3).   [29] *L'Orchestre à plectre* (1 Feb. 1936: 3).
[30] Bone (1972: 190–1); Wölki (1979a: 19); Janssens (1982: 38); and information supplied by Tetsuro Kudo.
[31] Müller (1991: 49).

4.3 *Japan*

The years immediately after World War I saw an increased interest in Western culture amongst the Japanese. The mandolin grew enormously in popularity, with dozens of plucked-string orchestras being formed all over the country: at Hokkaido University, the Aurora mandolini orchestra (later renamed the Circolo mandolinistico Aurora) was founded in 1922; in Tohoku in the same year, the orchestra Mandolinata de Hirosaki was formed; while by 1924, in the Tokyo area alone, there were eighteen mandolin ensembles (and several other mandolin clubs within colleges and universities), including the Orchestra Sinfonica Takei.[32] Adolfo Sarcoli, who remained in Japan at least until 1925, was the most important teacher in the country; his pupils included Seiichi Suzuki, founder of the Tokyo Plectrum Society (1921).[33]

The instrument received a tremendous fillip in 1924–5, when Raffaele Calace made an extensive tour of Japan, giving mandolin and liuto recitals in Tokyo (28 December 1924), Kyoto (17 January 1925), and Nagoya (18 January). At a later concert in Tokyo, given with the Orchestra Sinfonica Takei (31 January 1925, in the Hochi Kodo auditorium: Illustration 23), the programme included the Sonatina and Adagio by Beethoven, six of Calace's own pieces ('Pavana', Op. 54, Rondo, Op. 127, 'Serenata malinconica', Op. 120, 'Serenata gaia', Op. 75, 'Elegia', Op. 131 (first performance), and 'Danza spagnola', Op. 105), and two works by Takei (*La caduta della pioggia*, Op. 11, and *Dalla tristezza alla gioia*, Op. 9).[34] On 10 February, he performed before Prince Regent (later Emperor) Hirohito, after which he was awarded the Third Order of the Sacred Treasure. He also made several recordings for the Nîtto company,[35] and gave lessons to Suzuki (who later continued to study with him in Naples) before returning to Italy, sailing from Kobe on 14 February.

Although mutual mistrust amongst politicians from West and East had led to the partial isolation of Japan by the end of the 1920s, the legacy of Western

[32] *JMU Review* (Oct. 1978: 1; Apr. 1979: 2; and Oct. 1979: 5).

[33] *JMU Review* (Oct. 1978: 6). Sarcoli remained in Japan until his death in 1936, and is buried in the Catholic Fuchu graveyard in Tokyo. Tetsuro Kudo has sent me a photograph of his headstone, which states (in It.) that he was born in Siena, 6 Mar. 1867, and died in Tokyo, 12 Mar. 1936.

[34] A letter to me from Ken Tanioka of the Japan Mandolin Union mentions that the visit took place partly because the fiancé of Eleonora Calace (Raffaele's 3rd daughter) was then serving in Japan as an interpreter at the Italian Embassy. Raffaele had seven children: Vincenzo, Maria, Vittoria, Eleonora, Giuseppe, Bianca, and Giovanni.

[35] Details in Ch. 6.4.

Illustration 23. Raffaele Calace, Morishige Takei, and members of the Orchestra sinfonica Takei, Tokyo, December 1924 (photograph courtesy of the Japan Mandolin Union).

musical influences remained strong within the country. Suzuki was one of the most active mandolinists, conducting the Tokyo Mandolin Kyokai for several years from 1925 and broadcasting as a mandolin soloist on NHK radio. He also composed about ten romantic pieces for mandolin orchestra during the 1920s, often influenced by the scenery around Hokkaido (such as 'Ode to the Wild field', 1929) and by Western literature (a poem by Verlaine was the inspiration for 'Sky', 1927). He continued to write for mandolin orchestra during the 1930s, pursuing this activity alongside his career as a professional musician, first with the Victor Record Company and then, from 1936 onwards, with the Toho Motion Picture Company; he provided the music for (amongst others) many of the films of Akira Kurosawa. He also composed numerous works for symphony orchestra.[36]

Like Suzuki, Tadashi Hattori began his musical studies in Tokyo on the mandolin (with the Keio Mandolin Club of Keio University) and later followed a professional career as one of Japan's leading classical composers and conductors, while retaining a lifelong interest in plucked instruments. His operas and orchestral music were frequently performed in Japan, but the

[36] Full biog. and list of works for mandolin in *JMU Review*, Oct. 1978: 6–13.

compositions that concern us are his works for plectrum orchestra, beginning with 'Prelude' and 'Lyrical Scenery' (1929) and continuing with more than a dozen suites and sets of variations over the next decade.[37] Further south, Jiro Nakano founded the Nagoya Mandolin Orchestra (1928) and also a mandolin quintet, Club Domenica, which broadcast throughout Japan via the Nagoya Central Broadcasting Station during the 1930s. From 1931 onwards, he composed over a hundred works for plucked instruments, many of them (influenced by the example of Calace's preludes) for unaccompanied mandolin.[38] Between 1936 and 1948, he edited an occasional magazine, *The World of the Mandolin and Guitar* (Nagoya). Kinuko Hiruma, the daughter of Kempachi Hiruma, came to prominence during the 1930s as a mandolin soloist with NHK radio, and as an influential teacher, while Tsunehiko Tanaka, who studied the instrument in Italy during 1920–4 and 1927–31, became one of Japan's leading virtuosi.

Morishige Takei composed a total of 114 works for mandolin, many of which he recorded with his own orchestra. Most of these pieces have Italian titles, but their customary style is none the less unmistakably Japanese, adapted to fit Western scales and instruments. In 1927 and 1928 he organized competitions for new compositions for mandolin orchestra ('Sky' by Suzuki won the contest in 1927), and conducted performances of the winning pieces. Takei was in contact with mandolinists in many European countries, and compiled probably the world's largest private library of mandolin music and journals; complete runs of many European mandolin magazines can nowadays be found only in this collection.[39] His own publications included two journals: *Mandolin and Guitar* (Tokyo, 1916–23): and *Researches into the Mandolin and Guitar* (Tokyo, 1924–41).

4.4 *The USA, Britain, and Elsewhere*

The USA

The increased pace of life and changing tastes in commercial music after World War I led to a gradual decline in the fortunes of the mandolin as a popular

---

[37] Biog. and full list of works for mandolin in *JMU Review*, May 1978: 7–11.

[38] *JMU Review* (Dec. 1977: 8–9).

[39] Biog. and list of Takei's surviving works in *JMU Review*, Apr. 1979: 8–12. Takei's coll. is now housed in the music library of the Kunitachi College of Music, Tokyo.

urban instrument. Jazz and dance bands were the fashionable ensembles of the day and, although the banjo and guitar had a role in them, the mandolin was quite unsuited to such music. In an attempt to compensate for this, instrument-manufacturers promoted the banjolin (also called the mandolin-banjo), a small banjo with mandolin tuning originally designed in about 1900. The banjolin allowed mandolinists to produce a sound sufficiently loud to be heard in a large band, but lacked the delicacy and sensitivity of the mandolin. Although it enjoyed a limited vogue, fretted-instrument players in jazz and dance bands overwhelmingly preferred the banjo or guitar. As for mandolin journals, the *Cadenza* ceased publication in 1924, while the *Crescendo* disappeared in 1933.

The change in popular musical tastes and fashions was not, however, the only reason for the decline in the numbers of amateur mandolinists. A year before World War I, Clarence L. Partee had already identified a number of other elements that were conspiring to undermine home music-making in the USA (although some of these observations are overly simplified, others hold equally true for Britain and, to a lesser extent, most of the more prosperous European countries):

> Times have changed, and we, perforce, must change with them. Long, long years ago we had leisure for these things; but not now, unless it be at the concert or musicale, or on the vaudeville stage. We have reached the point of physical exhaustion where it seems too much like work to exert ourselves in an effort to produce music of our own making, when we can just as well hire some professional to provide the music for us, and thus save ourselves the exertion.
>
> Nowadays, the rendition of music is principally confined to the concert room and the theatre—all entertainments of a formal nature. The old time, informal, go-as-you-please, enjoyable home musicale is a thing of the past, relegated to oblivion, like the dodo and other extinct species.
>
> As to the causes of the decline mentioned, several factors loom large in the foreground. Of these, I believe the chief ones to have been: first, the bicycle craze which swept the country some twenty or more years ago; second, the advent of the phonograph or talking machine; third, the appearance of the mechanical player-piano and kindred instruments of the penny-in-the-slot variety; fourth, the advent and perfection of the automobile; fifth, the wonderful growth of the motion picture industry or photo-play shows; sixth, the general tendency to increased interest in athletics and outdoor sports, such as tennis, golf, cricket, football, yachting, and what not. (*BMG*, June 1913: 132–3.)

Although Lyon & Healy continued to manufacture round-back instruments, flat-back models now took the lion's share of the dwindling mandolin market.

In 1919, the catalogue of C. F. Martin & Co. still listed a single round-back model amongst the flat-backs; by 1935, only flat-backs remained. But it was the Gibson company, with its carved top and back instruments, which developed in the early 1920s what is now universally acknowledged to be the finest flat-back mandolin ever built: the F-5 (Illustration 21). This new instrument was largely the work of Lloyd Loar, a classical mandolin soloist and acoustical engineer who worked for the Gibson company between 1919 and 1924 (although the contribution of Guy Hart, who actually built the instruments, is often overlooked). Differences between the F-5 (introduced in 1922) and earlier Gibson instruments include the replacement of the round or oval sound-hole with violin-style f-holes, an elevated fingerboard, an adjustable bridge, and a longer neck and scale length. The result was an instrument with an extremely rich and powerful tone that Gibson were never consistently able to reproduce after Loar left the company in December 1924.[40] Loar had overseen the production and signed those instruments that satisfied him, barely 150 in total. Although Gibson instruments are anathema to many classical mandolinists, this combination of superb tone and extreme rarity has given an F-5 signed by Loar a commercial value above that of even an Embergher or Calace mandolin.

The most successful virtuoso to use a Gibson F-5 at this time was Dave Apollon, a Ukrainian from Kiev who emigrated to New York after the 1917 revolution and became a top vaudeville entertainer. His typical repertoire included Monti's 'Czardas' and pieces by Sarasate and Suppé, performed with a microphone and electronic amplification. He made numerous recordings (including a great deal of gypsy music, and some pioneering jazz-mandolin discs in the late 1930s), performed with the great jazz guitarist Django Reinhardt, and was also featured in several motion pictures.[41] Sol Goichberg, who had received a conservatoire training as a cellist, was another prominent soloist, whose performances on mandolin of violin music by Bach and Mozart, and his own original compositions—particularly his suite for solo mandolin *From the Forest* (1936)—earned him enthusiastic reviews for his New York concerts throughout the 1930s.[42]

While the mandolin's popularity was declining amongst the urban middle classes, it remained widely played within the Italian community, which was

[40] Siminoff (1975: 8–9) and information from Tony Williamson.
[41] Grisman (1977: 4–7). The actress Mae West, amused by Apollon's heavy Russian accent and unusual grasp of English, encouraged him to become a master of ceremonies in vaudeville. He became very popular in this role, but this success gradually overshadowed his fine mandolin playing.
[42] Gladd (1988: 4).

less susceptible to changes in musical fashions. One Italian performer with a successful recording career was Giovanni Vicari (he also used the Spanish form of his name, Juan Vicari); dozens of his discs were issued (mostly on the Columbia and Harmonia labels), playing popular music from Naples and Sicily and also South American tangos and sambas. Carlo De Filippis, born in Ariano (near Naples), made frequent radio broadcasts as a mandolin soloist, and also directed several ensembles in New York, including the Manhattan Mandolin Orchestra and the New York Plectrum Ensemble. His published compositions include several works for unaccompanied mandolin. Luigi Paparello, an important teacher in New York, organized a prominent mandolin orchestra which made several recordings from 1919 onwards (mostly medleys of Neapolitan songs). Amongst his original compositions is 'Bells of Night', a piece for unaccompanied mandolin with a recurring chime motif, played in harmonics.

Bernardo De Pace was undoubtedly the leading concert artist in New York; for many years he was mandolin soloist at the Metropolitan Opera (as well as a star performer in vaudeville), and his compositions include a mandolin concerto, although his recordings during the 1920s were mostly a mixture of light classical pieces and his own traditional Italian-style compositions. He also starred in three motion-picture soundtracks with synchronized discs: *Bernardo De Pace, The Wizard of the Mandolin Plays Morning, Noon and Night in Vienna* (Warner Brothers, 1927); *Bernardo De Pace, The Wizard of the Mandolin Plays Caprice Viennois (and Others)* (MGM, 1929); and *Bernardo De Pace, The Wizard of the Mandolin Plays Thaïs (and Others)* (MGM, 1929).[43]

Lastly, we should note the development of a form of country music where the mandolin has been used with great success—bluegrass. The most influential figure in its development was Bill Monroe from Kentucky, who began playing the mandolin as a child (unaware that it was no longer fashionable in northern cities) and used it to perform pieces based on traditional southern music, but played at a rapid tempo with brilliantly fast solo passages and with a pronounced blues influence (although the name itself comes from Kentucky's nickname, 'the blue grass state'). The standard line-up for bluegrass was (and still is) five unamplified instruments—mandolin, guitar, fiddle, banjo, and bass—and the style first came to national prominence when Monroe formed the Bluegrass Boys, who made their début appearance on 'The Grand Ole Opry' (a country-music programme broadcast by WLS, the world's largest

---

[43] I am grateful to Neil Gladd for informing me about these recordings, copies of which survive in the Library of Congress, Washington, DC.

radio station) in October 1939. Bluegrass is one form of music where round-back mandolins are generally admitted to be quite unsuitable, their delicate tone lacking the solid punch of a good-quality carved back and top instrument.[44] Ironically, although Lloyd Loar designed the Gibson F-5 specifically as a classical instrument (applying the principles of the Stradivarius violin to mandolin construction), it is in the performance of bluegrass music that it has found its most successful niche.

Britain

As in the USA, usage of the mandolin underwent a slow decline in Britain after World War I. The journal *BMG* and the organization that formed around it were both enthusiastically supported, but it was the banjo and guitar that interested most amateurs, especially in BMG orchestras, where the mandolin struggled to compete in volume against the banjo. The louder banjolin briefly became popular, but even an endorsement from Enrico Caruso failed to convince most players of its virtues.[45] The Luton Mandolin and Guitar Band (led by Bone) remained the best amateur British orchestra, and almost the only one to compete on the Continent during the 1920s; in 1923, it participated in the international concourse at Boulogne-sur-Mer, before a jury that included Emilio Pujol and Alexandre Georges.[46]

But although amateur interest was waning, artistic standards were raised to a new height in Britain with the arrival of Mario De Pietro (Illustration 24) from Naples. De Pietro had already achieved a considerable reputation in Italy (where he seems to have been taught by Calace), and his first major London recital, in the Aeolian Hall on 15 April 1921, brought him superb reviews:

> Sig. Mario De Pietro has been described in Italy (on native programmes) as 'The Paganini of the Mandolin' and, judging from his almost incredible technique, powerful tone production, and command over the instrument, this title would seem to be justly applied. (*BMG*, Apr.–May 1921: 38.)

---

[44] Tottle (1975: 109–11) and Evans (1977: 313–19). Grisman (1977–8: 4–7, 22) features a detailed interview with Bill Monroe.

[45] *BMG*, July 1914: 147 carried an advertisement for 'The Clifford Essex BANJOLIN. Powerful, sweet, musical, tuned and played like a mandolin. Signor Caruso writes: "I like very much the sound of this instrument."' Accompanying the text is a photograph of a banjolin; the instrument has been signed with the above message by Caruso, who has also drawn a face on the skin.

[46] *BMG*, Oct. 1924: 3–4 contains an interview with Bone and a photograph of the entire band.

SIG. MARIO DE PIETRO.

Illustration 24. Mario de Pietro with his favourite instrument, made by a luthier trained in the Calace workshop in Naples (from *BMG*, Apr.–May 1921: 45). Photograph courtesy of the British Library.

Most of his solos were well-known violin pieces like the 'Ballade and Polonaise' of Vieuxtemps, Wieniawski's 'Mazurka' and the Hubay arrangement of the Brahms' Hungarian Dances. These, with the other pieces he gave in acknowledgement of the enthusiasm of the audience, were played with all the effect they would have made if they were the work of a great violinist. Yet Signor Pietro retains the individuality of the instrument all through, just as his technique of right and left hand never fails. Highly esteemed in his native Naples, this performer is likely to win like renown in this country and at the same time to bring credit on a typical but much-misunderstood instrument. (*Morning Post*, quoted in Anson 1954*b*.)

It is doubtful if such playing has ever been heard in this country, and the artiste received quite an ovation *from a non-playing section of the public*. It seems difficult to believe that practically none of the recognised professors of the mandolin were present; but that, unfortunately, was the case. Recitals such as this are just what the mandolin requires in order to revive lost interest, but virtuosi cannot be expected to waste their time in a country where their efforts meet with such scanty support. (*BMG*, June–July 1921: 49.)

De Pietro chose to remain in London, giving a further recital at the Wigmore Hall on 18 June 1921 at which he performed the Concerto, Op. 76, by Bériot, a Bolero by Calace, and Wieniawski's *Scherzo e tarantella*.[47] He soon established himself as the country's leading teacher, conducting a mandolin orchestra, the Studientina, and also leading a vaudeville troupe, the Vesuvians, which became a popular musical act during the 1920s. His astounding virtuosity can be appreciated on the many recordings he made of classical mandolin works by Calace and Monti, his transcriptions of music by Kreisler, Mascagni, and Gounod, and his own light but brilliantly effective pieces (such as his march 'Viva la libertà!'). Many of these discs stand unrivalled for their phrasing, their cantabile tone, and the sheer *élan* of his performance of Italian pieces (especially of Calace's *Mazurka da concerto*, Op. 126, which was composed for him), although he occasionally let his dazzling technique override his better artistic judgement. He was also an excellent tenor banjo player, and made innumerable recordings on this instrument for many different companies, under a bewildering variety of pseudonyms.[48]

De Pietro was a celebrated radio performer on both mandolin and tenor banjo, giving many recitals for the British Broadcasting Company (BBC). His best-known pupil, Hugo d'Alton (Illustration 25), was a member of the Studientina, and also appeared frequently on radio. D'Alton formed the La Verne Quartet with other members of his family in 1928 (at a time when De Pietro had left Britain to make a tour of South Africa) and broadcast regular hour-long programmes from the Birmingham studios of the BBC (1928–36), usually accompanying opera singers.

Two other groups of mandolinists became well known during this period, mostly through playing light music in variety theatres. Fred Winslow's Serenaders were formed in 1920, with eight or nine performers (mandolins, mandolas, mandocello, and piano) playing works such as the *Poet and Peasant* Overture by Suppé and Brahms's Hungarian Dance No. 5. They re-formed in 1930 as a thirteen-strong ensemble, and were regular broadcasters on the BBC until

---

[47] *BMG* (Aug.–Sept. 1921: 71).

[48] Barry Pratt has provided me with a provisional list of these: Ken Darrell (on recordings for Coliseum), Pedro Ferrari (Metropole), Nix Ford (Beltona), Lew Nicholls (Adelphi), Louis Revell (Piccadilly), and Max Rickard (Guardsman). He also used the name Manuel Marini. Under his own name, he recorded for Beltona, HMV, Decca, Edison Bell, Meloto, Parlophone, Homochord, and Piccadilly.

Illustration 25. Hugo d'Alton with a Roman mandolin.

they disbanded at the outbreak of World War II. Winslow was also one of the few British makers of mandolins, building a number of shallow-bodied instruments that featured his own system of cross-stringing.[49]

More famous was Pasquale Troise, an Italian from the small fishing village of Minori (near Sorrento in the Gulf of Naples). He studied the mandolin and guitar, and played the clarinet in the junior village orchestra, before emigrating in 1911 to England, where he was initially employed as a waiter. After joining a ragtime band as a tenor banjo player, and broadcasting with the original 2LO Dance Orchestra, he formed the Selecta Plectrum Orchestra in 1930 (with Michele Fasano as leader) and made several recordings for Decca. Soon afterwards, he grouped together most of the professional mandolinists in the country and formed what became the best-known mandolin ensemble that has

[49] *BMG* (Aug. 1959: 277).

ever existed in Britain. The sixteen performers comprising Troise and his Mandoliers (conducted by Troise) made their public début on 9 January 1932 in the Central Hall, Westminster, and appeared regularly thereafter at concert-halls, cinemas, and music-halls, playing light music (often with Hawaiian, Cuban, or gypsy influences) and popular classical works such as Brahms's Hungarian Dance No. 5. Troise was, reputedly, not always the most congenial of conductors under whom to perform:

> Pasquale Troise was a perfectionist and a martinet at rehearsals. He would insist that his players be note-perfect and should any player fail to interpret the music as he wanted it he would snatch the instrument out of his hands and show him how he wanted it played. His fiery Italian temperament would flare up at the slightest provocation and a stream of invective would make it clear he was displeased if things went wrong. Once the broadcast or stage show was over, he was his usual affable self again. (*BMG* May 1957: 190–1.)

During and after World War II, Troise and his Mandoliers became stalwart performers on BBC radio programmes such as 'Variety Band Box' and 'Music Hall'. The same musicians also doubled on a range of banjos (all tuned like members of the mandolin family) and appeared under the name Troise and his Banjoliers.[50]

Elsewhere

In South America, the mandolin continued to be played in the large Italian immigrant communities that had grown up in many countries, but in Brazil it had by now achieved a wider usage, especially in the *choro* (a sophisticated form of street music). The most significant player was Luperce Miranda, who was born in Recife, studied with his father, and came to Rio de Janeiro in 1928, having been invited there by some of Brazil's leading musicians. He composed about 500 pieces and made a total of some 900 discs (mostly recordings of waltzes and *choros*), played, unusually, on a round-back instrument. A younger player just beginning to come to prominence in this period was Jacob Bittencourt, better known as Jacob do Bandolim (Illustration 26) and nowadays widely considered to be the greatest and most original player Brazil has yet produced. Jacob was self-taught and specialized in the *choro*, playing the bandolim in a way that combined jazz, classical, and native Brazilian styles.

---

[50] An obituary for Troise appeared in *BMG*, May 1957: 190–1.

Illustration 26. Jacob do Bandolim (photograph courtesy of Paulo de Sá).

He was already playing professionally at the age of 12, but later trained as an accountant and insisted throughout his life that he was an amateur musician, despite writing more than 150 compositions, giving innumerable performances, and making dozens of recordings.[51]

Elsewhere, the mandolin remained popular in countries with large Italian immigrant communities, and also in those that had been colonized by Western powers. For example, Algeria (under French rule) had a number of mandolin orchestras, some of which occasionally took part in European competitions. Orchestras could be found in the British Empire as far away as Kuala Lumpur. A photograph reproduced in *BMG* in 1923 featured an ensemble consisting of fifteen mandolins (and banjolins), fifteen violins, a double bass, a banjo, two flutes, drums, two guitars, a cello, a clarinet, and a piano. The conductor, Mr M. F. Gomes, seems to have been a European; all the instrumentalists appear to be native Malays.[52]

---

[51] I am indebted to Paulo de Sá for much of the information about Brazil. The bandolim is discussed further in the App.

[52] *BMG* (July 1923: 130).

5

1945 to the Present Day

5.1 *Europe*

In the decades immediately following World War II, the mandolin's profile throughout most of Europe was low. The infrastructure of many countries was so severely damaged that organized amateur music-making became a low priority for many years. The development of electronic amplification introduced new fashions in popular music, to which the mandolin was ill-suited. The poor construction of many turn-of-the-century instruments had by now rendered them unplayable, and they lingered on as unloved family heirlooms, consigned to the attic or hung on a wall. Those amateur orchestras that survived mostly became increasingly outmoded, their members preferring to play the same light Italian music that had first attracted them to the mandolin several decades earlier, thereby giving the mandolin an old-fashioned aura that unintentionally deterred younger musicians.

As for professional performers, the low status of the mandolin offered them few recital opportunities, the lack of academic recognition kept the instrument out of the conservatoires, and the decline of music-hall and vaudeville deprived them of their principal source of income. However, as we shall see, a few virtuosi kept the art of the mandolin alive during those years, many of them directing their own amateur plucked-string orchestras without payment and earning their living on the fringes of the musical establishment—playing on film soundtracks, accompanying popular singers, giving occasional radio broadcasts, teaching, and taking part in performances of new music by avant-garde composers who found the instrument well suited to their pointillist style. These mandolinists encouraged a new generation of performers to study the mandolin, and also persuaded many composers to write solo works for the instrument. Thanks to them, the mandolin is now enjoying a revival in virtually every area of music-making, and this chapter can give only a brief summary of the enormously varied usage of the instrument around the world during the past fifty years (mostly amateur, but with increasing numbers of professional musicians now playing in the instrument). The mandolin today is not as widely played as it was during its heyday a century ago, but the quality of composition and orchestral performance is perhaps higher now than it has been at any previous time in the instrument's long history.

Italy

Although innumerable informal groups continued to perform popular songs and melodies in and around Naples, the Calace family represented almost the sole continuation of the classical tradition in the south for many years after World War II. Maria, regarded as the country's premier performer, founded a school for young mandolinists in Naples and gave weekly radio recitals from 1945 onwards, both as a soloist and as the leader of the Calace Plectrum Quartet (in which her brother Giuseppe played the mandola). Giuseppe also continued the family manufacturing business, making fine mandolins and violins (mostly for export) until his death in 1968. Since then, his son Raffaele has been the principal luthier, equipping many mandolin orchestras throughout the world; currently, about 60 per cent of his instruments are exported to Japan and thirty per cent to Germany, while the remaining ten per cent are supplied mostly to Italian orchestras.[1]

Another fine virtuoso, Giuseppe Anedda, was born in Cagliari (Sardinia). He studied violin at the conservatoires of Cagliari and Padua before deciding to concentrate on the mandolin, becoming one of a very small number of internationally known professional mandolinists from the late 1950s onwards. His choice of repertoire is notable for the substantial amount of original eighteenth-century mandolin music he has performed and recorded—including concertos by Cecere, Gervasio, and Gabellone, at a time when these pieces were still almost unknown—as well as many of J. S. Bach's suites for unaccompanied violin, in particular the famous Chaconne in D minor. Anedda was also appointed '*maestro di mandolino*' at the Padua conservatoire, founding the only course in Italy where the instrument can be officially studied to a professional level.

The course at Padua continues today, currently being taught by Ugo Orlandi, a former Anedda student. In recent years, Orlandi has been a leading figure in the rehabilitation of the eighteenth-century mandolin repertoire, having

---

[1] Tyrell (1952–3: 107–8) and information supplied to me by Arena Anna ved. Calace. Raffaele is the father of Annamaria (b. 1980).

recorded many concertos from this period. He was also a founder member (in 1974) of one of Italy's leading mandolin ensembles, the Orchestra di mandolini e chitarre città di Brescia; he is currently its artistic director. Claudio Mandonico is its conductor, and also a composer of many complex and imaginative works for mandolin orchestra, including the *Suite per orchestra* (1985) and *Concerto in un solo movimento per flauto ed orchestra* (1990). Brescia is an important centre for the mandolin, being the home of the Federazione mandolinistica italiana (FMI, founded 1970) and of the quarterly journal *Plectrum*, which began publication in 1989. The instrument is often used by mainstream Italian composers, Goffredo Petrassi making significant additions to its repertoire with his *Serenata-trio* for mandolin, guitar, and harp (1962) and 'Sestina d'autunno' for viola, cello, double bass, mandolin, guitar, and percussion (published by Zerboni).

For many years, the leading teacher and performer in Milan was Bonifacio Bianchi. One of his pupils, Alessandro Pitrelli, has become a prominent concert performer and recording artist, his programmes often specializing in the eighteenth-century repertoire. In Rome, the Embergher style of mandolin-making was continued by Cerrone's pupil Pasquale Pecoraro. Pecoraro died in 1987 without a direct successor, but his family has since passed his tools into the hands of a Japanese luthier, Yoshihiko Takusari, who is now manufacturing Roman mandolins in the Embergher tradition in Japan.[2] In recent years, the classical mandolin in Italy has become increasingly popular, and its study is now well organized; in 1989, there were some sixty-six orchestras and ensembles affiliated to the FMI, with many more existing independently of the organization.[3]

Germany, Austria, and Eastern Europe

The organized performance of plucked-string music in Germany declined sharply during World War II (*Volksmusik* ceased publication on 18 February 1943, after the announcement of 'total war') and, in the years immediately after 1945, the membership of the D.M.G.B. (which stood at 5,000 in 1949) was initially unsure whether music composed during the Third Reich was any longer acceptable for performance. They briefly returned to the Italianate repertoire that they had played in the 1920s, until hindsight made it clear that Nazi

---

[2] *JMU Review* (May 1991: 8).   [3] *Plectrum* (June 1989: 14–15).

ideology had never permeated into the area of plucked-string music. Since the 1950s, mandolinists in Germany and elsewhere have again been eager to perform the distinctive, neo-Baroque music of Wölki, Ambrosius, and their contemporaries.

In 1948, Konrad Wölki helped to set up the Musikschule Berlin–Reinickendorf, one of a number of folk-music colleges established for amateur musicians after the war. As well as becoming the city's leading mandolin teacher (many of the next generation of German mandolinists studied with him), Wölki continued to explore the eighteenth-century repertoire, and composed a number of fine works in traditional style, many of them for full *Zupforchester*. One of his last pieces, the warmly romantic Concertino in D Minor for oboe and *Zupforchester*, Op. 97 (1979), is widely considered to be his best composition. Wölki was also important in bringing together former members of the DAMB and D.M.G.B. into a new organization, the Bund Deutscher Zupfmusiker (BDZ), in 1963. Since 1985, it has published *Zupfmusik* (edited by Rüdiger Grambow) as a regular quarterly journal, although the magazine first appeared as early as 1961. By the time of his death in 1983, Wölki was rightly regarded as the founding father of modern German plucked-string music.[4]

After the war, Hermann Ambrosius became a music producer with the radio station Leipziger Rundfunk, but continued to compose in his simple but appealing neo-Baroque style, with restrained use of tremolo. He wrote a total of about 500 works, most for conventional orchestral instruments, but including about thirty for plucked string ensembles. One of his last compositions, the *Finlandia Suite* (1972)—Entrata: Andante rhythmico, Vivo, Andante, Allegro vivace—has proved to be amongst the most popular of his works for *Zupforchester*. Perhaps his most frequently performed piece is the *Suite galante* for mandolin and guitar, a beautiful five-movement miniature, full of harmonic quirks and subtle jests, that none the less never loses its aura of graceful serenity. Amongst the many other German composers who have contributed to the repertoire for *Zupforchester* are Dietrich Erdmann, whose works include a mandolin concerto (1979), and Max Baumann, whose four-movement Concertino, Op. 38 No. 3, for recorder and *Zupforchester* is frequently performed.

The guitarist Siegfried Behrend was a pioneering figure in the composition and performance of avant-garde music for plucked strings. As conductor of Das Deutsche Zupforchester (DZO, founded 1967 and including many of Germany's

---

[4] Wölki (1979*b*: 31).

leading players), he directed performances of a wide variety of modern music for mandolins and guitars, including many of his own pieces. *Conserere* (1987) for guitar and *Zupforchester*, written after the death of Andrés Segovia, is typical of the experimental nature of much of his composition: the guitar plays from an intricately notated part while the orchestral performers have only approximate graphic symbols, which they must translate into precise musical sounds. Takashi Ochi, a Japanese mandolinist and guitarist who moved to Germany in 1961 (where, since 1979, he has taught both instruments at the Hochschule für Musik in Mannheim), has led the DZO for many years, together with his wife Sylvia. He has also written many pieces for plucked strings, including *SE'I-DOH* (1973) for unaccompanied mandolin, his idiosyncratic music often synthesizing traditional European and Japanese styles with radical, extended instrumental techniques.

The most influential German teacher of the present day is Marga Wilden-Hüsgen (a former pupil of both Hladky and Wölki), who runs a course for mandolinists at Wuppertal College (part of the University of Cologne), leading to a professional diploma. She is also an active performer and editor, especially of the early repertoire (including music for the six-course mandolino), and is author of *Mandolinen-Schule*, the first clear exposition of the modern German technique. One of her leading pupils is Gertrud Weyhofen-Tröster, whose concerts and recordings cover the entire spectrum of mandolin music; her recitals are usually given together with her husband Michael Tröster, former principal guitarist with the DZO. Detlef Tewes, another former Wuppertal student, has become one of the world's leading contemporary performers. He is presently conductor of the Mandolinen Orchester Bayer-Leverkusen, having inherited this post in 1990 from the influential teacher Fred Witt, who emigrated to Australia. One of the most highly respected mandolin-makers of the present day is Reinhold Seiffert, located near Frankfurt am Main; Keith Harris, who teaches at the Conservatorium Mannheim–Heidelberg, is amongst the many concert performers who use his instruments.

Of the hundreds of *Zupforchester* currently performing in Germany, two of the best-known internationally are the Badisches Zupforchester (BZO, founded 1971), directed by Wolfgang Bast, and the Hessisches Zupforchester (HZO, founded 1969), directed by Keith Harris. Bast was one of the original members of the BZO, and has also composed many works for plucked instruments in an advanced but accessibly tonal style, including Capriccio (1975) for unaccompanied mandolin. He was the principal mandola player with the

DZO (which has been defunct since Behrend's death). Harris, an Australian by birth and a graduate of Sydney University, has lived in Germany for many years (he was the first graduate from Wuppertal), and has directed the HZO since 1986. He has made numerous international tours, regularly performs and teaches in the USA and in many European countries, and is perhaps the best-known classical mandolin soloist of the present day. His recitals are usually given partly on the mandolin and partly on the domra, an Eastern European plucked instrument with four single strings.

Hans Werner Henze is the most celebrated contemporary German composer regularly to include the mandolin and guitar in his music. There are probably three contributory influences for this: their use by Schoenberg, a composer whose music strongly influenced Henze's own early style; their proletarian connotations, corresponding to Henze's own pronounced left-wing political leanings; and their Italian associations, Henze having lived mostly in Italy since 1953. His earliest use of the mandolin was in the lyric drama *Boulevard Solitude* (1952), and it has appeared since in at least seven other of his stage works—including *König Hirsch* (1956) and *Elegy for Young Lovers* (1961)—and several orchestral pieces. He has also composed *Carillon, Récitatif, Masque* (1974), a trio for mandolin, guitar, and harp. Two other significant orchestral works that include the mandolin are the Cello Concerto (1966) by Bernd Alois Zimmermann and the Sixth Symphony (1953) by Karl Amadeus Hartmann.

In Austria, Vinzenz Hladky became a teacher at the Vienna Musikakademie in 1955 (and a professor in 1960), specializing in the performance of chamber music for mandolin. For many years he directed a plucked-string orchestra consisting of about fifty-five graduate students (playing mandolins, mandolas, mandocellos, guitars, harps, and celeste), and also conducted performances and recordings of several eighteenth-century concertos, including those by Johann Nepomuk Hummel and Giovanni Hoffman. He played the liuto in a quartet devoted to the performance of works by eighteenth-century composers such as Hoffman and Giovanni Francesco Giuliani, and continued to edit and publish music from this period. He also continued to encourage contemporary composers to produce new works for mandolin. Most of these remain in manuscript form but, of the published pieces, several works by Hans Gál have proved particularly popular. They include a Capriccio (1949) for mandolin orchestra; a *Sonatine*, Op. 59 No. 1 (1952), for two mandolins; a Suite, Op. 59 No. 2 (1952), for three mandolins; and *Improvisation, Variations, and Finale on a Theme of Mozart*, Op. 60 ('Deh vieni alla finestra'), for mandolin, violin, viola, and liuto. The Romanian-born Armin Kaufmann composed several works, amongst them a mandolin concerto, but he is best remembered now for two short, exciting pieces for mandolin and piano, 'Burletta' and 'Mitoka Drogomirna'. From 1952 onwards, Kaufmann wrote many compositions for what were hitherto regarded primarily as folk instruments, in particular mandolin and zither. Since Hladky's death in 1979, Lieselotte Jancak has been one of the most prominent figures on the Viennese mandolin scene, while Ferdinand Zwickl directs the New Viennese Mandolin and Guitar Orchestra, whose many concerts have included tours of Japan and Australia.

The mandolin has continued to be played in many Eastern European countries, often to a very high standard, but until recently little information was available in the West. However, several works by the Czechoslovakian composer Theodor Hlouschek are regularly performed by players throughout the world, in particular his Six Duos for two mandolins (1952), which are full of haunting slow melodies and dissonant rhythmic passages recalling the violin duets of Bartók. Hlouschek's other compositions include a quartet for flute, mandolin, guitar, and accordion and a suite for unaccompanied mandolin (1951). Radim Zenkl (born in Czechoslovakia, but now resident in the USA) is an exciting young performer who has developed a highly idiosyncratic way of playing the unaccompanied (flat-back) mandolin, adapting classical and bluegrass styles to his own unusual tunings and unconventional techniques. For many years, the leading Russian performer was Emanuil Sheynkman from St. Petersburg, who studied domra first at the Mussorgsky Institute and then at the Rimsky-Korsakov Conservatoire, where he became professor of domra in 1967. As a mandolinist, he took part in the Soviet premières of Schoenberg's Serenade and Stravinsky's *Agon* and made the first Soviet recordings of the Vivaldi concertos. Sheynkman emigrated in 1978 to the USA, where he continues his concert career.

France

Maria Scivittaro remained the leading soloist in France after World War II, giving numerous recitals in Paris, Mulhouse, and Strasbourg and, in 1953, presenting the first French performance in modern times of Vivaldi's Mandolin Concerto in C major.[5] Her many recordings for Pathé display fine musicianship

[5] *Le Plectre* (Apr. 1992: 2–3).

and a superb technique, which she retained into old age. In July 1948 François Menichetti, now a civilian, published the first edition of *Le Médiator* (Épinay-sur-Seine), an occasional journal that contained a mixture of news and music; thirty editions had appeared by the time of his death in 1969. He composed a further twenty-six pieces for mandolin and guitar or *orchestre à plectre* after World War II, as well as founding and directing his own *Estudiantina*—also called Le Médiator—with which he recorded for Barclay, Decca, and other gramophone companies.

André Saint-Clivier played in Menichetti's orchestra, and was also soloist with two other prominent orchestras, the Estudiantina de la SNCF and the Mandolin Club de Paris. When Scivittaro moved into semi-retirement in about 1960, Saint-Clivier became France's leading soloist, performing not only brilliant virtuoso showpieces (such as the Caprice No. 20 for unaccompanied violin by Paganini) but a great deal of new, experimental music as well. In particular, he was an early member of the Ensemble InterContemporain—founded at the Institut de Recherche de Coopération Acoustique Musical (IRCAM) in Paris in 1977—under the direction of Pierre Boulez, a musician whose advanced compositional style and pointillist technique is well suited to the bright, percussive sounds of plucked strings. Saint-Clivier thus became the first mandolinist to tackle the tremendous technical difficulties and musical complexity of Boulez's work—in *Éclat* and *Pli selon pli*—an experience that later persuaded him to write (with the collaboration of the acoustical laboratory of IRCAM) *Art contemporain du plectre,* the first thesis comprehensively to analyse the movement of the plectrum and the wide range of sonorities that the instrument is capable of producing. Saint-Clivier also founded and taught mandolin classes at the conservatoire in Longjumeau (1967) and at the Schola Cantorum in Paris (1983).

Another important figure was Mario Monti who, in 1950 formed the Estudiantina d'Argenteuil (also called the Estudiantina de l'Île-de-France). As well as directing and teaching this orchestra, Monti published modern editions of many of the eighteenth-century mandolin duets and sonatas which are housed in the Bibliothèque Nationale in Paris.[6] Maurice Totain was an important teacher and performer in Paris (he was mandolin soloist at the Opéra for many years), while Sylvain Dagosto (who moved to Paris from Algeria following the civil unrest of 1962) has been a leading player, teacher, and

---

[6] Pub. by L'Orchestre à plectre.

conductor there for many years. Since the 1970s, Christian Schneider (a former pupil of Scivittaro and member of Menichetti's orchestra) has become an active figure in Parisian mandolin life, joining the Ensemble InterContemporain, teaching at the Schola Cantorum, making numerous solo and ensemble recordings, and also running the city's principal mandolin store and publishing house, L'Orchestre à plectre. Jean Françaix is perhaps the most eminent French composer to have written for *orchestre à plectre*, composing a single short piece originally for the enthronement ceremony of Prince Rainier of Monaco (1949).

The most important recent development for the mandolin in France has been the appearance of the quarterly journal *Le Plectre* (Mirecourt), which began publication in 1992. As well as Schneider, the editorial staff include Didier Le Roux and Jean-Paul Bazin, both of whom played in the Estudiantina d'Argenteuil under Monti, specialize in the authentic performance of the early repertoire (in the Ensemble Gabriele Leone), and have made a detailed study of the history of the mandolin in France. Although intended primarily for French mandolinists, the excellent presentation, high standard of scholarship, and cosmopolitan editorial stance of *Le Plectre* make it amongst the most impressive and comprehensive of the hundreds of mandolin periodicals that have been published throughout the world during the past hundred years.

Britain

Hugo d'Alton, who began his solo career in 1946, became Britain's leading classical mandolinist after the death of Mario De Pietro in 1945. His many performances (given, since the early 1950s, on Embergher instruments) have included a major London concert at the Wigmore Hall on 8 October 1949, numerous radio recitals for the BBC (during one of these, he gave the first British broadcast performance of Hummel's Mandolin Concerto in 1953), and countless film soundtracks recorded during the 1950s and 1960s. These recitals have included many of the most difficult works in the mandolin repertoire (such as Ranieri's Concerto, and the 'Corale' and Preludes Nos. 2 and 10 by Calace), as well as several of the Bach suites for unaccompanied violin. Amongst the composers who have written works specially for him is William Bardwell, whose music often makes striking use of oriental influences and ostinatos; his compositions include the *Little Serenade* for piccolo, xylophone, and mandolin (1953) and the Concerto for mandolin and small orchestra (1956). D'Alton also took part in the first performance of the frenetic but exhilarating *Concert for 8* (1962) by Roberto Gerhard, a Catalan composer who spent much of his life at Cambridge University.

Apart from d'Alton, there were, until recently, very few professional British players. Troise and his Mandoliers continued to perform light music, but after Pasquale's death in 1957, only a handful of amateur BMG orchestras made much use of the classical mandolin. By 1978, when the firm of Clifford Essex closed (the magazine *B.M.G.* having already ceased publication in 1976), the instrument seemed to be in almost terminal decline. However, during the 1980s a small group of young mandolinists was taught by d'Alton, many of them students at Trinity College of Music, London, or in university music departments. At present, two of these former pupils—Nigel Woodhouse and Alison Stephens—are amongst the leading British concert mandolinists. At about the same time, the American early-music specialist James Tyler (then resident in London) drew attention to the large amount of seventeenth- and eighteenth-century music for the six-course mandolino, and encouraged lutenists to take up the study of this instrument, something that they have done in considerable numbers. The British composer Eileen Packenham (encouraged by Philip J. Bone's daughter, Irene) has produced a large number of light but interesting pieces: three volumes of duos for mandolin and piano, several works for mandolin orchestra, and a demanding mandolin duet, 'Lark's Song' (1975), often performed by the Danish Mandolin Duo.

Although the mandolin and mandola are only rarely used in modern-day pop or rock music, flat-back instruments have both been incorporated successfully into British and Irish folk-music since the 1960s. The instruments are occasionally fitted with electronic pick-ups, but more commonly they are amplified via a microphone. It should be noted that round-back mandolins are amongst the most difficult of all instruments to amplify electronically, because of the great number of high harmonic partials they produce; flat-back mandolins, which produce fewer high harmonics, are far more tractable in this respect.

Elsewhere in Europe

With the death of Ranieri in 1956, Franz De Groodt became the leading Belgian mandolinist, working as an orchestral soloist in Brussels and Antwerp, teaching at the music academy in Deurne, and leading the Antwerps Plectrum Kwartet. One of his pupils, Robert Janssens, founded the Braasschaats Mandoline-Orkest in

1955, and also published *Geschiedenis van de mandoline* (1982), a fascinating book containing biographical information on hundreds of players, composers, and makers. In Antwerp, Henri Gamblin has directed the ensemble La Napolitaine since the death of Romain Van den Bosch in 1949. Currently, the orchestra's leading soloist is Ralf Leenen. In Malmédy, where a mandolin orchestra was founded in 1922, a festival was held biennially between 1982 and 1990, attracting soloists and orchestras from around the world. The repertoire played in Belgium includes many works by German composers, and a similar influence can be observed in Holland where, amongst approximately 100 flourishing ensembles, the best-known is the sixty-strong Estrellita (Breda).

The instrument remains popular in Switzerland, with the Zupforchester Luzern (founded in 1900) being amongst the oldest surviving mandolin orchestras anywhere in the world. In Geneva, Danièle Meyer is the leading soloist, while in Zurich, Armin Keller has established a private museum, collecting all types of mandolin from the late seventeenth century onwards. In Sweden, Ebbe Grimsland has been a prominent orchestral soloist since 1940, and has also composed for the mandolin in a tonal, but often rhythmically complex style; his works include a Concertino for mandolin and ten instruments, a *Canzona* for three mandolins (1981), and *Tonal dialog för 3 mandoliner + litet slagverk* (1972). In Linköping (Sweden), Lars Forslund established Musica Festiva as a Baroque mandolin ensemble in 1979; their concerts have included an extended tour of Japan in 1988. Västeras has one of the largest and most influential orchestras in Sweden. In Denmark, the leading players for many years have been Kurt Jensen (who studied with Bracony, and subsequently became a soloist with many Danish orchestras) and his former pupil Tove Flensborg. They formed the Danish Mandolin Duo in 1983, and their regular duet concerts have included annual appearances at the Tivoli concert-hall in Copenhagen. Jensen is now resident in Australia. In Norway, the Oslo Mandolin Orchestra celebrated its thirtieth anniversary in 1990; there are at least five other flourishing ensembles in the country, including orchestras in Bergen, Vardo, and Stavanger. Although the mandolin is not widely played in Spain (the bandurria being more popular in that country), mandolin orchestras from throughout the world attend the plucked-instrument festivals which are held periodically in Logroño. In Greece, there are currently about ten orchestras, including the Plucked Strings Orchestra of the Municipality of Patras (founded 1985), which has commissioned over twenty new works from Greek composers.

I have been able to list only a few of the most significant names connected with the mandolin in Europe, and I apologize to all those fine players, orchestras, and composers whom considerations of space have precluded me from mentioning. However, we should not end this section without noting the use of the mandolin by perhaps the greatest composer of the twentieth century, Igor Stravinsky, who first adopted it in his ballet *Agon* (1957). It plays in several movements in this work, including a prominent role in the beautiful 'Gailliarde', where it is used to suggest the presence of medieval minstrels. In 1962, when he revised his first edition (1921) of his opera *Le Rossignol*, he also added a tremolo mandolin to the entrance of the Chinese Emperor in Act II; the instrument reappears later in Act III (again playing tremolo), making brief comments during the nightingale's song to death.

5.2 *Japan*

Although Japan was more severely damaged by World War II than almost any other country, its economic and social revival was under way by the early 1950s, and accelerated throughout that decade. Several hundred mandolin groups and orchestras were formed during these years, mostly performing light pieces by European composers. However, as standards of performance improved, many Japanese composers regained an interest in writing for plucked strings, producing works that have more recently also found favour with Western orchestras. A number of Japanese mandolin orchestras include wind and percussion (and occasionally brass) sections, giving them a wide range of expression and allowing them to perform transcriptions of symphonic music.

Between the end of World War II and 1966, Seiichi Suzuki wrote almost exclusively for films and the theatre (including making many arrangements of American jazz for the broadcasting company NHK), although he did compose a few works for mandolin orchestra, notably a fantasy, 'Vision of Bali Island' (1947, based on a gamelan theme), and a caprice, 'Native Song of Jitsugetsutan' (1947, using Taiwanese folksong), both of which were given first performances by the Tokyo Mandolin Society. But, from 1966 onwards, he devoted himself primarily to the mandolin, composing about thirty works for plucked-string orchestra, as well as teaching and directing dozens of ensembles. His works from this final period include a *Cantata Requiem* (1966), three Spanish suites (1966–8), and several symphonic poems and fantasies, of which the finest is perhaps *Silk Road* (1967), an eight-part work depicting the perilous journey of ancient merchants from China to Rome.[7]

In 1946, Tadashi Hattori became a conductor of, and arranger for, the Nippon (now NHK) Symphony Orchestra (and professor of composition at Kunitachi College of Music, Tokyo), but he continued to write for plectrum instruments as well. In 1956, when the Keio Mandolin Club was reorganized as a giant plectrum orchestra with over a hundred members, he began to compose a series of musical fantasies, such as 'Cinderella' (1956) and 'Kerib the Guitar Player' (1960); under his direction, the Keio Mandolin Club made several tours of the USA (1964, 1973, and 1976) and a particularly successful visit to Australia (1975).[8] Jiro Nakano's Nagoya Mandolin Orchestra continued to broadcast regularly on NHK; his original compositions include 'La iglesia sobre la colina' and 'Una notte di villaggio pescatori'.[9] Amongst his pupils are Kizoh Sakakibara, winner of Japan's Third Mandolin Solo Performers' Contest (1972) and a noted concert artist, and Hirokazu Nanya, founder of the Ghifu College Mandolin Club (1962) and the Arte Mandolinistica music school (1986). Kinuko Hiruma remained an important performer and teacher, giving recitals throughout Japan and training many of the nation's leading young players, including the internationally known performer Yasuo Kuwabara and perhaps the most famous soloist in Japan, Ikuko Takeuchi, a frequent broadcaster on Japanese television and radio and leader of her own group, the Takeuchi Mandolin Ensemble (founded 1961, and renamed the Tokyo Mandolin Ensemble in 1972). In 1961, Siegfried Behrend invited Hiruma to teach the mandolin at a course in Saarbrücken, together with one of her students, Takashi Ochi. While there, Hiruma and Ochi recorded Vivaldi's Concerto for two mandolins (with the Saarbrücken Mandolin Orchestra, conducted by Behrend) and became popular performers. Hiruma subsequently returned to Japan, but Ochi has remained in Germany ever since.[10]

In 1968, the Japan Mandolin Union (JMU) was founded, with Tsunehiko Tanaka as its first president, and it began to organize competitions for performers and composers. The winner of the Second Mandolin Solo Performers' Contest (1970) was Masayuki Kawaguchi, a versatile musician, and founder of the KaVa san Trio (1987; mandolin, guitar, and cello); professional soloists who were once his pupils include Takayuki Ishimura (who also studied with Orlandi in Padua) and Goshi Yoshida (who later studied in Wuppertal, and

[7] *JMU Review* (Oct. 1978: 6-13). I would like to thank Tetsuro Kudo for his helpful additions to this section.
[8] *JMU Review* (May 1978: 7–11). [9] *JMU Review* (Dec. 1977: 8–9). [10] *JMU Review* (Oct. 1978: 3–5).

Illustration 27. Some notable mandolinists and composers from Japan: *a* Kempachi Hiruma; *b* Jiro Nakano; *c* Tadashi Hattori; *d* Seiichi Suzuki; *e* Kinuko Hiruma; *f* Hisao Itoh (left) and Yoshihiko Takusari.

often performs on an eighteenth-century mandoline). Since 1977, the JMU has published an annual or biannual magazine in English (as well as a bimonthly newsletter in Japanese), something that has helped to forge closer links with players in the West. Since 1972 the president of the JMU has been Hisao Itoh, conductor of the Ghifu Mandolin Orchestra (which he founded in 1954) and a musician who has helped to forge close links between German and Japanese mandolinists.

Outside Germany, the mandolin is probably played to a higher standard in Japan than anywhere else in the world (helped by the periods of study which many Japanese have spent at Wuppertal), and it has a large and enthusiastic following throughout the islands. For example, in 1980, in the Tokyo area alone, there were 45 amateur groups with about 1,200 members in all (these groups date back as far as 1915, but most were formed during the 1950s and 1960s), 33 company groups with 579 members (mostly formed by employees during the 1960s, and acknowledged by the companies as an off-duty activity), 72 ensembles with 3,432 members in colleges and universities (most were formed during the 1960s, but the Waseda University group has been in existence since 1914), and 38 ensembles in high schools. In the same year, there were eighteen mandolin teachers in the Tokyo area registered with the JMU.[11] There are also many fine mandolin-makers in Japan, including Yoshihiko Takusari, who continues to make Roman mandolins in the Embergher style. Sanae Onji of Takarazaku City is one of the many fine soloists who have used his instruments which, like almost all mandolins from Japan, are made with traditional round backs.

5.3 *The USA and Elsewhere*

Until the 1980s, the classical mandolin had few exponents in the American concert-hall. Sol Goichberg retired from playing for many years, although he made a brief comeback in the early 1960s, forming the MandoArt Quartet and giving performances of the Vivaldi concertos with several orchestras in New York. Samuel Firstman, a leading mandolinist and conductor in the city, made many orchestral arrangements which remain popular today. Howard Frye, a former student of Paparello, became a notable soloist in New York from the late 1950s onwards. His repertoire was a mixture of original Italian works (by Calace, Munier, and their contemporaries), arrangements of folk-songs and gypsy music, and pieces from the classical violin repertoire. His surviving recordings confirm that he was a remarkably charismatic performer, although his tone-production could, at times, be surprisingly harsh. Two years before his untimely death in 1967, Frye announced a competition for new mandolin music, resulting in the composition of the first known American mandolin sonata—the *Sonata: Variations* for mandolin and piano (1965) by Carman Moore.[12] On the West Coast, Rudy Cipolla has been an important influence throughout this period, while Dave Apollon also remained a popular figure,

[11] *JMU Review* (Oct. 1980: 2–12).   [12] Gladd (1988).

but for financial reasons he tended to perform and record primarily popular, sentimental music, becoming a much-sought-after entertainer in the plusher venues of New York and Las Vegas.

A number of amateur classical orchestras were meeting and performing during these decades, including the Long Island Mandolin and Guitar Orchestra and the Los Angeles Mandolin Orchestra (both founded in the mid-1950s), but these existed primarily for the benefit and enjoyment of their own members, and had a low public profile. Within the Italian communities of major cities, mandolinists continued to play from the same sheet music that their grandparents had bought half a century earlier. In Philadelphia, for example, the Munier Mandolin and Guitar Orchestra (founded 1957, but previously existing as a quartet) consisted mainly of professional people from the local Italian-American community; it performed a repertoire of music by Italian and French composers, mostly dating from the years around 1900 and preserved in a private collection originally established by the father of one of its members.[13]

The mandolin fared much better outside the classical world, especially as an integral part of bluegrass music. Bill Monroe has continued to be one of its finest exponents, but Jesse McReynolds evolved a very different method of playing in the early 1950s, imitating the cross-picking technique of finger-style banjo players and developing a syncopated arpeggio across three strings that came to be known as the 'McReynolds' Roll'. At speed, this is an extraordinarily effective and exhilarating technique, and completely unaccompanied pieces can be played in this style, with melody and accompaniment emerging clearly from a seemingly endless cascade of notes. Elements of bluegrass can be found in the playing of David Grisman, but traces of jazz, blues, folk, and classical music have also been synthesized into the distinctive style he calls 'Dawg' music. Grisman has collaborated with musicians as diverse as the jazz violinist Stephane Grappelli, the Grateful Dead rock band, and the Kronos String Quartet; he was also editor and publisher of *Mandolin World News* (San Rafael, California, 1976–82, and a further four issues, Wisconsin, 1984), a quarterly journal that featured interviews with contemporary mandolinists of all styles, biographies of celebrated classical figures, and a wealth of technical and practical information for players. A regular columnist in this journal was Jethro Burns, a noted Nashville session musician whose laconic humour

---

[13] Hambly (1977*b*: 21–2). Another important ensemble is the Takoma Mandoleers, led for many years by Herman Von Bernewitz.

brought him national success as one half of Homer and Jethro, a celebrated pair of comics and musical parodists.

Interest in the classical mandolin started to reawaken in the early 1980s. Neil Gladd, now based in Washington, DC, has been a significant figure in this revival, in particular through his championing of the unaccompanied mandolin. Many of his recitals (usually given on a Seiffert round-back instrument) consist entirely of unaccompanied pieces, a typical programme including a Bach violin partita, a set of variations by Leoné, a bravura piece by Stauffer, and one of his own compositions, such as the *Partita a dodici toni* (1984) or the *Sonata 1 for Solo Mandolin* (1980–3). He has also made an extensive study of the history of mandolin recordings and of published mandolin music. In Providence, Rhode Island, the tradition begun by Pettine and Place has continued uninterrupted through to the present day, via Place's pupil Hibbard Perry, who founded the Providence Mandolin Orchestra and in turn became the mentor of the Mair–Davis Duo—Marilynn Mair and Mark Davis (mandolin and guitar respectively)—who have performed throughout the world and for whom many duets have been composed from the early 1980s onwards.

The catalyst for this revival has been Norman Levine who, after hearing the Malmédy Mandolin Orchestra in Belgium in 1981 and organizing the Malmédy Festival 1982, established the firm of Plucked String in Arlington, Virginia, to publish classical music for mandolin. He also organized the Festival of Mandolins in the USA in 1984 to encourage new works for the instrument, a competition that produced two important additions to the mandolin's repertoire: *Three Movements* for mandolin and guitar—Fantasia, Song, Dance—by Will Ayton, a work whose accessible American style is tinged with pentatonic, oriental overtones, reflecting the composer's early years in China and Taiwan; and the *Sonatinetta* for mandolin and guitar—Toccata (Ex. 11), Elegia, Menuetto—by Brian Israel, which makes great use of mixed metres and ends with a deliberately grotesque parody of a graceful minuet. Israel, a professor of composition at Syracuse University, became particularly interested in the mandolin, composing a concerto (for Gladd) and the bizarre *Surrealistic Serenade* for mandolin and euphonium before his premature death from leukaemia in 1986. Levine was also instrumental in establishing the Classical Mandolin Society of America (CMSA), which in 1987 began publishing a quarterly newsletter; this journal has since carried many fascinating historical articles on the development of the mandolin in the USA.

Many other players and composers are now actively involved with the

Ex. 11. Israel: *Sonatinetta*, Toccata, bars 1–17 (Courtesy of Norman Levine publications)

classical mandolin, but space allows me to mention only a few of them here. In Maryland, David Evans has become a leading figure, both as soloist and as the conductor of the Baltimore Mandolin Orchestra. Emanuil Sheynkman has continued a successful career as a mandolinist, although it is his balalaika playing that has made him especially popular with Soviet *émigrés*. The Modern Mandolin Quartet (based in Berkeley, California), has made several fine recordings, mostly performing orchestral transcriptions, such as the overture to Mozart's *Magic Flute*. The members of the quartet all play flat-back instruments, many of them made by John Monteleone, whose modern replicas of a Gibson F-5 have won him a high reputation. Radim Zenkl emigrated to the USA from Czechoslovakia in 1989, and quickly established himself as a highly original performer with an entirely unconventional approach to the mandolin. Lastly, the remarkable Evan Marshall has developed the duo-style of playing to a very sophisticated degree, enabling him to perform such works as Brahms's Hungarian Dances Nos. 5 and 6 entirely without accompaniment.

Of the many contemporary orchestral composers who have incorporated the mandolin into their works, two are especially noteworthy: David Del Tredici has frequently used it, as part of a folk ensemble, in the beautiful series of orchestral works (based on the Alice stories of Lewis Carroll) which he wrote during the 1970s; and George Crumb included the mandolin in *Ancient Voices of Children* (1970), requiring the performer to produce many unusual and unconventional sounds from the instrument. Ernst Krenek's last composition, the three-movement Suite for mandolin and guitar, Op. 242 (1989— Overture, Intermezzo I, Scherzo, Canon, Soliloqui, Intermezzo II, Mini-Opera) was commissioned by the Mair–Davis Duo, who gave its first performance in 1993.

Elsewhere

Gustavo Batista from Puerto Rico has acquired an outstanding international reputation as a concert performer, in addition to directing his own quartet and mandolin orchestra. A popular item in his repertoire is *El Turia*, a medley of waltzes for mandolin and piano composed by Denis Granada, leader of the Spanish Students during their famous American tour in 1880. Batista's concerts are usually a mixture of unaccompanied works and pieces with piano or guitar. They generally include at least one composition by his teacher, the late Jorge Rubiano.

In Brazil, Jacob do Bandolim remained the most celebrated player, beginning his recording career in 1947 and continuing to perform right up until his death in 1969. Throughout his life he composed and performed *choro* music, his brilliant technique and powerful tone reawakening general interest in the bandolim in Brazil. The composer Radamés Gnattali (formerly conductor of the Radio Nacional Orchestra, Rio de Janeiro) has written a concerto for him and another for Joel Nascimento, perhaps the leading player of the present day.

In Israel, the Romanian-born mandolinist Abraham Leibovitz is the leading player and teacher in Tel Aviv. He has published a four-volume mandolin method and recorded several concertos, including Bach's Double Violin Concerto in D Minor. There are also a few mandolin ensembles in other countries in the Middle East, notably an all-girl orchestra in the Yemen which visited Britain in 1989.

Finally, Australia (where the German influence is particularly strong) has produced a number of important players in recent years. We have already noted Keith Harris, who began playing in a BMG orchestra in Sydney during the 1960s (his teacher there was Phil Skinner, MBE) before studying music at Sydney University and embarking on a career as a concert soloist based in Germany. Adrian Hooper and his Sydney Mandolins have commissioned and recorded many contemporary works for the instrument, while Robert Schulz has written many works for his own Western Australian Mandolin Orchestra. Several fine players have also been produced by the Melbourne Mandolin Orchestra, in particular Stephen Morey, who formed the trio i mandolini in 1982 to play early mandolin music on authentic instruments, and was also a member for many years of one of the continent's foremost new-music groups, Elision.[14] He has made a specialist study of seventeenth- and eighteenth-century mandolins surviving in museums, and organized the Melbourne International Mandolin Festival in 1993.

[14] A hand injury unhappily forced Stephen Morey to terminate his playing career in 1993.

6

Practical Information for Players and Composers

The following chapter aims to provide the reader with useful information about the Neapolitan mandolin, an introduction to some aspects of technique (with observations from some eminent performers), and details on how to contact various organizations, publishers, and suppliers throughout the world. It is *not* intended to serve as a tutor for the instrument. There are many excellent and detailed methods currently available in print, although, as with the serious study of any instrument, there is no substitute for an experienced teacher.

6.1 *Instruments, Strings, and Plectrums*

Although there are many fine players of flat-back (and, more especially, carved top and back) mandolins, round-back instruments have always been the preferred choice of the vast majority of classical players throughout the world. As we have seen, the deep, punchy tone of a Gibson mandolin is ideally suited to bluegrass and Irish and South American folk-music, but it lacks the high harmonics and ringing, soprano timbre that are an essential feature of the authentic Italian round-back instrument. The warm and expressive tone produced by such ensembles as the Mair–Davis Duo and the Modern Mandolin Quartet (all of whom play on instruments with flat backs) should serve as a warning against excessive dogmatism on this point, but it remains generally true that the music of Calace, Munier, and their contemporaries is more effective when performed on the type of mandolin for which it was originally composed.

Given the enormous numbers of Neapolitan (and Roman) mandolins that were made and sold during the instrument's heyday, it is comparatively easy to find one in an antique shop almost anywhere in northern Europe, often at a modest price. Owning a century-old Italian mandolin undeniably has a certain aesthetic attraction but, unless the buyer is fortunate enough to find a top-quality instrument—an Embergher, Calace, Vinaccia, De Meglio, or one of a surprisingly small number of other superior names—he or she will almost certainly be purchasing a musical disaster. Most surviving instruments from this period are the cheap and shoddy souvenirs of Naples about which Calace once complained so bitterly, and time has not improved them. Their machine heads are usually faulty, their fretting is often inaccurate, the wood and workmanship involved in their construction are likely to be of poor quality, and their necks and tables will almost invariably have been distorted by years of excessive string tension. Unless a competent repairer can be found, such instruments will prove impossible to play in tune, and in any case will probably produce a disappointingly weak sound.

With these potential pitfalls in mind, it is prudent for beginners to seek expert advice before buying a mandolin, and to expect to pay a substantial amount for the instrument, be it new or old. Although Embergher and Calace mandolins have not (yet) attained the astronomical figures demanded nowadays for Stradivarius violins, a great deal of skilled craftsmanship and expensive wood is involved in the manufacture of any good-quality stringed instrument, and this is reflected in the price.[1]

Finding suitable strings is not an easy matter, as many of the most common brands lack homogeneity of tone across the four courses. Worse, the combination of thick cores and windings frequently used to make the lower strings (and the way that these strings are manufactured) tends to make the g string (in particular) sound sharp in higher positions, unless the bridge is adjusted to compensate for this. Many leading players use Maxima strings (manufactured in Germany), which give a bright and consistent tone across the instrument's entire range. D'Addario strings (made in the USA) are favoured by many players, especially those who play mandolins with carved top and back. The strings manufactured by Dr Thomastik-Infeld (in Austria) give a somewhat duller tone than Maxima, which makes them less well suited to the virtuoso music of Calace and Munier; however, their timbre is more appropriate when performing eighteenth-century repertoire on a modern instrument, and also suits much twentieth-century German music. It is important

---

[1] In the absence of a local expert, any of the suppliers whose addresses are given later in this chapter will be able to supply information about old and new instruments.

always to fit strings of the correct tension, appropriate to the weight and design of the mandolin. Although too low a string tension will make an instrument sound dull and lifeless, great care must be taken not to place too much tension on it in a quest for extra volume or brilliance, as it can quickly become permanently damaged in the process. In general, carved top and back instruments require higher-tension strings than do round-backs.

Steel strings were first fitted to the mandolin more than a hundred and fifty years ago, but, at the time of writing, it is still almost impossible to purchase an entirely satisfactory *a'* string. The great majority of manufacturers supply bare steel second strings, which are necessarily thin (to counteract the stiffness of the material) but are therefore under-tensioned and prone to go out of tune when struck firmly. Attempts earlier this century to make wound *a'* strings met with failure, because the very thin and brittle windings that were then used disintegrated after just a few hours' playing, as Adelstein noted ruefully:

> The covered *a'* string is not the success it was hoped for. The covering is necessarily so thin that it wears off in a very short time, especially with continuous playing ... It is one of the strange phenomena of the [bare steel] *a'* string of most mandolins that while in continued forte passages on the *e''*, *d'* and *g* strings the instrument will stay in comparatively good tune, it is most provoking to find that the *a'* string will not stand in tune—one, or often both, will become sharp right in the middle of a passage. (Adelstein 1905: 25–6.)

Although the bare steel used today is of a superior quality to that which caused Adelstein such vexation, the *a'* remains the mandolin's problem string. Far more resilient materials for making wound strings exist nowadays, but few string manufacturers have yet experimented with them. Thomastik-Infeld is one of the very few commercially available brands of string made with wound second strings, but, as we noted earlier, many players find their tone rather dull. For many years, the English mandolinist Hugo d'Alton produced his own hand-made strings with bright, resonant, and extremely durable wound second courses, but these are, sadly, not commercially available at the present time.[2]

Neapolitan and Roman mandolins have movable bridges, and care should be taken when tightening the strings, since there is a tendency for the bridge to move very slightly as the tension increases. To ensure that the bridge is in

---

[2] Since 1992, when Hugo d'Alton retired, Barry Pratt has been making these strings. However, being entirely hand-made, they are currently manufactured in strictly limited quantities.

precisely the correct position, check that the twelfth-fret harmonic on each string produces exactly the same pitch as the stopped note. We have already noted that, on most brands of string, the lowest course tends to sound sharp; because of this, many makers compensate by designing the bridge with an angled saddle, so that the effective playing length of the fourth course is very slightly longer than that of the first.[3] Lastly, it is essential that the bridge sits absolutely flat on the table when the instrument is brought up to pitch, in order to prevent a groove being worn in the table, and to ensure maximum transmission of string-vibration to the table.

Plectrums are largely a matter of personal choice. Traditionally, most performers have chosen tortoiseshell for its combination of strength and flexibility. Unfortunately, this material is obtainable only from the carapace of the hawksbill turtle, which is now an endangered species; all international trade is currently banned, although music shops are still allowed to sell any existing stocks that they may possess. Many players briefly hold a lighted match beneath the upper (non-playing) edge of a new tortoiseshell plectrum, causing a slight bubbling of the surface which makes it easier to grip; this is also a simple (but irreversible) way to detect a counterfeit material, since a celluloid plectrum will instantly flare up. It is important to polish the playing edge of a tortoiseshell plectrum on a hard surface before use, so as to avoid producing a scratching sound against the strings.

Nowadays, plectrums are also manufactured from a variety of plastic materials, and many players use these in preference to tortoiseshell. They are made in hundreds of different shapes and sizes, all of which subtly affect both tone and technique. Most players choose a plectrum about an inch in length, but Ranieri used one several times longer throughout his life, and achieved the highest artistic and technical results with it. The plectrum has to be pointed enough to allow for its intricate movement between the strings, but if it is too narrow then the tone can become rather thin and weak. It also has to be sufficiently rigid to produce a crisp attack on each note, but pliant enough to allow for a smooth tremolo. Many of these points were summarized by Mario De Pietro in a short article (originally written before World War II) concerned with the basic prerequisites of good tone-production:

---

[3] The design and method of manufacture of the d'Alton string eradicates this problem, although, to obtain perfect intonation, these strings should only be used on mandolins with uncompensated bridges. The exact method of manufacture is a trade secret, but Barry Pratt intends to publish an article which will discuss in detail the design of these strings.

The first essential is to use strings that are not too thin. I use strings that are fairly stout and that can be played forcibly without sacrificing quality of tone. Moreover, I change them very frequently because a stretched string soon begins to lose its elasticity and consequently its tone; this applies more particularly to the third and fourth covered strings. The second essential is to vibrate the strings with a suitable plectrum which should be of tortoiseshell and not too large—not more than an inch in length. The plectrum I use is of medium pliability, just sufficiently stout to allow of the strings being struck forcibly without any 'flapping' effect from the plectrum. I have always found that a flexible plectrum with a nicely polished and bevelled playing edge produces far more volume than does a hard plectrum, and it gives the player a finer degree of sensitivity during the playing of a solo. Another important point is that the mandolinist's right wrist must be arched, because this gives a much greater control over the strings. The player must also see that he always strikes both strings of a pair. I have been surprised to find how many mandolinists often strike only a single string instead of double strings. (De Pietro 1975: 9.)

6.2 *Positions and Techniques*

Although some performers (especially bluegrass and folk musicians) like to play standing upright—holding the mandolin against the chest and (usually) supporting it with a leather strap around the neck—most classical mandolinists favour the sitting position for the greater stability it affords. Conventionally, the right leg is either crossed over the left or raised on a small footstool, while the bowl of the mandolin rests on the right thigh and chest, held in place by the right forearm and balanced by the left hand. The neck of the instrument is slightly raised, and a chamois-leather is often placed beneath the bowl of the instrument, to prevent it from slipping against the player's clothes. A few solo performers combine these two positions, standing upright but placing the right foot on a high stool, so that the right thigh is parallel to the ground; this gives them a commanding stance over an audience, but also ensures the absolute stability of the instrument.

The neck of the mandolin rests between the thumb and forefinger of the left hand (although the hand must remain perfectly free to move up and down the fingerboard). Each left-hand finger drops on to the fingerboard from above, with the fingertip holding down a pair of strings just behind the appropriate fret (it is important that the lowest joint does not collapse when doing this).

Many players adopt a guitar-like left-hand posture (with their fingers parallel to the frets), as this facilitates chordal playing; however, many virtuoso performers find that a violin-like hand posture (with the fingers pointing down the neck) allows them to perform scale passages more rapidly, especially when playing in higher positions on the fingerboard. Left-hand positions on the mandolin are exactly the same as on the violin—in Position I the first finger covers *f″* and *f♯″* on the first string, in Position II it covers *g″* and *g♯″*, and so on—and many mandolinists develop their left-hand technique by using classic sets of violin studies, such as those by Kreutzer and Rode. Arabic numerals are used to indicate left-hand fingering; roman numerals indicate positions.

The standard position for the right hand involves resting the right forearm on the edge of the mandolin (near the hitch-pins) and arching the right wrist[4] so that the plectrum—which is held lightly but firmly between the thumb and (curved) forefinger—attacks the strings perpendicularly. Many mandolinists also like to glide the tip of the little finger lightly across the table of the instrument as they play; this gives them a constant reference point, enabling them to judge the precise position of the tip of the plectrum *vis-à-vis* the strings more easily and making intricate right-hand work less prone to error. The strings are usually struck above the scratchplate, midway between the bridge and the soundhole, the sound being sweetened by moving the plectrum towards the soundhole, or made more metallic by striking the strings nearer to the bridge. All plectrum-movement should originate from the wrist, with the arm providing only secondary motion.

Those who take a violinistic approach to the mandolin tend to regard it as an instrument on which the left hand is dominant, with the right hand performing most passages with simple, alternate down strokes (∧) and up strokes (∨).[5] But the majority of specialist mandolin virtuosi, from Branzoli onwards, have always stressed that the right hand is the dominant partner, requiring greater study, versatility, and flexibility than the left. These two approaches towards technique are often called, respectively, the 'French' and 'Italian'

---

[4] Although the arched-wrist position is favoured by most performers, and has been recommended by most of the great players of the past, there are a number of first-rate mandolinists (especially in Italy) who play with a flat wrist. However, these remarks by Samuel Siegel undoubtedly represent the general consensus on the subject: 'I find that the arched wrist *permits greater freedom and a larger scope as regards tonal qualities.*... The elevation of the wrist from the mandolin should under no circumstances strain or cramp any of the wrist muscles. A height of one and one-half to three inches, depending upon the physique of the player, is sufficient.' (*BMG*, July 1923: 135.)

[5] Other symbols are occasionally used, but this is by far the most commonly encountered notation.

schools,[6] although both styles of playing have long coexisted in France, Italy, and almost everywhere else where the mandolin is studied seriously. There is, in reality, not quite as much difference between the two approaches as is sometimes claimed, because most scale passages are executed in exactly the same way by adherents of either school (with alternate down and up strokes), as is most triplet arpeggio movement (usually performed with one of a number of idiosyncratic plectrum patterns). However, it is undoubtedly true that certain Italian virtuoso showpieces require plectrum movements that initially seem awkward and unnatural to those trained exclusively in the French school, and can be performed with greater ease and fluency by those who have thoroughly mastered the Italian school.

Tremolo is indisputably the most contentious aspect of mandolin technique. Some regard it as the very soul of the instrument, others as an annoying affectation that prevents the mandolin being taken more seriously by the musical establishment at large. A more constructive viewpoint lies somewhere between these two extreme positions: tremolo is a perfectly legitimate means for a plucked instrument to prolong the notes of a melodic phrase, but an uneven or poorly executed tremolo is as unmusical as it is relentless. A late nineteenth-century orchestral tutor gives an even-handed and objective opinion of the technique:

> A plectrum of quill, bone or tortoiseshell is thrummed upon the strings with a rapid *tremolo*, not easy to learn, and the sounds thus acquire an almost continuous or sustained character. If exceedingly well done, this is agreeable, but unless the *tremolo* is of the utmost rapidity and evenness, it is irritating beyond description . . . It is not now the custom to write out the tremolos; but all notes are supposed to be played in tremolo unless otherwise indicated (by staccato dots) . . . Because of its being a *quasi*-sustaining instrument, the Mandoline may with advantage be used in numbers. (Corder 1896: 80.)

Corder was referring to the Italian style of playing, where tremolo is the normal method of performing the longer notes of a melodic phrase, and is rarely notated. In this style, the performer conventionally leaves a very short gap at the end of each note, unless a slur is placed over two or more notes

---

[6] The violinistic style is probably known as the French school because the Neapolitan virtuoso De Cristofaro popularized it in Paris during the 1880s; the more complex Italian school of plectrum technique descends from Branzoli and Munier. However, the more advanced sections of De Cristofaro's method show that he, too, was well acquainted with complex movements of the plectrum, and that his own technique was by no means restricted to straightforward up and down movements.

Ex. 12. Tremolo notation

to indicate that they should be tied together, as in Ex. 12. A more pronounced separation between notes is indicated by a horizontal line above each one.

Nowadays, most composers indicate in words when they require a note or phrase to be played tremolo, and otherwise expect each note to receive a single plectrum-stroke. Sometimes (especially in orchestral scores) tremolo passages are notated in full, usually as lines of continuous demisemiquavers. However, unless a strictly rhythmical effect is specifically required, most experienced players will ignore this notation and perform the tremolo at a speed that produces a smooth cantabile tone; in other words, although a minim might be written out as sixteen demisemiquavers, the mandolinist might actually play a completely different number of strokes while performing that minim. The ideal tremolo is one that is completely fluid and gives the illusion of a single sustained sound, rather than a series of rapid percussions (which is why the precise number of strokes is not important); to this end it is imperative that it is perfectly even, with the down and up strokes both as smooth and regular as possible, and that plectrum noise is kept to an absolute minimum. Otherwise, the end result can be profoundly unappealing, as Sgallari once lamented, when describing the poor state of many of the amateur orchestras he encountered when he first arrived in London:

In place of a fine tremolo—a thing as exquisite as the vibration of any well-poised machine—they scratch out a noise like that of a hen on the ground in a farmyard. Consequently, even when accurately interpreted, their pieces are not elegantly produced, for they sound ponderous and not nice. It is this type of playing which does such harm to the popularity of the mandoline. I have noticed that the majority of people who consider themselves quite competent players and who perform in orchestras ought to be taking lessons ... Divergence of style, lack of freedom of wrist, lack of attention to the stroke, all serve to produce that sound of nutmeg grating which disfigures so many orchestras. (Sgallari 1903: 11.)

In accompanied playing the mandolinist usually tremolos a single line, but many unaccompanied solos make extensive use of duo style, a technique developed principally by American mandolinists in the late nineteenth century. Bickford once gave the following description of the style:

Probably the one thing that has done most to elevate the mandolin in the eyes of musicians, at least in my own country, is the introduction and development of the duo style of playing. This style really comprises several distinct species within itself, but they are usually all gathered under one heading. For example, there is the melody sustained by the tremolo on one string, while another melody or an accompaniment is picked on a lower string, or two or three of the lower strings may be used for a chord accompaniment. Then the melody may be played tremolo on a lower string, while the accompaniment is picked on the higher strings, or the tremolo may be used on the middle strings, while the accompaniment is distributed both above and below. (Bickford 1909: 131.)

Because duo style requires the player to interrupt the tremolo in order to play the notes of the accompaniment, it is essential that it is performed as smoothly as possible, with the smallest possible gaps, so that the sustained part appears continuous. Samuel Siegel, one of the first players to popularize this style, emphasized the importance of slow and careful practice of this technique:

Very few mandolinists have as yet learned to play the duo form correctly. They try to learn it too quickly and without first practising the necessary preliminary exercises. They at once attempt to sustain a tremolo and at the same time play the lower or accompaniment notes staccato. The general result of such an attempt shows a perceptible (in many instances quite marked) pause in the tremolo, when the pick is reaching for the note to be played staccato. (Siegel 1901: 4.)

When playing in duo style, performers give an exact and measured number of strokes to the tremolo, so that the notes of the accompaniment can be played strictly in time. Although it is a very difficult technique to perform convincingly, it is an extremely impressive and effective way of playing an

Ex. 13. Duo-style notation

unaccompanied solo when done well. Duo-style passages are sometimes written out in full, but are more commonly notated as in Ex. 13.

In addition to duo style, some players developed the technique of playing tremolo on three or four courses simultaneously (known as trio and quartet style respectively). When expertly performed, this can produce a shimmering sound somewhat like the *vox humana* stop on an organ, but great technical mastery is required in order to fuse the various parts together convincingly and to minimize plectrum noise. An effective use of trio and quartet style is found in a work by Calace, inspired by a fragment of Gregorian Chant: the *Corale: imitazione delle 4 voci*, Op. 123 (Ex. 14), a piece which he dedicated to Takei and performed during his tour of Japan in 1924–5.

The topic of ornamentation is too vast to deal with in detail here. Eighteenth-century players of the mandoline and mandolino (which have low-tension strings) performed many ornaments with the left hand alone, but this technique is less successful when attempted on a modern instrument with high-tension strings. Most authorities recommend that each note of an ornament should receive a separate plectrum-stroke, to ensure that it is clearly heard. However, some very brief ornaments (especially acciaccaturas) can be performed successfully by hammering or pulling the strings with a left-hand finger. Every note of a turn or trill must be individually stroked by the plectrum, otherwise it soon becomes inaudible.

Ex. 14. Calace: *Corale*, bars 1–11

Scordatura tunings have been used primarily by performers when composing unaccompanied virtuoso showpieces for themselves. A favourite altered
tuning for the eight strings is *g–b♭–d′–f′–a′–a′–e″–e″*, allowing performers to
play six-note chords, and rapid runs in minor thirds on each of the lower two
courses. Because of the risk of damage to the instrument caused by the increased
string tension (and also of the strings themselves breaking), it is often advisable to lower all the strings by a semitone to *f♯–a–c♯′–e′–g♯′–g♯′–d♯″–d♯″*. Michele
Ciociano (an Italian soloist and composer who spent some thirty years in
England) used this lowered tuning for his unaccompanied solo 'Le Village:
printemps' (Ex. 15), so that the sounds produced are radically different from
(and harmonically much richer than) the written notes.

Several modern composers, including George Crumb, have experimented
with the dissonant effect of tuning pairs of strings a quarter-tone apart. Radim
Zenkl, on his album of unaccompanied solos *Galactic Mandolin* (1992), has
gone further, basing an entire series of thirteen compositions around scordatura tunings. The first piece uses conventional tuning, the second piece lowers one string from each pair by a semitone (*g♭–g–d♭′–d′–a♭′–a′–e♭″–e″*), the
next lowers them by a further semitone (*f–g–c′–d′–g′–a′–d″–e″*), and so on
until, by the thirteenth piece, the two strings in each pair are an octave apart.

Although the mandolin is, by definition, a pizzicato instrument, a distinction is made between conventional plectrum-strokes and the more muffled
sounds produced by the fingers of either hand. Left-hand pizzicato (×) is

Ex. 15. Ciociano: *Le Village*, bars 1–8

occasionally used, mainly to pluck open strings while accompanying a tremolo melody (as in Abt's Impromptu, Ex. 10), and produces a soft but distinctive tone. Right-hand pizzicato (✳) is particularly effective when the thumb
brushes lightly across the strings (as in the opening of Rocco's Serenade, Ex.
7), but is also occasionally used when an extremely soft tone is required for
a simple passage. The extract from a piece by Dounis shown in Ex. 16 contains both left- and right-hand pizzicato.

Harmonics are used less on the mandolin than on most other plucked-string
instruments, because the shorter string length makes it more difficult to artic-
ulate them clearly. However, they can with practice be produced by both the
right and left hands. The usual way of sounding a natural harmonic is to touch
a pair of strings directly above the appropriate fret with a left-hand finger,
while plucking the strings with the plectrum. Alternatively, this can be done
by extending the second finger of the right hand (or, the index finger, in which
case the plectrum is held between thumb and second finger) and touching the
strings with the tip, simultaneously giving a plectrum-stroke. Harmonics on

Ex. 16. Dounis: *Rêve oriental*, bars 20–9

(✻) Pizz. R.H.
(✕) Pizz. L.H.

open strings sound most clearly at the twelfth and nineteenth (or seventh) frets, but, depending on the strings and the instrument used, the first five or six notes of the harmonic series can often be produced with surprising clarity by either method (especially if the plectrum strikes the strings near to the bridge).

Other notes can be produced as artificial harmonics, again by two methods. The clearest technique is to fret a note with the left hand, touch the strings twelve frets higher (directly over the fret) with the second finger of the right hand, and simultaneously sound the note with the plectrum. It is also possible to produce artificial harmonics by using a violin technique—fingering a note with the first finger of the left hand and touching the strings five frets higher with the little finger of the left hand while giving a plectrum stroke—but it is extremely difficult to get them to speak clearly and consistently in this way. Ex. 17 shows the opening of Siegel's unaccompanied 'Harmonic Waltz: The Bells', which makes extensive use of both natural and artificial harmonics. It is customary nowadays to write all harmonics with diamond-shaped heads.

6.3 *The Mandolin Quartet and the Mandolin Orchestra*

The Romantic Quartet—two mandolins, octave mandola, and guitar (or, very occasionally, liuto)—has been perhaps the most popular type of mandolin ensemble over the past hundred years. A more sophisticated form of the mandolin and guitar duos that were once part of everyday life in southern Italy,

Ex. 17. Siegel: *The Bells*, bars 1–8

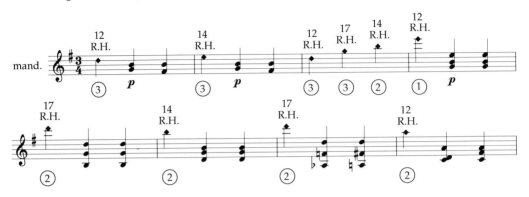

it is capable of performing music of great depth and complexity and, in an intimate venue, can produce an impressively wide range of dynamics and tone-colours, from an ethereal whisper to an imposing fortissimo. Almost a century after they were written, the three Munier quartets remain landmarks in the development of the Romantic Quartet, demonstrating for the first time that mandolins and guitars could produce music of great expressive power, and that they had the tonal resources to perform extended works. An enormous amount of music has since been written for this instrumentation (mostly by Italian, French, and German composers), the quartets by Ambrosius being especially attractive and enjoyable to play. In addition, many compositions for full mandolin orchestra can be satisfactorily reduced to four quartet parts.

Because of the different natural strengths of the four instruments, music written for Romantic Quartet often gives the impression of two mandolins and a mandola being accompanied by a guitar. The guitar, being plucked with the fingers, cannot sustain melodies as easily as can a plectral instrument, but it is particularly well suited to playing full chords and arpeggios, its soft tone providing a rich harmonic base for the plectrum trio. However, continual use of the guitar in an accompanying role is musically unsatisfying and can become tedious for the player; therefore imaginative composers, such as Munier and Ambrosius, ensure that the guitar is also given melodic lines and occasional solo passages, thus becoming a full and equal member of the quartet.

Guitarists should also be aware that it was formerly common practice for publishers to issue several versions of the same composition, so that a work for mandolin and piano might also appear in an arrangement for mandolin and guitar (with optional parts for second mandolin and mandola). In many cases, the piano score has simply been adapted into a guitar part by the publisher, rather than being reconceived for the guitar by the composer, and frequently sits poorly on the instrument, rarely venturing beyond first position and sounding rather ponderous. When performing such pieces, guitarists may find it rewarding to compare their part with the original piano version; moving passages up an octave and reworking the spacing of chords can, if sensitively handled, greatly improve the overall texture of a piece. In quartets that originally included a liuto, the published edition often has a guitar part instead, usually constructed by combining the mandola and liuto parts. Thinning out the guitar part, so that it doubles the mandola line only at key moments, is advisable.

Music originally written for string quartet seldom transfers well to the Romantic Quartet, primarily because the natures of the cello and the guitar are very different. Replacing the guitar with the liuto (as Munier did in his Florentine Quartet) will solve this problem, but, even so, viola parts are not ideally suited to the octave mandola. A better solution was found in the development of the Classical Quartet; by incorporating a mandoliola and a mandoloncello, the entire string quartet repertoire was opened up to players of fretted instruments, once they had learned to read the alto and bass clefs. One of the most notable of all Classical Quartets was the one led by Silvio Ranieri in Brussels during the 1910s and 1920s (Illustration 19).

Although an octave mandola can be turned into a mandoliola simply by restringing and retuning it, there is a fundamental difference between the two instruments in conception. Whereas the octave mandola is simply a slightly larger mandolin, the mandoliola (as designed by Embergher and Maldura) is built in exact proportion to the mandolin, relative to its lower pitch. Consequently, although the tuning of the octave mandola is lower than that of the mandoliola, the former is usually the smaller of the two instruments. The short string length of the octave mandola used to give rise to complaints that it lacked volume; correctly strung, however, it is an extremely powerful instrument (even on its lowest notes), and can easily dominate a Romantic Quartet unless played with restraint.

The arrival of the tenor mandola and mandocello in the USA led, indirectly, to the introduction of one of the most absurdly flawed but widely disseminated systems of music printing ever devised—Universal Notation. Although the appeal of the new instruments was that they could open up the treasures of the string quartet repertoire to mandolinists, many amateurs were unwilling to spend time learning to master the alto and bass clefs. Initially, therefore, transposed parts in the treble clef were published for the two instruments (written a fifth and a twelfth higher than pitch, respectively), so that performers could play on the larger instruments as though they were mandolins.

In 1907, the American Guild (which to a great extent reflected the business interests of major companies such as Gibson) adopted the tenor mandola and mandocello as the 'correct' instruments for the mandolin orchestra. For several years, publishing houses continued to issue transposed parts for the two instruments but, in 1913, it was decided to adopt a newly invented system of Universal Notation instead. Under this system, all music was henceforth to be published in the treble clef, no matter whether it was intended for mandolin or mando-bass; it would be written at the correct pitch (that is, a written *c* would always sound *c*), but not necessarily at the correct octave; one or two diagonal lines through the treble clef indicated the number of octave transpositions.

Advocates of Universal Notation claimed that, because three courses (*g–d′–a′*) on the tenor mandola were the same as on the mandolin, players would be able to sight-read easily on the new instrument. Critics rightly pointed out that none of these courses was in the same place on the two instruments (therefore none of the notes had the same fingerings), and that players would find it far less confusing simply to learn to read the alto and bass clefs. Many publishers, however, approved of the system, realizing that once players had begun to use it, they would have to keep buying music printed in Universal Notation, as they would be incapable of reading anything else. Over the next decade, as much as half of all mandolin music published in the USA appeared in this new system, and marginalized a generation of mandolinists as effectively as the over-reliance on tablature had marginalized lutenists several centuries earlier. Eventually, mandolinists began to realize that the only sensible course was to master the alto and bass clefs, but by then the musical aspirations of many amateurs had already been seriously damaged.

Fortunately, the farce of Universal Notation had little impact outside the USA, partly because the octave mandola and guitar remained more popular in Europe than the tenor mandola and mandocello. Many of the earliest European compositions for mandolin orchestra were almost indistinguishable from music for Romantic Quartet, and in France the term *Estudiantina* could be applied to ensembles with as few as four members, and to others which had dozens of performers, all playing the same four basic parts. Gradually, however, other instruments were added, the number of parts increased, and the music became truly orchestral in character. Harps, double basses, and percussion (including piano) were the most frequent additions from the late nineteenth century onwards, with entire wind sections often appearing after World War I. Mandoloncello, liuto, mandoliola, and third mandolin parts were also added to many scores. In France, this expansion of the basic *Estudiantina* was eventually acknowledged by the adoption of the term *orchestre à plectre* (OAP).

During the early part of the twentieth century, various attempts were made to perfect a bass member of the mandolin family.[7] Most of these instruments were shaped like huge mandolins, and often had to be played in an awkward standing position, since many were far too large to be accommodated on the lap. Tremolo was achieved either by rapidly plucking the strings with the index and middle fingers, or by striking them with a large leather plectrum (even small hammers were tried). While some of these instruments were very effective in quiet passages, none of them possessed sufficient volume to produce a convincing forte, and most lacked very low bass notes. Many mandolinists were initially extremely reluctant to use the orchestral contra-bass, considering it a bowed intruder in the world of plucked-string music, but its sheer flexibility, versatility, and, above all, audibility soon led to its widespread adoption. The double bass is predominantly played pizzicato in mandolin orchestras, but the bow is often used in forte passages for the greater sonority it can provide.

Modern-day mandolin orchestras still contain the four basic sections—first and second mandolins, octave mandola, and guitar—but are often augmented in various ways. In Japan, for example, the mandolins are usually divided into two or three sections, the octave mandolas and guitars are occasionally divided, and mandoloncellos and double basses are almost always added. Wind and brass sections are frequently included, and the percussion section can be as extensive as that found in a full symphony orchestra, with timpani, drums, cymbals, tubular bells, Chinese gongs, and keyboard instruments. The relative seating arrangements of the various sections are absolutely vital, in order to balance the overall sound. In particular, it is important that the mandolas and mandoloncellos are not muffled by other players being seated immediately in front of them, and that the guitarists are centrally placed for maximum audibility.[8]

---

[7] Some of these are discussed in the App.

[8] Matsomoto (1985, 1986) discusses the relative merits of different layouts in great detail.

In Europe, most ensembles nowadays contain only plucked strings (preferring to model themselves on string orchestras rather than full symphony orchestras), but greater use is made of divisi sections and of solo passages, giving great tonal variety and allowing dense, complex music to be performed. Occasionally, a third mandolin part (often played on a small, high-pitched instrument) is added, used sparingly in imitation of a woodwind section. In Britain and the USA, attempts have been made over the past century to incorporate members of the banjo family into the mandolin orchestra, in imitation of a brass section (such orchestras were sometimes called 'Plectrophonic'). Transforming the mandolin orchestra into a quasi-symphony orchestra remains a fascinating challenge for a number of players and conductors, yet many others would assert that the most artistically satisfying results are still obtained from the simple, traditional resources—guitars and the members of the mandolin family.

6.4 *Useful Addresses*

Although there are dozens of societies, publishers, and retailers devoted to the mandolin world-wide, they mostly survive outside the musical mainstream and can therefore be extremely difficult to locate. The following section gives addresses for some of them but, because many of the businesses and societies are small-scale, their addresses are subject to periodic change. Readers wishing to pursue their interest in the mandolin further are therefore advised to contact as many as possible.

Journals and Societies

Classical Mandolin Society of America (CMSA)

PO Box 124
Merrick, NY 11566–0124
USA

publishes the quarterly *Classical Mandolin Society of America* newsletter which gives details of recent publications, recordings, and concerts.

Japan Mandolin Union (JMU)

c/o Mr. Rikio Ichige
4–11, Takaido-Higashi 3-chome
Suginami-ku, Tokyo
Japan

publishes the annual English-language *JMU Review*, which gives details of competitions, reviews of concerts, and general articles.

Association PROMIFI

470, rue de Mirecourt-Poussay
88500 Mirecourt
France

publishes the quarterly French-language journal *Le Plectre*, which contains some excellent historical articles as well as reviews of concerts, publications, and recordings, and contemporary domestic news.

Federazione mandolinistica italiana (FMI)

via San Faustino 41
I-25122 Brescia
Italy

publishes an irregular Italian-language magazine, *Plectrum*, with articles on the development and history of the mandolin and details of events in Italy.

Zupfmusik, a quarterly journal devoted to the guitar and mandolin, can be obtained from:

Zupfmusik Magazin,
Huulkamp 26
D-2000 Hamburg 65
Germany

All of these journals will provide readers with up-to-date addresses of makers, publishers, and suppliers, as well as details of new publications, recordings, and compositions. They have also acted in recent years as one of the primary means of dissemination of scholarly work about the mandolin. There is also a Federation of Australasian Mandolin Ensembles (FAME), which can be contacted at 16 Fyfe Circle, Bull Creek, WA 6149 Australia.

Publishers, Makers, and Suppliers

The complete works of Raffaele Calace, edited by Toshimichi Hibino (a Buddhist Priest), are available in nine volumes, published by Suiseisha Music Publishers, Tokyo. The Calace family still publishes many of his compositions individually. These are obtainable from:

Ditta Raffaele Calace & figlio
via S. Domenico Maggiore 9
80134 Naples
Italy

Many works by Munier (including his Concerto and two of his three quartets), Marucelli, Leonardi, and their Italian contemporaries are obtainable from:

Edizioni Ditta R. Maurri
via del Corso, 1 (17 r.)
Florence
Italy

Heinrichshofen's Verlag of Wilhelmshaven, Germany, publishes chamber music with mandolin, including works by Gál, Kaufmann, Uhl, and Sprongl. The catalogues of Zimmermann (Frankfurt), Vogt & Fritz (Schweinfurt), and Grenzland-Verlag (Aachen) also contain many interesting items.

In the first instance, however, most readers will probably find it easier to contact one of the specialist mandolin retailers listed below. They have expert knowledge of what music is currently available in print, and will be able to obtain most pieces without difficulty.

Joachim Trekel Verlag
Postfach 620 42B

22404 Hamburg
Germany

is the largest modern-day publisher of mandolin music (from solo to full *Zupforchester*). Its catalogue, mainly of works by German composers, includes many pieces by Ambrosius and Wölki. The firm can also obtain works for mandolin issued by many other publishing houses throughout the world.

Plucked String
PO Box 11125
Arlington, VA 22210
USA

also publishes mandolin music (including works by Ayton, Gladd, Goichberg, and Israel), and is expert at locating almost anything ever written for the mandolin, in or out of print.

Both Joachim Trekel Verlag and Plucked String are retailers of instruments, strings, and other accessories, and will be able to advise on suitable purchases. They also offer a postal service.

Those interested in bluegrass and folk music may wish to contact:

Mandolin Central
Rt. 3, Box 503
Siler City, NC 27344
USA

British readers will find a limited selection of instruments, strings, and sheet music at:

John Alvey Turner
36 New Road
Ware
Herts. SG12 7BY

It is beyond the scope of this book even to attempt to catalogue the immense amount of mandolin music published since the late nineteenth century and preserved in various national libraries around the world. The British Library, London, alone contains thousands of pieces, the American

Library of Congress, Washington, DC, has many times more, and the total number of individual pieces for mandolin published since 1880 undoubtedly runs into many hundreds of thousands. Similarly, the number of sound recordings (historic and contemporary) is too vast a subject to be addressed here.[9] Many countries now have a national sound archive, and the chances of finding recordings there by some of the performers listed in this book are very high. The National Sound Archive in London, for example, has copies of the following acoustic recordings which Raffaele Calace made of his own works in Japan in 1925:

Raffaele Calace—mandolin (with Hakujiró Kondo—piano)
    Rondo, Op. 127: Nittô 1461A
    'Danza del nani': Nittô 1461B
    Tarantella, Op. 18: Nittô 1462A
    'Pavana', Op. 54: Nittô 1462B

Raffaele Calace—liuto
    Prelude No. 9: Nittô 1463 (both sides)

The Library of Congress, Washington, DC, holds many recordings, including cylinders and discs by Abt, De Pace, and Place, and possibly the first mandolin recording ever made, a seven-inch disc of 'Nearer my God to Thee' performed by Samuel Siegel (Berliner 01141G).

---

[9] Neil Gladd has made a specialist study of early sound recordings by mandolinists, and has located thousands of individual discs and cylinders.

APPENDIX

The Mandolin and Related
Instruments: Brief Definitions

This section gives short descriptions of some of the many different plectrum instruments that the reader might encounter in the literature of the mandolin (more detailed information on the most important instruments can be found elsewhere in this book). The late nineteenth century and early twentieth century were times of great innovation and development in the field of fretted instruments, with hundreds of makers inventing their own types of mandolin, most of which have since disappeared without trace. This list, therefore, can include only some of the most frequently encountered instruments, and is concerned only with the late nineteenth century and the twentieth century. It should be noted that mandolin-makers have often appropriated names formerly used for completely different instruments. The late nineteenth-century additions to the mandolin family known as the liuto and chitarrone, for example, are quite unrelated to the better-known Renaissance and Baroque instruments of the same name. Those instruments still commonly encountered today are referred to in the present tense; those that have largely disappeared are described in the past tense.

Arcichitarra: see *Chitarrone*.

Bandola: (i) John H. Parker was granted an American patent for this instrument on 7 August 1894. His bandola was a mandolin-style instrument with twenty-two frets and standard tuning. It was widely advertised in the USA at the beginning of the twentieth century. (ii) a combination instrument, made from a banjo neck and a Gibson Florentine body. It had a fingerboard with thirty-six frets and produced a tone that blended with other plucked strings more readily than that of the banjo. (iii) the tenor member of a family of flat-back fretted plucked instruments of Portuguese and Brazilian origin. They include the bandolineta (high soprano), the bandolim (soprano), the bandoleta (alto), and the bandoloncello (cello). They are modelled on the members of the violin family, but probably also derived from the Neapolitan mandolin family. (Hambly 1977*a*: 512–13, and information provided by Paulo de Sá.)

Bandolim: a flat-backed variant of the mandolin, widely played in Brazil and Portugal.

Bandurria: a plucked, fretted, flat-back instrument of Spanish origin, the Iberian equivalent of the Neapolitan mandolin. It has a small but deep body and a very short string length (about ten and a half inches), allowing its first course to be tuned to a high pitch. Its twelve strings (arranged in six pairs) are tuned entirely in fourths—$g\sharp$–$c\sharp'$–$f\sharp'$–b'–e''–a''—a tuning that has been standard since the eighteenth century. Nowadays, it usually has metal strings (see Illustration 4). As with the mandolin, there is an entire family of bandurrias, ranging from soprano to bass. For its earlier history, see Tyler and Sparks (1989: 52–3).

Banjeaurine: a small banjo, tuned a fourth above the standard, full-size banjo: c'''–f'–c''–e''–g''. It was invented by the American manufacturer S. S. Stewart in 1885 to take the lead in banjo club orchestras, and was popular in Britain and the USA until the banjolin superseded it.

Banjolin: also known as the mandolin-banjo, this is a small banjo with a short neck and either four or eight strings, tuned like a mandolin but producing a loud banjo tone. Of little value as a solo instrument, its main purpose was to allow mandolinists to strum chords in dance bands during the ragtime era.

Banjulele: also known as the ukulele-banjo, this was a banjo version of the Hawaiian ukulele. It had four single gut or nylon strings, tuned *a'–d'–f♯'–b'*, and was strummed either with the right-hand fingers or with a plectrum. It was frequently used by popular entertainers during the 1920s and 1930s to accompany their own singing.

Chitarrone: in about 1890, Monzino of Milan invented the arcichitarra, known more commonly as the chitarrone (moderna). It had the tuning of a conventional bowed double bass, but was always played pizzicato, tremolo being achieved by plucking the strings with the index and middle fingers alternately. It lacked the power of the plectrum-played mandolin and, because orchestras invariably had far more mandolins than chitarroni, could not be heard in rapid passages or full, loud textures. It was, however, much more effective in pianissimo passages and in detached slow movement (Ranieri 1925: 1994).

Contra-bass banjo: a very large, very loud, three-stringed banjo, tuned *E,–A,–D*. Made mostly of wood, and played with a leather plectrum, it measures about five feet in length from the tailpiece to the peg-head. It was often used instead of (or in addition to) an orchestral double bass in BMG orchestras.

Cremonese mandolin: also known as the Brescian mandolin, this has four single gut strings and a fixed bridge, and is effectively a Milanese mandolin with Neapolitan tuning. It was originally popularized in Vienna in the early nineteenth century by Bartolomeo Bortolazzi, and was quite widely used in Germany at the beginning of the twentieth century. For its earlier history, see Tyler and Sparks (1989: 139–40).

Domra: a mandolin-like instrument whose origins can be traced back to the Slavic and Russian peoples some four centuries ago. Most domras have three single strings tuned in fourths, but a four-string version is favoured by a number of mandolinists, most notably Keith Harris.

Florentine Mandolin: (i) see *Tuscan mandolin*. (ii) the name given by the Gibson company to some of the carved back and top mandolins in its A- and F-series.

Liola: invented by the Vinaccia family in Naples, this was a bass instrument for use in mandolin orchestras, and was also known as the mandolone. Much larger than the liuto, and with a flat back, it had four heavy wound strings, tuned *A,–D–G–c*.

Liuto: also known as the liuto moderno, this is a Neapolitan instrument whose design was perfected by Raffaele Calace (Illustration 9). Early models resembled large mandolins, measured about thirty-nine inches from the end of the head to the hitch-pins, and had twenty frets (with an extension for the top course). The five pairs of strings are tuned *C–G–d–a–e'*. In ensemble playing, liuto parts are usually written in the bass clef; solo parts are written out like those for guitar—in the treble clef, but sounding an octave lower than written. The liuto is seldom heard nowadays, which is a great pity since it has a rich, deep, powerful tone and offers even greater possibilities as a solo instrument than does the mandolin. Raffaele Calace preferred the liuto to the mandolin, and wrote many of his unaccompanied preludes for it. On 4 May 1980, a rally for players of the liuto was held in Shimonoseki city, Japan, and the instrument is frequently encountered in Austria.

Lombardian mandolin: see *Milanese mandolin*.

Mando-bass: a very large bass mandolin with three (occasionally four) strings, tuned *E,–A,–D(–G)*, usually held upright and supported on a spike. It was used in mandolin orchestras and was played with a leather plectrum, either staccato or tremolo. Like other types of bass mandolin, it lacked sufficient power to be heard clearly in rapid or forte passages.

Mandola: (i) often called the octave mandola, this is a large mandolin tuned an octave lower than the standard mandolin. Its music is written in the treble clef, exactly like that for mandolin, and it is played in precisely the same way. (ii) see *Mandoliola*.

Mandolinole: this twelve-string instrument was a combination of mandolin and mandola, and was developed by the Neapolitan maker Mariani in about 1904. Fantauzzi (1904) recommended it as being very useful for *Estudiantinas*.

Mandoliola: more commonly known as the tenor mandola, this instrument is a mandolin with viola tuning, developed by Maldura and Embergher as part of their conscious decision to emulate the bowed string quartet. Its music is usually written in the alto clef, but transposed parts (written a fifth higher than they sound) were also published during the early twentieth century. Although Embergher perfected the instrument, various makers were designing similar instruments throughout the 1890s.

Mandoloncello: often called simply the mandocello, this instrument was perfected by Maldura and Embergher to complete their plucked equivalent of the string quartet. Tuned like the cello, it was to be found in most mandolin orchestras during the early decades of the twentieth century. Nowadays it is widely used in Japan, and to a lesser extent in Europe. Its music is usually written in the bass clef, but transposed parts in the treble clef (an octave and a fifth above pitch) were published during the early twentieth century.

Mandolone: see *Liola*.

Mandolira (or *mandolyra*): invented by Raffaele and Nicola Calace, this had a round back, a neck with twenty frets, and a flat top with two outspread wings like a lyre. It was strung and tuned like a conventional Neapolitan mandolin, and had the advantage that it could be played in high positions very easily. The Calace brothers claimed that it had a sweeter sound than a conventional mandolin, but it never became popular outside Naples.

Milanese mandolin: developed by the Monzino family in Milan (and also known as the Lombardian mandolin), this is the modernized version of the mandolino. It is shorter and wider than a Neapolitan mandolin, has a shallow back, six single strings tuned $g–b–e'–a'–d''–g''$ (three of gut and three of silk covered with wire), and up to twenty frets. The spaces between the frets are slightly concave. During the 1890s, the Italian maker Casini produced a variant with twelve metal strings, tuned in the standard Lombardian manner.

Neapolitan mandolin: the standard form of the mandolin, developed by Pasquale Vinaccia of Naples in about 1835. It is overwhelmingly the most common of the many forms of mandolin played throughout the world; consequently, it is usually referred to simply as 'the mandolin', no further designation being necessary.

Octave mandola: see *Mandola* (i).

Octavin: a very small mandolin, using the same tuning and notation as the standard instrument, but producing notes an octave higher. Its high, penetrating tone was useful in mandolin orchestras, where it took on a role somewhat like that of a piccolo, contributing shrill flourishes to the overall texture.

Piccolo mandolin: a rather vague term that was used to describe almost any small, high-pitched mandolin, although the most common tuning was a fourth above the standard instrument. They are still occasionally met with, primarily in the hands of small children whose fingers are too small to cope with a full-size instrument.

Quartini: a small mandolin, tuned a fourth above the standard instrument, and used in mandolin orchestras in a role rather like that of a woodwind instrument. Although a concert mandolin with extended fingerboard could produce the same notes as a quartini, it was favoured for the piercing shrillness and brilliance of its timbre. According to Ranieri (1925: 1993), it was developed by the Vinaccia family.

Roman mandolin: a modified version of the standard mandolin, considered by many to be its perfected form. The classic Embergher form, developed in about 1890, has a narrow, slightly rounded and extended fingerboard (like a violin), a bridge raised on the bass side, and a scrolled head with mechanized tuning-keys and tuning-barrels.

Tenor mandola: see *Mandoliola*.

Terzini: a small mandolin similar to the quartini, but tuned a minor third higher than the standard mandolin. Ranieri (1925: 1993) credits Embergher with creating this instrument.

Tuscan mandolin: also known as the Florentine mandolin, this was constructed like a Lombardian mandolin, but with only four strings (two of gut and two of wound silk), and was tuned like a Neapolitan instrument. It was similar to the Cremonese mandolin, but was built in the Roman manner, with a convex, violin-style neck. According to Pisani (1913: 135–6), the first one was built by Lybert & Maurri in Florence during the 1890s, in response to a request from a mandolinist who wanted to produce the sweet sound of gut strings from a Roman mandolin. Sachs (1913: 252) gives a completely different definition of the Florentine mandolin. I have become extremely sceptical of most of the regional variants listed by Sachs, since in many cases they totally fail to correspond with the documentation found in primary sources dating back to the eighteenth century.

Bibliography

ACTON, HAROLD (1961). *The Last Bourbons of Naples (1825–1861)* (London).

ADELSTEIN, SAMUEL (1905). *Mandolin Memories: A Descriptive and Practical Treatise on the Mandolin and Kindred Instruments* (San Francisco).

ANGER, DAROL, and RICE, TONY (1977–8). 'Tortoise-Shell Picks', *Mandolin World News* (winter), 15–18.

—— and GRISMAN, DAVID (1978). 'Hugo d'Alton Interview', *Mandolin World News* (summer), 4–8, 23–5.

ANSON, JOHN (1954a). 'Mandolin Masters (2)', *BMG* (Sept.), 292–3.

—— (1954b). 'Mandolin Masters (3)', *BMG* (Oct.), 16–17.

BAILY, LESLIE (1966). *Leslie Baily's BBC Scrapbooks* (London).

BAINES, ANTHONY (1966). *European and American Musical Instruments* (New York).

—— (1984). 'Mandoline', *The New Oxford Companion to Music* (Oxford).

BELL, JOSHUA, ed. (1993). *Mandolin Music in America: 3,800 Pieces for Mandolin and Where to Find them* (Arlington, Va.).

BELLOW, ALEXANDER (1970). *The Illustrated History of the Guitar* (New York).

BERLIOZ, HECTOR (1843). *Grand traité d'instrumentation* (Paris).

BICKFORD, ZARH MYRON (1909). 'The Mandolin Duo', *BMG* (June), 131.

—— (1920). 'A Brief History of the Mandolin and its Development', *The Bickford Mandolin Method* (New York).

BLACK, BOB (1976). 'Sources', *Mandolin World News* (Spring), 7–10.

BODIN, L. (1906). 'L'Art de la mandoline', *L'Estudiantina*, 8 (1 Apr.), 2.

BONE, PHILIP J. (1909). 'The International Mandolin Contests at Boulogne, France', *BMG* (July), 150; (Aug.), 166, 171.

—— (1972). *The Guitar and Mandolin* (1st edn. 1914; London).

BORTOLAZZI, BARTHOLOMEO (1805). *Anweisung die Mandoline von selbst zu erlernen* (Leipzig).

BRANZOLI, GIUSEPPE (1875). *Metodo teorico-pratico per mandolino napolitano o romano* (Rome).

BREMER, FREDRIKA (1861). *Two Years in Switzerland and Italy,* trans. Mary Hewitt (London, 2 vols).

BRUCE, DIX (1979). 'David Grisman Interview', *Mandolin World News* (spring), 5–8, 32–8.

—— (1981). 'The Electric Mandolin', *Mandolin World News* (spring), 22–8.

—— (1982). 'Keith Harris Interview', *Mandolin World News* (spring), 5–13.

BRUEN, BOB (1978). 'Jesse McReynolds Interview', *Mandolin World News* (autumn), 4–7.

BUCHNER, ALEXANDER (1958). *Musical Instruments Through the Ages* (London).

—— (1973). *Musical Instruments: An Illustrated History* (New York).

BUSCH, HANS, ed. (1988). *Verdi's Otello and Simon Boccanegra (Revised Version) in Letters and Documents* (Oxford, 2 vols.).

BUSCH, NOEL F. (1972). *A Concise History of Japan* (London).

CALACE, RAFFAELE (1908a). 'Il mandolino ed il liuto in orchestra', *Musica moderna* (Feb.).

—— (1908b). 'La costruzione degli strumenti a plettro', *Musica moderna,* (Mar.), 1–2.

—— (1908c). 'La nuova scuola del mandolino', *Musica moderna* (Apr.), 1–2.

—— (1908d). 'Gli albori di una vittoria', *Musica moderna* (Nov.), 1–2.

CAMPBELL, RICHARD (1980). 'Mandolin', in *The New Grove Dictionary of Music and Musicians* (London).

CASTERAS, SUSAN P. (1987). *Images of Victorian Womanhood in English Art* (Cranbury, NJ).

CHARNASSÉ, HÉLÈNE, and VERNILLAT, FRANCE (1970). *Les Instruments à cordes pincées* (Paris).

CHASE, GILBERT (1959). *The Music of Spain* (New York).

CLARKE, MICHAEL (1991). *Corot and The Art of Landscape* (London).

COLERIDGE, A. D., ed. (1873). *Life of Moscheles* (London, 2 vols.).

CORDER, FREDERICK (1896). *The Orchestra and How to Write for it* (London).

CROCE, BENEDETTO (1929). *A History of Italy 1871–1915*, trans. Cecilia Mary Ady (Oxford).

DAGOSTO, SYLVAIN (1981). 'Qu'est-ce qu'un "orchestre à plectre"?', in Domergue, ed. (1981), 37–8.

DEBLAIVE, JULES (1906). 'Mandoline et mandolinistes', *L'Estudiantina* (1 Feb.), 2.

DE PIETRO, MARIO (1975). 'Mandolin Tone', *BMG* (June), 9 (written before 1939).

Dictionnaire de biographie française, ed. Roman d'Amat (Paris, 1933–).

Dizionario biografico degli italiani (Rome, 1973–).

DOMERGUE, MARCELLE, ed. (1981). *La Mandoline: Exposition musicale au musée Comtadin de Carpentras* (Carpentras).

DUCHARTRE, PIERRE LOUIS (1929). *The Italian Comedy* (London; repr. New York, 1966).

EIDSON, KEN (1977). 'Jethro [Burns] Interview', *Mandolin World News* (summer), 6–9, 18, 24.

EITNER, ROBERT (1900–4). *Biographisch-bibliographisches Quellen-Lexikon* (Leipzig; repr. New York, 1945).

Encyclopaedia Britannica, 9th edn. (Edinburgh, 1883).

Encyclopedia della musica (Milan, 1963).

ESCUDIER, LES FRÈRES (1854). *Dictionnaire de musique* (1st edn. 1844; Paris).

L'Estudiantina (Paris, 15 Dec. 1905–1939; retitled *L'Orchestre à plectre* in 1934).

EVANS, TOM and MARY ANNE (1977). *Guitars: Music, History, Construction and Players from the Renaissance to Rock* (New York).

FANO, FABIO (1971). *Musica e teatri* (Naples).

FANTAUZZI, LAURENT (1904). 'Mandolines et cordes', *Le Plectre* (1 Nov.), 4.

FÉTIS, FRANÇOIS JOSEPH (1873a). *Biographie universelle des musiciens* (Paris).

—— (1873b). *Curiosités historiques de la musique* (Paris).

FOUCHETTI, GIOVANNI (1771). *Méthode pour apprendre facilement à jouer de la Mandoline à 4 et à 6 Cordes* (Paris; repr. Geneva, 1984).

FRANCIA, LEOPOLDO (1896). 'Remarks on the Interview of Señor Lopez', *Banjo World* (Dec.), 21.

—— (1897). 'History of the Mandoline', *Banjo World* (June), 132, (July), 150.

GAINHAM, SARAH (1979). *The Habsburg Twilight* (London).

GAISBERG, FRED (1946). *Music on Record* (London; 1st pub. as *The Music goes Round*, New York, 1943).

GALLENGA, A. (1875). *Italy Revisited* (London, 2 vols.).

GERHART, PAUL CESSNA (1897). 'A Few Facts Concerning the Mandolin', *Musical Courier* (New York, 10 Feb.), 36.

—— (1900). 'The Artistic Pre-eminence of the Mandoline', *Banjo World* (July), 132–42 (1st pub. in *Cadenza* (Nov.–Dec. 1899), 5–6).

GEVAERT, F. A. (1863). *Traité général d'instrumentation* (Paris).

GILL, DONALD (1984). 'Mandolin', in *The New Grove Dictionary of Musical Instruments* (London).

GLADD, NEIL (1987a). 'The Classical Mandolin: An Attempted Definition', *Classical Mandolin Society of America*, 1 (3), 8–11.

—— (1987b). 'The Classical Mandolin in America Pt. 1', *Classical Mandolin Society of America*, 1 (4), 7–11.

—— (1988). 'The Classical Mandolin in America Pt. 2', *Classical Mandolin Society of America*, 2 (2), 4–7.

Grand Larousse encyclopédique (Paris, 1964).

GRISMAN, DAVID (1976–7). 'The Mandocello', *Mandolin World News* (winter), 12–14.

—— (1977). 'The Dave Apollon Story Part I', *Mandolin World News* (autumn), 4–7.

—— (1977–8). 'Bill Monroe Interview', *Mandolin World News* (winter), 4–7, 22.

—— (1980). 'Dave Apollon Part II', *Mandolin World News* (autumn), 17–27.

GROVE, GEORGE (1878–90). *A Dictionary of Music and Musicians*, 1st edn. (London).

Grove's Dictionary of Music and Musicians, 5th edn. (London, 1954).

GUTMAN, F. O. (1906). 'The Slur', *American Music Journal* (June), 32.

HAMBLY, SCOTT (1977a). 'Mandolins in the US since 1880' (PhD diss., Univ. of Pennsylvania).

—— (1977b). 'The Munier Mandolin and Guitar Orchestra [Philadelphia]', *Mandolin World News* (summer), 21–2.

HANSLICK, EDUARD (1869). *Geschichte des Concertwesens in Wien* (Vienna).

HANSON, ALICE M. (1985). *Musical Life in Biedermeier Vienna* (Cambridge).

HARDING, JAMES (1965). *Saint-Saëns and his Circle* (London).

HARICH-SCHNEIDER, ETA (1973). *A History of Japanese Music* (London).

HARRISON, FRANK, and RIMMER, JOAN (1964). *European Musical Instruments* (London).

HARRISON, RICHARD (1898). 'Mandoline Making in Italy', *Musical Opinion* (July); repr. in *Banjo World* (Oct. 1898), 159.

HENKE, MATTHIAS, ed. (1993). *Das Grossbuke der Zupforchester* (Munich).

HEPOKOSKI, JAMES A. (1987). *Giuseppe Verdi: Otello* (Cambridge).

HIBBERT, CHRISTOPHER (1969). *The Grand Tour* (London).

HIPKINS, ALFRED JAMES (1954). 'String', in *Grove's Dictionary of Music and Musicians*, 5th edn. (London).

HUCK, OLIVER (1990). 'Gitarre und Mandoline im Septett', in *Zupfmusik*, 3, 106–10.

HUNT, CHARLES (1981). 'History of the Mandolin', *Mandolin World News* (autumn), 8–12.

HYNES, SAMUEL (1968). *The Edwardian Turn of Mind* (London).

JANSSENS, ROBERT (1982). *Geschiedenis van de mandoline* (Antwerp).

JENKINS, JEAN (1977). *International Dictionary of Musical Instrument Collections* (Netherlands).

KASTNER, JEAN GEORGES (1837). *Traité général d'instrumentation* (Paris).

LANSING, GEORGE L. (1921). 'Banjoists Round Table: The Standard Banjo (cont.)', *Crescendo* (May), 22.

LAROUSSE, PIERRE (1873). *Grand dictionnaire universel du XIXme Siècle* (Paris).

LAUGHLIN, CLARA E. (1928). *So you're Going to Rome!* (London).

LAVIGNAC, ALBERT, ed. (1925). *Encyclopédie de la musique et Dictionnaire du Conservatoire* (Paris).

LEEDS, CHRISTOPHER (1974). *The Unification of Italy* (London).

LE ROUX, DIDIER (1981). 'La mandoline, instrument de l'orchestre', *Confédération Musicale France*, Jan. 1981; repr. in Domergue, ed. (1981), 18–21.

LEVINE, NORMAN (1989). 'Recent Activities in the World of Classical Mandolin', *Lute Society of America Quarterly* (Aug.), 18–19.

LIVERMORE, ANN (1972). *A Short History of Spanish Music* (London).

LOESSER, ARTHUR (1954). *Men, Women and Pianos: A Social History* (New York).

LONGWORTH, MIKE (1975). *Martin Guitars: A History* (Cedar Knolls, NJ).

LOO, ESTHER VAN (1957). 'La Mandoline', *Musica* (Sept.). 36–40.

MANN, H. MABEL (1899). 'Mandolines, and Where they Grow', *Banjo World* (Aug.), 161–2.

MARCUSE, SIBYL (1975). *A Survey of Musical Instruments* (New York).

MARSH, JAN, and NUNN, PAMELA GERRISH (1989). *Women Artists and the Pre-Raphaelite Movement* (London).

MASTROIANNI, FRANCO (1993). 'I liutai di Arpino e il museo della liuteria Embergher-Cerrone', *Plectrum*, 1, 6.

MATSOMOTO, YUZURU (1985). 'Layout of the Mandolin Orchestra, parts 1, 2, & 3', *JMU Review*, 10, 7–12.

—— (1986). 'Layout of the Mandolin Orchestra, parts 4 & 5', *JMU Review*, 11, 6–9.

MENDELSSOHN-BARTHOLDY, FELIX (1864). *Letters from Italy and Switzerland*, 3rd edn., trans. Lady Wallace (London).

MONTAGU, JEREMY (1979). *The World of Baroque and Classical Musical Instruments* (London).

MONTGOMERY, JOHN (1968). *1900: The End of an Era* (London).

MÜLLER, METTE, ed. (1991). *Mandolin i Danmark: Musikhistorik Museum og Carl Claudius' samling* (Copenhagen).

MUNIER, CARLO (1895). Scuola del mandolino: metodo completo per mandolino (Florence).

—— (1909). 'Amateurs et défenseurs de la mandoline', *Le Plectre* (Dec.), 4.

Die Musik in Geschichte und Gegenwart (Kassel, 1949–68).

MUSSELMAN, JOSEPH A. (1971). *Music in the Cultured Generation: A Social History of Music in America* (Evanston, Ill.).

NEDEROST, EDITHA (1921). *Die Mandoline in der Wiener Volksmusik* (Vienna).

The New Grove Dictionary of Music and Musicians (London, 1980).

The New Grove Dictionary of Musical Instruments (London, 1984).

ODELL, H. F. (1903). 'The Proper Instrumentation for Mandoline Clubs and Orchestras', *Banjo World* (Apr.), 84–5.

O'DONOVAN, DENIS (1859). *Memories of Rome* (London).

OSBORNE, CHARLES (1969). *The Complete Operas of Verdi* (London).

The Oxford Companion to Music, 10th edn., ed, Percy A. Scholes (Oxford, 1970).

PARTEE, CLARENCE L. (1901). 'Popular Illusions Concerning the Guitar and Mandolin', *Cadenza* (May), 3–4, (June), 5–6.

—— (1902). 'The Mandolin', *Cadenza* (Apr.), 17–19, 40–1 (first pub. in *Men's Magazine*, New York).

—— (1912). 'The Mandolin in America', *BMG* (July), 148–9.

PASCAL, ROY (1973). *From Naturalism to Expressionism* (London).

PEARSALL, RONALD (1975). *Edwardian Popular Music* (Rutherford).

PENNELL, JOSEPH and ELIZABETH ROBINS (1887). *An Italian Pilgrimage* (London).

The Penny Cyclopaedia of the Society for the Diffusion of Useful Knowledge (London, 1833–46).

PICARD, G. HENRI (1901). 'Suggestions for Mandolin Instruction' *Cadenza* (Sept.), 15.

PIETRAPERTOSA, JEAN (1892). *Méthode de mandoline* (Paris).

PISANI, AGOSTINO (1913). *Manuale teorico pratico del mandolinista* (1st edn. 1898; Milan).

POST, CHARLES N. (1903). 'The Origin and Growth of the Guitar, Mandolin, and Banjo Industry in America', *Music Trades* (New York), 26 (24), 77.

PRAT, DOMINGO (1933). *Diccionario de Guitarristas* (Buenos Aires).

QUIEVREUX, LOUIS (1956). 'Silvio Ranieri est mort', *La Lanterne* (28 Nov.), 2.

RANIERI, SILVIO (1925). 'La Mandoline', in Lavignac, ed. (1925).

REINHARD, KURT (1949–68). 'Mandoline', in *Die Musik in Geschichte und Gegenwart* (Kassel).

RICHARDSON, JOANNA (1971). *Verlaine* (London).

RIPM (*Répertoire Internationale de la Presse Musicale*): *La musica* (Maryland, 1992).

SACHS, CURT (1913). *Real-Lexicon der Musikinstrumente* (Berlin).

—— (1920). *Handbuch der Musikinstrumentenkunde* (Leipzig).

SAINSBURY, JOHN (1825). *A Dictionary of Musicians* (London).

SAINT-CLIVIER, ANDRÉ (1960). 'Trois siècles de mandoline', in Domergue, ed. (1981), 22–4.

SCHERILLO, MICHELE (1917). *L'opera buffa napoletana* (Palermo).

SCHILLING, GUSTAV (1835–40). *Encyclopädie der musikalischen Wissenschaften oder Universal Lexicon der Tonkunst* (Stuttgart).

SCOTT, MICHAEL (1988). *The Great Caruso* (London).

SEWARD, DESMOND (1984). *Naples, a Traveller's Companion* (London).

SGALLARI, GIUSEPPE (1903). 'How to Play the Mandoline', *BMG* (Oct.), 11.

SHARPE, A. P. (1957). 'Troise Dies', *BMG* (May), 190–1.

SIEGEL, SAMUEL (1900). 'The Advance of the Mandoline', *Banjo World* (Jan.) 38.

—— (1901). *Siegel's Special Mandolin Studies* (New York).

SIMINOFF, ROGER (1975). 'The Gibson Story: The Early Years', *Pickin'*, 2 (5), 5–15.

SPAETH, SIGMUND (1948). *A History of Popular Music in America* (New York).

STARKIE, WALTER (1936). *Don Gypsy* (London).

STENDHAL (1956). *Life of Rossini*, trans. Richard N. Coe (London; trans. of *Vie de Rossini*, Paris, 1824).

STREATFIELD, R. A. (1895). *Masters of Italian Music* (London).

SUTTON, KEITH (1962). *Picasso* (London).

TERZI, BENEVENUTO (1937). *Dizionario dei chitarristi e liutai italiani* (Rome).

TILL, NICHOLAS (1983). *Rossini: His Life and Times* (New York).

TOTTLE, JACK (1975). *Bluegrass Mandolin* (New York).

TRAPANI, FRANCAMARIA (1982). 'Partono i mandolini per terre assai lontane', *Gente*, 26 (20), 165–70.

TRUESDELL, W. PORTER (1901–2). 'An Historical Essay on the Mandolin, with an Introduction on Music in General', *Cadenza* (Nov.–Dec. 1901, Jan.–Apr., Nov. 1902), 10–11, 10–12, 38–40, 10–12, 10–12, 12–15.

TYLER, JAMES, and SPARKS, PAUL (1989). *The Early Mandolin* (Oxford).

TYRELL, R. M. (1939a). 'The Mandolin—its History and Development', *BMG* (Feb.), 117–18.

—— (1939b). 'More Mandolin History', *BMG* (Oct.), 7.

TYRELL, E. J. (1952–3). 'Mandolin Miscellany [The Lives of Raffaele and Maria Calace]', *BMG* (Dec. 1952) 50–1, (Jan. 1953), 107–8.

VANNES, RENÉ (1951). *Dictionnaire universel des luthiers* (Brussels).

VAN VECHTEN, CARL (1920). *The Music of Spain* (London).

VINCENZI, MARCELLA (1984). *La musica a Napoli* (Naples).

VITTORI, GIOVANNA (1927). *Margherita di Savoia* (Milan).

WALLACE, WILLIAM KAY (1917). *Greater Italy* (London).

WEYHOFEN, GERTRUD (1989). 'Analyse der Spieltechniken anhand romantischen Schulwerke für Mandoline (1860–1920)' (diss., Hochschule für Musik, Cologne).

WÖLKI, GERDA, ed. (1994). *Konrad Wölki: Werkverzeichnis* (Berlin).

WÖLKI, KONRAD (1979a). *Zupfmusik-Journale* (Hamburg).

—— (1979b). *Entwicklungsphasen des Zupforchesters* (Hamburg).

—— (1984). *History of the Mandolin*, trans. Keith Harris (Arlington, Va.; as trans. of *Geschichte der Mandoline*, Berlin, 1939).

ZIMMERN, HELEN (1906). *The Italy of the Italians* (London).

ZUTH, JOSEF (1926). *Handbuch der Laute und Gitarre* (Vienna; repr. Hildesheim, 1972).

—— (1931). 'Die Mandolinehandschriften in der Bibliothek der Gesellschaft der Musikfreunde in Wien', *Zeitschrift für Musikwissenschaft*, 19.

Periodicals Consulted

Allgemeine musikalische Zeitung (Leipzig, 1798–1848).

L'Art musical (Paris, 1860–70, 1872–94).

BMG (London, Oct. 1903–76).

The Banjo World (London, Nov. 1893–Feb. 1917).

The Cadenza (New York and Boston, 1894–1924).

Classical Mandolin Society of America (Arlington, Va., 1987–).

Il concerto (Bologna, 1897–1934).

The Crescendo (Boston, 1908–33).

Dallas' Musical Monthly and Advertiser (London, 1908–14).

Gazzetta musicale di Firenze (Florence, 1853–5).

The Harmonicon (London, 1823–33).

JMU Review (Tokyo, 1977–).

Journal de Musique (Paris, 1770–7; repr. Geneva, 1972, 3 vols.).

Keynotes (London, 1907–14).

Mandoline: Internationales Musik-Journal (Leipzig, 1904–10).

The Mandoline and Guitar (London, Oct.–Nov. 1906).

Il mandolino (Turin, 1892–1937).

Moderne Musik (Zurich, 1911–14).

Musica moderna (Naples, 1905–10).

The Music Students' Magazine (London, 1906).

Le Plectre (Marseille, 1903–27).

Le Plectre (Mirecourt, 1992–).

Il plettro (Milan, 1906–43).

Zupfmusik (Hamburg, 1985–).

Index

The birth and death dates given below have been compiled from numerous sources, including correspondence with many mandolinists throughout the world. Even so, it has not always been possible to obtain exact dates and, in some cases, there are discrepancies between various sources; in such cases, only the most plausible date is shown. Because many instruments (especially those of the mandolin family) are mentioned repeatedly throughout the book, the index relates only to sections where they are discussed in detail. For the same reason, only detailed references to mandolin journals are included.